W9-BBA-233

PE

not

2007

The
Vocab
Vitamins
Vocabulary Booster

The
Vocab
Vitamins
Vocabulary Booster

Julie Karasik & Colin O'Malley

LIBRARY
NSCC - STRAIT AREA CAMPUS
226 REEVES ST.
PORT HAWKESBURY NS
B9A 2A2 CANADA

New York   Chicago   San Francisco   Lisbon   London   Madrid   Mexico City
Milan   New Delhi   San Juan   Seoul   Singapore   Sydney   Toronto

The **McGraw·Hill** Companies

Library of Congress Cataloging-in-Publication Data

Karasik, Julie.
    The vocab vitamins vocabulary booster / Julie Karasik and Colin O'Malley.
       p.   cm.
    ISBN 0-07-145811-5 (alk. paper)
    1. Vocabulary.   I. O'Malley, Colin.   II. Title.

PE1449.K327   2006
428.1—dc22   2005058009

Copyright © 2007 by Julie Karasik and Colin O'Malley. All rights reserved. Printed in the United States of America. Except as permitted under the United States Copyright Act of 1976, no part of this publication may be reproduced or distributed in any form or by any means, or stored in a database or retrieval system, without the prior written permission of the publisher.

1 2 3 4 5 6 7 8 9 10 11 12 13 14 15 DOC/DOC 0 9 8 7 6

ISBN-13: 978-0-07-145811-5
ISBN-10:   0-07-145811-5

Illustrations copyright © 2007 by Adam Neumann
Interior design by Think Design Group

McGraw-Hill Books are available at special quantity discounts to use as premiums and sales promotions, or for use in corporate training programs. For more information, please write to the Director of Special Sales, Professional Publishing, McGraw-Hill, Two Penn Plaza, New York, NY 10121-2298. Or contact your local bookstore.

Note: Example quotations are copyright by their respective authors. The original spellings and punctuation have been retained where possible.

This book is printed on acid-free paper.

To our parents and

grandparents, for all your love,

guidance, and inspiration.

Contents

Preface

Our brains have a very clever way of sifting through the millions of stimuli they receive on a daily basis and deciding which are truly important enough to remember. If somebody with stature—like your boss—says something really loudly while turning red and foaming at the mouth, your brain marks that bit of information down with a fat highlighter.

Three of the most important attributes for creating long-term knowledge are relevance, frequency, and context. Baseball fans are often able to rattle off statistics with a level of detail that nonfans find astonishing; they can do this because the information is relevant to them. We know the main streets of the city we live in because we come into contact with their names frequently on street signs and maps and in conversations and traffic reports. Context allows us to relate new knowledge to things we already know. Armed with this, a reader who may not immediately know a word used in a text can make an educated guess from the surrounding words and general meaning of the sentence. The reader can then connect the new word to another, well-known word and remember them as synonyms.

In our six years of teaching vocabulary online, we have developed a model that thousands are using to fold useful and interesting words into their active vocabularies. This book, the culmination of our experience on effective and efficient vocabulary building, contains a selection of advanced words in a format with relevance, context, and veiled repetition to give your brain the best possible shot at retaining them.

How This Book Is Organized

There are nine groups of twenty-five words, each called a Vocab Vitamin Pack. Within each pack are five themes, each with five words. These groupings are designed to create meaningful links between our words and to tell a bit of a story as we introduce each of them in turn. Vocab Vitamin Packs begin with a summary page that presents the central concept behind the pack and lists each word with several corresponding and similar words. Every theme is presented with an original illustration that acts as a mental bookmark, bringing to life the thematic concept with visual flair.

We present each word along with a pronunciation guide, the part of speech, an in-depth definition, word origin, and usage examples. We've excerpted contemporary media sources, famous quotes, and literature to provide you with interesting examples of each word in action. Most examples include the surrounding text to give the full context in which the word is being used and to show the word integrated into interesting discussions on a variety of subjects. Please keep in mind that we don't necessarily agree with what's being said in each selection. The criteria for inclusion are (1) quality of word usage and (2) value of the text as a thought-provoking or amusing piece. One other note: some of our example sentences come from Commonwealth nations whose spellings may differ from American English. In the spirit of accuracy, we've kept those spellings as they appear in the original.

Finally, each Vocab Vitamins Pack ends with one or more fun exercises to help you practice the words. And don't worry— these are not the exercises you had to do back in school!

Our approach uses the same three important attributes for creating long-term knowledge that we mentioned earlier—relevance, frequency, and context—but it wouldn't mean much if it wasn't also fun and stimulating and made for great reading. We've operated a word-of-the-day mailing list for more than five years, and we've learned how to teach in a manner that is respectful, engaging, and never stuffy. We're confident that if you stick with us, you'll soon have these words down pat.

An Explanation of the Icons

Our usage examples are introduced with little icons that correspond to the general topical category to which they belong.

LEGEND

Film and Television

Music and Dance

People and Society

Science, Medicine, and Technology

Funny and Ironic

Frivolity, Gossip, and Chatter

Sports and Recreation

Challenging, Thought-Provoking, and *Deep*

Around the World

Writing and Literature

Love, Flirtation, and Food

Bonus Words

Each word has one or more friends. These bonus words are related to the original word in one of the following ways:

- origin: shared root or word origin
- sound: sound alike or often confused
- synonym: actual synonym or word that conveys a similar meaning
- antonym: actual antonym or word that conveys an opposite meaning
- continuum: on the same meaning continuum (for example, *cold* and *tepid*)
- related: related word, usually related by subject (such as, *horse* and *buggy*)

VocabVitamins.com

Our webste has bonus book content! You can hear audio pronunciations of every single vocabulary word in this book on the VocabVitamins.com website. You are also entitled to six months of free access to our premium service. Don't miss out! Go to www.vocabvitamins.com/book and enter 1MGHB9120623.

Acknowledgments

Many sincere thanks to:

Our friends and families, for your love, support, and much-needed merry diversions and for helping us keep our feet on the ground and our chins up

Adam, for your tireless, hilarious, and brilliant work

Holly, for your enthusiasm and knowledge

Yunee, Jeannice, Wes, Zeph, and Patrick, for your technical wizardry

Daniel Humphrey, Deborah Bial, Matt Blumberg, and Hans Peter Brondmo, who make up our advisory board, for believing in us and throwing us our first breaks

All the publications and authors that have allowed us to demonstrate words in the context of wonderful writing

The VocabVitamins member community, for the support and feedback that fuels everything we do

The
Vocab
Vitamins
Vocabulary Booster

[vo·cab]
VITAMINS

....

PACK 1

....

DO IT
WITH FEELING
THIS TIME!

PROTECTION SEALED PROTECTION SEALED FOR PROTECTION SEALED FOR PROTECTION

THEME 1
Acting with Passion

SIMILAR TO:

fervid	hot, passionate, burning
impetuous	impulsive, violent, rash
irascible	angry, irate, short-tempered
precipitant	rushed, impulsive, abrupt
tempestuous	stormy, gusty, turbulent

THEME 2
Always Look on the Bright Side

SIMILAR TO:

revelry	fun, celebration, festivity
mollify	ease, soothe, soften
levity	lightness, buoyancy
copacetic	fine, OK, splendid
jaunty	lively, brisk, crisp

THEME 3
In Anger

SIMILAR TO:

acrimony	bitterness, dislike
apoplexy	hemorrhage, fit
dudgeon	angry, sullen mood
ebullition	boiling, violent emotion
irate	mad, angry, enraged

THEME 4
Sweet and Sappy

SIMILAR TO:

confection	candy, sweet, chocolate
maudlin	sentimental, cheesy, mushy
mawkish	gushy, sappy, cloying
saccharine	sugary, overly sweet
simper	smile, guffaw

THEME 5
Your Conscience Talking

SIMILAR TO:

chagrin	embarrassment, annoyance
compunction	regret, shame, pang of guilt
contrition	remorse, repentance
expiate	pay for, absolve, atone
qualm	nausea, unease, compunction

Acting with Passion

THEME 1

fervid

impetuous

irascible

precipitant

tempestuous

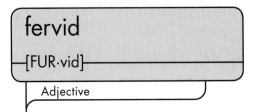

fervid

[FUR·vid]

Adjective

1. characterized by intense emotion; heated and passionate: "In addition to his now famous love of beer, Samuel Adams was a fervid American patriot and one of the first governors of Massachusetts."
2. extremely hot; burning or glowing

ORIGIN

Approximately 1599; borrowed from Latin, *fervidus*: glowing, burning, from *fervere*: to boil.

BONUS WORD   Origin

fervor: heat, intense emotion

IN ACTION

"They raise their minds by brooding over and embellishing their sufferings, from one degree of **fervid** exaltation and dreary greatness to another, till at length they run amuck entirely, and whoever meets them would do well to run them thro' the body."

Thomas Carlyle (1795–1881). Scottish essayist and historian. [Referring to the Romantics.]

"Everything in the neighbourhood of this city exhibits the appearance of life and cheerfulness. The purity of the air, the brilliancy of the unspotted heavens, the crowd of moving vessels, shooting in various directions, up and down and across the bay and the far-stretching Hudson, and the forest of masts crowded round the quays and wharfs at the entrance of the

East River. There is something in all this—in the very air you breathe, and the fair and moving scene that you rest your eye upon—which exhilarates the spirits and makes you in good humour with life and your fellow creatures. We approached these shores under a **fervid** sun, but the air, though of a higher temperature than I had ever before experienced, was so entirely free of vapor, that I thought it was for the first time in my life that I had drawn a clear breath."

Frances Wright (1795–1852). Scottish-born U.S. social reformer and author. Entry for September 18, 1818, from Views of Society and Manners in America *(1821).*

impetuous

[im·PECH·oo·ahs]

Adjective

1. of, or characterized by, undue haste; sudden, rash, and assertive emotion or action; full of passion: "His impetuous decision last night to withdraw from the competition will probably cost him in the long run."
2. marked by violent force; moving with great impetus and momentum: "The impetuous waves heaved all around us, and for the first time we realized just how much we were at their mercy."

ORIGIN
Approximately 1398; from Latin, *impetus*: impetus.

BONUS WORD   Origin

impetus: stimulus, force

IN ACTION

"In the life of children there are two very clear-cut phases, before and after puberty. Before puberty the child's personality has not yet formed and it is easier to guide its life and make it acquire specific habits of order, discipline, and work: after puberty the personality develops **impetuously** and all extraneous intervention becomes odious, tyrannical, insufferable. Now it so happens that parents feel the responsibility towards their children precisely during this second period, when it is too late: then of course the stick and violence enter the scene and yield very few results indeed. Why not instead take an interest in the child during the first period?"

Antonio Gramsci (1891–1937). Italian political theorist. Letter to his brother (August 25, 1930).

"For the most part, our leftover Puritanism doesn't condone exhibiting ourselves to each other naked before we've kissed and fondled first. There is an etiquette, a protocol, even in **impetuous**, runaway sex. But kissing can happen right away, and, if people care for each other, then it's less a prelude to mating than a sign of deep regard."

Diane Ackerman. "Touch," A Natural History of the Senses (1990).

irascible

[i·RAS·ah·bahl, eye·RAS·ah·bahl]

Adjective

1. quickly aroused to anger; temperamental: "The irascible sergeant would send us to do push-ups if anyone showed even the slightest hesitance fulfilling his orders."

2. characterized by, or the product of, temper and anger: "Her irascible response was so harsh, it bordered on violent."

ORIGIN

Approximately 1398; borrowed from Late Latin, *irascibilis*, from *irasci*: to grow angry, from *ira*: anger.

BONUS WORD   Continuum

LESS EXTREME . . .   **. . . MORE EXTREME**

volatile   ⟶   irascible

volatile: varying widely, inconstant, explosive

IN ACTION

"I have never known anyone worth a damn who wasn't **irascible**."

Ezra Pound (1885–1972).
U.S. poet and critic. Remark (1917).

"Closely related to the North African ass is the Asiatic ass, also known as the onager. Since its homeland includes the Fertile Crescent, the cradle of Western civilization and animal domestication, ancient peoples must have experimented extensively with onagers. . . . However, all writers about them, from Romans to modern zookeepers, decry their **irascible** temper and their nasty habit of biting people. As a result, although similar in other respects to ancestral donkeys, onagers have never been domesticated."

Jared Diamond. Guns, Germs, and Steel:
The Fates of Human Societies *(1999).*

precipitant
[pri·SIP·i·tahnt]

Adjective

1. falling into something without control; headlong: "Her precipitant descent into an affair with her boss led to all of the well-known complexities and frustrations that she had been warned of."
2. done with very great haste; without due deliberation; rushed, impulsive, or rash: "Arturo had a habit of making precipitant stock purchase decisions, often based on a single favorable headline, and this was beginning to eat a hole in his portfolio."
3. unexpected and sudden, or abrupt

ORIGIN
Approximately 1550; from Latin, *praecipitans*, present participle of *praecipitare*: to throw headlong, to be hasty.

BONUS WORD Antonym

circumspect: prudent, heedful of consequences

IN ACTION
"An additional, important characteristic of true migraines is that they have a definite **precipitant**. The most common precipitants are foods: chocolate, coffee or red wine being the most likely culprits; and emotional stresses such as anxiety or sleep deprivation. Some women suffer from menstrual-induced migraines, and a subset of sufferers, including Lexi and me, have exercise-induced migraines."

Dr. Jeff Sankoff. "Ask the Tri Doc: Post-exertional migraines," triathletemag.com/Triathlete magazine (November 24, 2005).

". . . and we in the haste of a **precipitant** zeal shall make no distinction, but resolve to stop their mouths, because we fear they come with new and dangerous opinions, as we commonly forejudge them ere we understand them, no less than woe to us, while thinking thus to defend the gospel, we are found the persecutors."

John Milton (1608–74). English poet.
Areopagitica (1644).

tempestuous
[tem·PES·choo·ahs]
Adjective

1. showing violence resembling the nature of a fierce windstorm, often accompanied with hail, snow, or rain (a tempest): "As the sea began to rock our boat with larger waves, and the wind developed a tempestuous ferocity, we decided to head indoors to the relative shelter of our quarters."
2. turbulent, tumultuous; with ongoing difficulties: "Their relationship had always been tempestuous, but I had always thought that their bedrock of trust and mutual admiration would hold it together."

ORIGIN
Approximately 1385; from Late Latin, *tempestuosus*: stormy, turbulent, from *tempestas*: tempest, related to *tempus*: time, season.

BONUS WORD　Related

blitzkrieg: sudden military attack

IN ACTION

"Even when Odets was an adult, L.J. continued to belittle him as 'big boy.' 'My father [is] driving nails into my head,' Odets wrote to a friend. Although he offered L.J. substantial financial assistance—between 1935 and 1950, he gave him more than a hundred thousand dollars—the harangues continued. Trying to persuade Odets to employ him as his manager in 1935, L.J. wrote, 'Tell me young man, where have you gotten all the experience in the world, you think you have? I have seen men that was raised higher than you, and then seen them drop lower than that. . . . Yes, you are still the "White Hope" but you are dropping.' When, in 1937, L.J. learned that Odets had separated from Luise Rainer, the two-time Academy Award-winning actress, with whom he had a **tempestuous** three-year marriage, he sounded off in all his brutishness: 'I'm ashamed of you. You are the dummist [sic] chunk of humanity I have ever come in contact with' . . . Odets internalized this constant excoriation, berating himself in his journal as a 'pig,' a 'pissant,' an 'idiot,' a 'loafer,' and 'twice an ass.' He wrote, 'It is the father you have incorporated, his characteristics and hated elements—that is the father to be afraid of!'"

John Lahr. *"Stage Left: The Struggles of Clifford Odets,"* New Yorker (April 17, 2006).

"Romance is **tempestuous**. Love is calm."

Mason Cooley (b. 1927). *U.S. aphorist. City Aphorisms, Eighth Selection, New York (1991).*

Always Look on the Bright Side

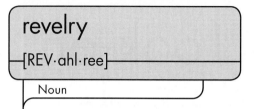

revelry

[REV·ahl·ree]

Noun

1. unrestrained merrymaking; raucous and lively celebration: "Sarah successfully lobbied her father to suspend her curfew on prom night, as time constraints would deny her of the night of revelry that was every teen's birthright."

ORIGIN

Approximately 1410; borrowed from Old French, *reveler*: to be disorderly, to make merry; from Latin, *rebellare*: to rebel.

BONUS WORD Origin

reverie: daydreaming, musing

IN ACTION

Midnight shout and **revelry**,
Tipsy dance and jollity.

John Milton (1608–74). English poet. Comus *(1634).*

"He did everything well; he sang charmingly, sketched with spirit, wrote verses, and was a very fair actor. He was only twenty-eight, and he was already a kammer-yunker, and had a very good position. Panshin had complete confidence in himself, in his own intelligence, and his own penetration; he made his way with light-hearted assurance, everything went smoothly with him. He was used to being liked by every one, old and young, and imagined that he understood people, especially women: he certainly understood their ordinary weaknesses. As a man of artistic leanings, he was conscious of a capacity for passion, for being carried away, even for enthusiasm, and, consequently, he permitted himself various irregularities; he was dissipated, associated with persons not belonging to good society, and, in general, conducted himself in a free and easy manner; but at heart he was cold and false, and at the moment of the most boisterous **revelry** his sharp brown eye was always alert, taking everything in. This bold, independent young man could never forget himself and be completely carried away. To his credit it must be said, that he never boasted of his conquests."

Ivan Turgenev (1818–83). Russian novelist, dramatist, and short-story writer. From Chapter 4 of A Nest of Gentlefolk *(1859).*

mollify

[MOL·ah·fie']

Transitive Verb

1. to calm, soothe, or assuage, as the temper or emotion of an upset or excited individual; to pacify: "To mollify and reassure him, Sharon covered her son's flushed cheeks with her hands and gently kissed his nose."
2. to make less intense; to temper
3. to make less rigid or stiff; to soften: "to mollify the soil"

ORIGIN

Approximately 1392; from Late Latin, *mollificare*: to make soft (Latin, *mollis*: soft + *facere*: to make).

BONUS WORD Sound

mollycoddle: to pamper, overprotect

IN ACTION

"'How come you've never mentioned her before if you're such good friends?'

"'Well, we're old friends,' I said. 'I don't see her that much. I ran into her the other day in the Marina. But she laughs easily. She likes cultural things, just like you. Believe me, she's a piece of ripe fruit, ready to be plucked.'

"This seemed to **mollify** him. I heard his beeper go off as he wrote down Penny's number and we hung up. Seconds later, my phone rang. 'I forgot to ask you,' Oliver said. 'What kind of fruit?'

"I considered. 'A peach.'"

Courtney Weaver. *"Unzipped: Yenta Out of Shape,"*
Salon.com *(March 5, 1997)*.

"The ordinary politician has a very low estimate of human nature. In his daily life he comes into contact chiefly with persons who want to get something or to avoid something. Beyond this circle of seekers after privileges, individuals and organized minorities, he is aware of a large unorganized, indifferent mass of citizens who ask nothing in particular and rarely complain. The politician comes after a while to think that the art of politics is to satisfy the seekers after favors and to **mollify** the inchoate mass with noble sentiments and patriotic phrases."

Walter Lippmann (1889–1974). U.S. journalist.
"The New Congress," New York Herald Tribune
(December 8, 1931).

levity
[LEV·i·tee]
Noun

1. behavior or remarks that are light or comical, especially when inappropriate considering the seriousness of the occasion; frivolity: "Justin was genuinely concerned about the characters loitering across the street from us, and my levity only heightened his anxiety."
2. lack of steadiness; inconstancy; fickleness
3. the quality of being light in weight, especially relative to another substance; buoyancy

ORIGIN
Approximately 1564; borrowed from Latin, *levitas*: lightness, frivolity, genitive *levitatis*, from *levis*: light in weight.

BONUS WORD   Continuum

MORE SERIOUS . . .   **. . . LESS SERIOUS**

gravity   ⟶   levity   ⟶   frivolity

gravity: seriousness, importance

frivolity: triviality, silliness

IN ACTION

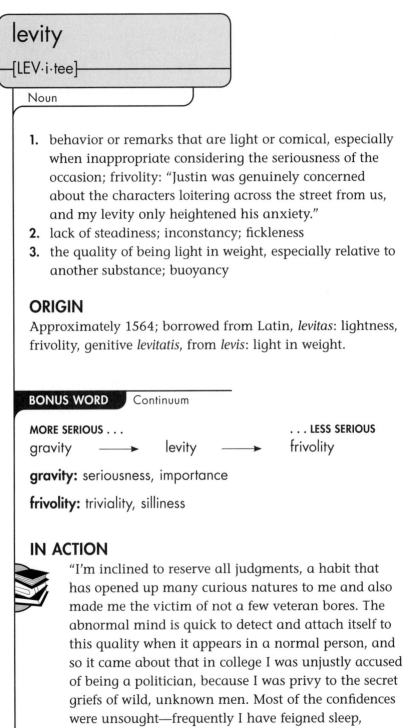

"I'm inclined to reserve all judgments, a habit that has opened up many curious natures to me and also made me the victim of not a few veteran bores. The abnormal mind is quick to detect and attach itself to this quality when it appears in a normal person, and so it came about that in college I was unjustly accused of being a politician, because I was privy to the secret griefs of wild, unknown men. Most of the confidences were unsought—frequently I have feigned sleep, preoccupation, or a hostile **levity** when I realized by some unmistakable sign that an intimate revelation was quivering on the horizon; for the intimate revelations of young men, or at least the terms in which they express them, are usually plagiaristic and marred by obvious suppressions."

> F. Scott Fitzgerald (1896–1940). U.S. novelist
> and short-story writer. From Chapter 1 of
> The Great Gatsby (1925).

copacetic

{koe'·pah·SET·ik}

Adjective

1. completely satisfactory; quite acceptable; fine: "Gerry was indignant that his best friend's girlfriend would set him up with a blind date, until he saw her, at which point everything was copacetic."

ORIGIN

Approximately 1919; from American English, *copasetic*: very good, all right, possibly originating among southern blacks in the nineteenth century.

BONUS WORD   Sound

ascetic: self-denying, austere

IN ACTION

"I once heard someone use **copacetic** as a slang term for 'drunk' and I thought That's me. With a buzz on, I'm first rate. Alcohol is my sealant. When I'm painted, nothing can penetrate my essence. My best friend can call me *bitch*. The boy who is brushing my thigh with the back of his hand can tell me I'm only pretty when he's drunk. In the moment, these sentiments just bead up and roll off me."

Koren Zailckas. Smashed: Story of
a Drunken Girlhood *(2005)*.

"After raising prices and decreasing fares, you'd think that with ridership going up, everything in MUNI-land would be **copacetic**, right? Wrong. Those ever increasing gas prices are affecting MUNI in that after all that number crunching, spreadsheet summing, and budget rearranging, they still might be four to five million in the red. Also causing a budget crunch is the fact that MUNI is receiving less money in parking fines than they had expected. Yep, the very fact that more people are getting out of their cars and taking MUNI is actually hurting MUNI. Kind of ironic, don't cha think?"

Jon Shurkin. "Who Reads Yesterday's Papers?"
SFist *(October 24, 2005)*.

jaunty

[JON·tee, JAWN·tee]

Adjective

1. having a buoyant, lighthearted, or self-confident air: "The recent bout with unemployment had been difficult for Ariel, but her jaunty walk and gleaming smile were still intact."
2. smart and dapper in appearance or manners

ORIGIN

Approximately 1662; borrowed from French, *gentil*: nice, pleasing; from Old French, *gentil*: noble.

BONUS WORD   Related

spry: lively, vigorous

IN ACTION

"A rather **jaunty** sign advertising the grimmest of tasks was pinned up on a small notice board labeled 'Human Shields' in the airy lobby of the Andalus Hotel Apartments here this morning.

"It sought three additional volunteers to join the 13 already committed to living at the Baghdad South Power Plant to try to prevent its being bombed in the event of war. 'There is no more important place for a shield to be,' the notice read."

Neil MacFarquhar. "Human Shields, No Résumé Needed," New York Times (February 20, 2003).

In Anger

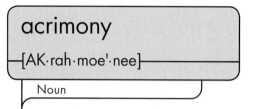

acrimony

[AK·rah·moe'·nee]

Noun

1. a sharp and bitter manner, especially as exhibited in speech or other behavior: "Her retort was so charged with an acrimony that took us off guard and left us speechless."

ORIGIN

Approximately 1542; from Latin, *acrimonia*, from *acer* or *acris*: sharp, sour + *monia*: suffix meaning an action or state.

BONUS WORD Origin

acropolis: fortified high ground, citadel

IN ACTION

"'The squabbling has unquestionably hurt the stock,' said Paul Kelly, a biotech analyst with ING Barings in San Francisco. 'The Human Genome Project began in the early '90s. Its leaders now for a decade have all envisioned their names on that seminal paper in biology and here this somewhat of a maverick, Craig Venter, is just kind of scooping them and the antipathy and the animosity is unbelievable.'

"But that may no longer be the case.

"'This is all part of an effort to take these announcements and not have the **acrimony** and backbiting that has characterized this whole effort for years. Both research groups want peace,' said a government official who asked not to be named."

Kristen Philipkoski. "Genome Mappers to Make Amends," Salon.com (June 22, 2000).

"Mr. Barry acknowledged that the incident had 'caused deep divisions and **acrimony** among the District's residents.' The incident also appears to have created a rift between Mr. Barry and his wife, Cora Masters Barry, who stood by him in 1992 after he was released from jail on misdemeanor drug charges. She said she had moved out of their home in Washington and was taking time to evaluate her life.

"Mr. Barry was elected to his last term as mayor in 1994, four years after being videotaped by federal agents smoking crack cocaine in a hotel room."

"Washington Ex-Mayor Ends Campaign After Drug Incident," New York Times (April 5, 2002).

apoplexy

[AP·ah·plek'·see]

Noun

1. a sudden loss of consciousness resulting from the rupture or occlusion of a blood vessel and a lack of oxygen in the brain; a stroke
2. an effusion of blood into the substance of an organ or tissue
3. a fit of extreme anger or rage: "Alex had wrung himself dry over his paper for Professor Lopez, and his poor grade sent him into apoplexy."

ORIGIN

Approximately 1390; from Late Latin, *apoplexia*; from Greek, *apoplexia*, from *apoplessein*: to disable by a stroke (*apo*: away from + *plessein*: to strike).

BONUS WORD   Related

spleen: anger, bad temper

IN ACTION

"A cluster of men gathered in a tight circle in the plaza of Central Park [near Old Havana]. Judging from the boisterous shouts and shaking fists, they were watching a brawl. Closer, I saw that the crowd was focused on two men faced off like cocks in a pit.

"A black man in a faded yellow tank top pushed his face to within inches of his opponent's nose. His brown eyes widened. Smooth features contorted. One palm extended outward, as if pleading for reason. The other hand flapped like a bronco. His point made, the aggressor planted his feet and folded his arms.

"The adversary, a stocky man in a checkered shirt, sprang to life. Arms spread, veins popping, he launched an oral bombardment that looked likely to end in fisticuffs or **apoplexy**. Communism versus capitalism? Is there a God? The chainsaw buzz of their Spanish made it impossible for me to tell the stakes.

"I turned to a sturdy youth who was also watching the debate . . .

"'What are they arguing about?'

"'Baseball.'"

Christopher Hunt. Waiting for Fidel *(1998).*

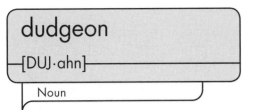

dudgeon

—[DUJ·ahn]—

Noun

1. a feeling of intense indignation or resentment, usually prefaced with *high*, as in *high dudgeon*; anger: "Uncle Jerry stormed off in high dudgeon when I mistook his home-fried chicken recipe for an order from KFC."

ORIGIN
Approximately 1570; origin uncertain.

BONUS WORD   Sound

bludgeon: club, to hit with a heavy club

IN ACTION

"In the boom years of the 1990s, America's business magazines often served as fawning cheerleaders for the hotshot capitalists of the dot-com era, publishing countless puff pieces portraying them as brilliant, altruistic, heroic geniuses.

"Now, after the boom has busted and Enron has collapsed in scandal, business magazines have turned into pit bulls, printing stories excoriating these once-deified entrepreneurs as crooked, mendacious, rapacious robber barons.

"Particularly enjoyable are two recent pieces. One, published in *Fortune*, is an enraged exposé of our criminal justice system's 'coddling' of white-collar crooks. . . . *Fortune*'s excellent exposé appeared in the March 18 issue, which, alas, departed from most newsstands yesterday. Its premise was hyped in headlines that made this venerable old business mag read like the *Daily Worker* in highest **dudgeon**. The cover screamed: 'It's time to stop coddling white-collar crooks. Send them to jail.' Inside, the headline read: 'White-Collar Criminals: They Lie, They Cheat, They Steal and They've Been Getting Away With It for Too Long.'"

Peter Carlson. "Post-Enron, a Reversal of Fortune," Washington Post (March 26, 2002).

ebullition

{eb'·ah·LISH·ahn}

Noun

1. the state or process of a liquid boiling or bubbling up
2. a sudden burst or violent display, as of emotion, such as ill temper or grief; an outburst: "I wasn't anywhere near the events that took place that September, but the ebullition of grief and anger that rippled through our country was palpable for me nonetheless."

ORIGIN

Approximately 1530; from Latin, *bullitus*, past participle of *bullire*: to boil or bubble.

BONUS WORD   Sound

abolition: the act of ending or annulling

IN ACTION

"I hesitated long before I put this theory to the test of practice. I knew well that I risked death; for any drug that so potently controlled and shook the very fortress of identity, might by the least scruple of an overdose or at the least inopportunity in the moment of exhibition, utterly blot out that immaterial tabernacle which I looked to it to change. But the temptation of a discovery so singular and profound, at last overcame the suggestions of alarm. I had long since prepared my tincture; I purchased at once, from a firm of wholesale chemists, a large quantity of a particular salt which I knew, from my experiments, to be the last ingredient required; and late one accursed night, I compounded the elements, watched them boil and smoke together in the glass, and when the **ebullition** had subsided, with a strong glow of courage, drank off the potion."

Robert Louis Stevenson (1850–94).
Scottish novelist, poet, and essayist. The Strange
Case of Dr. Jekyll and Mr. Hyde *(1886).*

"The captain ground his teeth. Spectre-monk, phantom, superstitions—all were forgotten at this moment. He saw only a man and an insult.

"'Ha—very good!' he stammered, his voice choking with rage, and he drew his sword, still stammering—for passion makes a man tremble as well as fear. 'Draw,' he cried, 'here—on the spot—draw and defend yourself! There shall be blood upon these stones!'

"The other never stirred. Then, as he saw his adversary on guard and ready to run him through—'Captain Phœbus,' said he, and his voice shook with bitterness, 'you are forgetting your assignation.' The angry fits of such men as Phœbus are like boiling milk of which a drop of cold water will stay the **ebullition**. These few words brought down the point of the sword which glittered in the captain's hand."

Victor Hugo (1802–85). French poet, novelist,
playwright, and essayist. Notre Dame de Paris *(1831).*

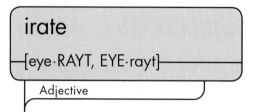

irate

—[eye·RAYT, EYE·rayt]—

Adjective

1. extremely angry or incensed; enraged: "Trevor was irate to find his employees smoking in the small stockroom, in the midst of the new season's clothing line, fresh from the warehouse."
2. characterized by extreme anger: "Nora was fuming over the editor's skewed portrayal of events, so she loaded her thoughts into an irate letter and mailed it immediately."

ORIGIN

Approximately 1838; from Latin, *iratus*, past participle of *irasci*: to grow angry, from *ira*: anger, rage.

BONUS WORD   Antonym

blithe: carefree and happy

IN ACTION

"Reveling in meeting and chatting to new people ('If we do not pass on, I shall soon pass out,' her husband once said as Elizabeth persisted in chatting at a public appearance), she was also eternally tactful and diplomatic. At a luncheon on a trip to South Africa, she once listened patiently as an **irate** Afrikaaner mayor complained about the indignities his countrymen had suffered at the hands of the English. 'Oh, I do understand so well,' Elizabeth responded. 'That's just how we feel about them in Scotland.'"

Sarah Lyall. "Britain's Beloved 'Queen Mum,' a Symbol of Courage, Dies at 101," New York Times (March 31, 2002).

Sweet and Sappy

THEME 4

confection

maudlin

mawkish

saccharine

simper

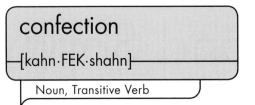

confection
[kahn·FEK·shahn]

Noun, Transitive Verb

Noun
1. the act or process of combining elements or materials, or the result of it; confecting: "Sally's confection of newspaper clippings, illegible scribbling, and artwork did not earn her a passing grade for the final project."
2. a sweet food made with a mixture of ingredients, such as fruit, nuts, or sugar
3. a medicinal compound that has been sweetened

Transitive Verb
4. to make into a confection

ORIGIN
Approximately 1387; from Middle English, *confeccioun*: something prepared by mixing ingredients; from Latin, *conficere*: to put together, to prepare.

BONUS WORD   Synonym

concoction: an unusual mixture

IN ACTION

"The kiss. There are all sorts of kisses, lad, from the sticky **confection** to the kiss of death. Of them all, the kiss of an actress is the most unnerving. How can we tell if she means it or if she's just practicing?"

Ruth Gordon (1896–1985). U.S. playwright and actor.
[Benjy, in] The Leading Lady (1948).

"Americans, unhappily, have the most remarkable ability to alchemize all bitter truths into an innocuous but piquant **confection** and to transform their moral contradictions, or public discussion of such contradictions, into a proud decoration, such as are given for heroism on the battle field."

James Baldwin (1924–87). U.S. author.
"Many Thousands Gone," Partisan Review
(November–December 1951).

"In February, the Cherry Pie Three were sentenced to six months in jail for their November 1998 pieing of San Francisco mayor Willie Brown. The pastry tossers rejected an offer of probation on the grounds that it would interfere with their continued activism.

"In a related development, the Biotic Baking Brigade whacked Chevron CEO Kenneth Derr with a pie in March. According to a BBB press release, Derr was targeted to protest Chevron's human rights abuses in Nigeria. Before hurling the **confection**, one of the pie throwers reportedly shouted, 'Do people really kill Nigerians for oil? People do!'"

Jennifer Barrios. "Pie-Pie," Mother Jones Magazine
(May/June 1999), ©1999,
Foundation for National Progress.

maudlin

—[MAWD·lin]—

Adjective

1. excessively or tearfully sentimental, especially as a result of alcohol: "I knew the staff had loved working for Jerry, but I wasn't expecting his farewell party to be such a maudlin affair."

ORIGIN

Approximately 1607; from Middle English, *Maudelen,* derived from *(Mary) Magdalene,* the repentant sinner forgiven by Jesus, often portrayed weeping in repentance; from *Magdala,* a town on the sea of Galilee.

BONUS WORD   Sound

mandolin: a stringed instrument related to the lute

IN ACTION

"But none of this makes 'Tuesdays With Morrie' a good play; none of this makes it anything but a **maudlin**, manipulative tear-jerker with the subtlety of a children's bedtime story and a complete absence of tension and conflict that, from an audience perspective, keeps Morrie alive much longer than it has to."

> Bruce Weber. *"A Life Examined as Death Inches Closer,"* New York Times (November 21, 2002).

"It is a **maudlin** and indecent verity that comes out through the strength of wine."

> Joseph Conrad (1857–1924). English novelist of Polish descent. *A Personal Record* (1912).

mawkish
[MAW·kish]

Adjective

1. overly sentimental, especially in a contrived or objectionable manner: "To set the tone before she took to the stage, Claire had arranged for the screening of a

mawkish short film covering her political career to date, complete with a dramatic musical score."

2. bland or nauseating in taste

ORIGIN

Approximately 1668; from dialectal *mawk*: maggot, from Middle English, *mawke*, of Scandinavian origin + suffix *-ish*.

BONUS WORD   Sound

brackish: slightly salty

IN ACTION

"Tuckett had no intention of turning the project into infomercials for the league or the military. 'I felt strongly it couldn't be a recruiting commercial,' he said. 'We didn't want them to be **mawkish** or maudlin. I wanted them to tell their own stories and somehow capture the essence of what was going on over there.'"

Leonard Shapiro. "NFL Delivers American Postcards,"
Washington Post (November 22, 2002).

"If this bureau had a prayer for use around horse parks, it would go something like this: Lead us not among bleeding-hearts to whom horses are cute or sweet or adorable, and deliver us from horse-lovers. Amen. . . . With that established, let's talk about the death of Seabiscuit the other night. It isn't **mawkish** to say, there was a racehorse, a horse that gave race fans as much pleasure as any that ever lived and one that will be remembered as long and as warmly."

Walter Wellesley (Red) Smith (1905–82). U.S. author,
sports columnist, and reporter. "A Horse You
Had to Like," New York Times (May 20, 1947).

saccharine

[SAK·ahr·in, SAK·ah·reen', SAK·ah·rine']

Adjective

1. of, pertaining to, or characteristic of sugar or saccharin: "a saccharine taste"
2. cloyingly sweet and ingratiating in attitude or tone: "Earl would telegraph his sales pitches with a saccharine smile, which usually killed the deal before he had a chance to speak a word."
3. excessively sentimental

ORIGIN

Approximately 1674; from Medieval Latin, *saccharum*: sugar, from Latin, *saccharon*, from Greek, *sakcharon*, from Pali, *sakkhara*, from Sanskrit, *sarkara*: gravel, grit, sugar.

BONUS WORD   Continuum

LESS SWEET . . .   **. . . MORE SWEET**
saccharine   ⟶   cloying

cloying: overly sweet

IN ACTION

"But Wonderland's most dangerous specter is not the predatory stranger, or even the reader who thrills guiltily to tales of predation, but the forthright curiosity of Alice herself. Unlike the oysters, she knows the rules. Before accepting the invitation of a bottle to 'Drink Me,' she makes sure it's not marked 'Poison.' Having obtained this rather minimal assurance, however, she goes on to partake eagerly of every size-altering substance she is offered, not to mention taking advice from disappearing cats, smoking caterpillars and cracked eggs. In fact, she enters into the hallucinatory logic of Wonderland and its size-altering potions with the gusto of a college freshman discovering the mind-bending possibilities of dope. The faint menace of her foolhardiness and her surroundings prevent Alice from developing the **saccharine** poisoning that can afflict icons of girlish innocence (think Shirley Temple)."

Laura Green. "Alice in Mirrorland,"
Salon.com (July 30, 1997).

"Television programming for children need not be **saccharine** or insipid in order to give to violence its proper balance in the scheme of things. . . . But as an endless diet for the sake of excitement and sensation in stories whose plots are vehicles for killing and torture and little more, it is not healthy for young children. Unfamiliar as yet with the full story of human response, they are being misled when they are offered perversion before they have fully learned what is sound."

Dorothy H. Cohen. U.S. educator and child
development specialist. "Beyond the Home to School
and Community," The Learning Child (1972).

simper
[SIM·pahr]

Intransitive Verb, Transitive Verb, Noun

Intransitive Verb
1. to smile in a silly, coy, and affected or self-conscious manner

Transitive Verb

2. to say or express something with such a smile: "They simpered good-bye as their date came to a close, and they wondered if they would ever see each other again."

Noun

3. a silly, coy, and affected or self-conscious smile

ORIGIN

Approximately 1563; perhaps of Scandinavian origin, akin to dialectal Danish, *semper, simper*: affected, coy, prudish.

BONUS WORD　Sound

simian: relating to an ape

IN ACTION

"Stupid, cheesy, idiotic lines drip from the lips of every single actor—ape and human. At one point an orangutan, played by Paul Giamatti, actually utters the line 'Can't we all just get along?' Rodney King should sue. Another **simpering** female chimp laments that she's 'having a bad hair day,' as she pats her coif. These comments—along with many others— cross that fine line between laughing with a character and laughing at one. And consider these other memorable lines: 'Look!' 'Run!' and 'Follow me!'"

Paul Clinton. "Review: Monkey See, Monkey Run from 'Apes,'" CNN.com (July 26, 2001).

Your Conscience Talking

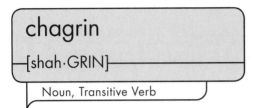

chagrin

[shah·GRIN]

Noun, Transitive Verb

Noun

1. a strong feeling of vexation or embarrassment due to disappointment or failure: "When pressed, Garrison admitted with chagrin that he hadn't locked the car door and offered to replace any stolen items."

Transitive Verb

2. to cause to feel vexed or embarrassed, as through disappointment or failure; to mortify

ORIGIN

Approximately 1717; borrowed from French, *chagrin*: melancholy, anxiety; possibly related to Old North French, *chagreiner*: to become gloomy, to distress.

BONUS WORD   Related

faux pas: a social mistake

gaucherie: a tactless act

IN ACTION

"Family membership is not the super-deal we sometimes suppose it is for nannies, either. When I called Ali last week to get her perspective for this column, I expected her to remember working for our family with pleasure and pride. She did. But she also gently reminded me that I had never paid her overtime. To my **chagrin**, I remembered that I had compensated her with time off, usually within a few days. I gave her what I would have chosen for myself, but I was presuming too much about what she wanted, just the way your sister or your mother might think she knows, without asking, where you want to vacation or the way you like your tuna fish sandwiches."

Ellyn Spragins. "Of Good Fences and Good Nannies," New York Times (May 4, 2003).

Sweet is death forevermore.
Nor haughty hope, nor swart **chagrin**,
Nor murdering hate, can enter in.
All is now secure and fast.

Ralph Waldo Emerson (1803–82). U.S. essayist, poet, and philosopher. "The Past," May-Day and Other Pieces (1867).

compunction

[kahm·PUNGK·shahn]

Noun

1. anxiety or deep uneasiness arising from a sense of guilt: "compunctions of conscience"
2. a twinge of misgiving or conscience; scruple; qualm: "There I was, finally at the front of the line, about to order my morning coffee, when a lady walks through the door, maneuvers in front of me, and orders, showing no compunction."

ORIGIN
Approximately 1340; from Latin, *compungere*: to prick severely, to sting (*com-*: thoroughly + *pungere*: to prick).

BONUS WORD　Related

sordid: filthy or dirty

IN ACTION

"For some, just being in the military fulfills a desire to give something back to a country that gave them freedom. 'I owed this country something, and I thought, "Let me go pay that debt,"' said 1st Lt. Arkadiy Baumval, 34, a physician's assistant here and also in his civilian life back home in Brooklyn, N.Y.

'So I joined.'

"The soldiers often affectionately call Baumval 'the crazy Russian,' because he is one of the most animated members of the 384th—performing traditional Russian dances and breaking into falsetto without **compunction** is a tough act to pull off on a military base.

"But earlier, when he lived in Belarus under Soviet rule, he and his family faced discrimination because they are Jewish. . . . 'They called it nationality. They didn't call it religious preference because we didn't have any religion in Russia,' Baumval said. 'But they kept track of it—who is what. They made a line called nationality in your passport, and they labeled you as a Jew.'"

John Fritze. "Foreign-Born Soldiers Value Liberty,"
Indianapolis Star (April 29, 2003).

"Men who have been raised violently have every reason to believe it is appropriate for them to control others through violence; they feel no **compunction** over being violent to women, children, and one another."

Frank Pittman. U.S. psychiatrist and family therapist.
Man Enough (1993).

contrition

─[kahn·TRISH·ahn]─

Noun

1. deep and genuine remorse for sin or wrongdoing; repentance: "Hugh tried everything to convey his contrition, but Kayla wasn't sure if she could fully trust him again."

ORIGIN

Approximately 1303; from Latin, *contritionem*, from *conterere*: to wear down, to crush (*con-*: thoroughly + *terere*: to rub, to grind).

BONUS WORD   Sound

contrive: to work out a plan for

IN ACTION

"By the end of that month, public officials and colleagues were beginning to challenge his reporting. By November, the investigation has found, he was fabricating quotations and scenes, undetected. By March, he was lying in his articles and to his editors about being at a court hearing in Virginia, in a police chief's home in Maryland and in front of a soldier's home in West Virginia. By the end of April another newspaper was raising questions about plagiarism. And by the first of May, his career at *The Times* was over.

"A few days later, Mr. Blair issued a statement that referred to 'personal problems' and expressed **contrition**. But during several telephone conversations last week, he declined repeated requests to help the newspaper correct the record or comment on any aspect of his work. He did not respond to messages left on his cell phone, with his family and with his union representative on Friday afternoon."

Dan Barry, David Barstow, Jonathan D. Glater,
Adam Liptak, and Jacques Steinberg. "Times Reporter
Who Resigned Leaves Long Trail of Deception,"
New York Times (May 11, 2003).

"I shall never send for a priest or recite an Act of **Contrition** in my last moments. I do not mind if I lose my soul for all eternity. If the kind of God exists Who would damn me for not working out a deal with Him, then that is unfortunate. I should not care to spend eternity in the company of such a person."

Mary McCarthy (1912–89). U.S. author. [Raised in
a strictly religious, unsympathetic Irish-Catholic
home, McCarthy had become an unbeliever.]
Memories of a Catholic Girlhood (1957).

expiate

[EK·spee·ayt']

Transitive Verb, Intransitive Verb

Transitive Verb

1. to make amends for, as by suffering appropriate penalty; to atone for: "Rico hoped his leap into strict vegetarianism would expiate a long history of lustful, carnivorous endeavors."

Intransitive Verb

2. to make amends; to atone

ORIGIN

Approximately 1600; borrowed from Latin, *expiatus*, past participle of *expiare*: to make amends (*ex-*: completely + *piare*: to appease, from *pius*: faithful, loyal, devout).

BONUS WORD Sound

expatriate: voluntarily absent from home or country

IN ACTION

"A man with a talent does what is expected of him, makes his way, constructs, is an engineer, a composer, a builder of bridges. It's the natural order of things that he construct objects outside himself and his family. The woman who does so is aberrant...We have to **expiate** for this cursed talent someone handed out to us, by mistake, in the black mystery of genetics."

May Sarton (1912–95). U.S. poet and novelist.
[Hilary Stevens, in] Mrs. Stevens Hears
the Mermaids Singing (1965).

qualm

[kwawm]

Noun

1. a sudden sensation of nausea
2. a sudden feeling of anxiety or apprehension: "The frequent travel required in Carmen's job no longer seemed exciting, and she felt intense qualms of homesickness when unpacking into large, empty hotel rooms."

3. uneasiness about the fitness or propriety of an action; misgiving

ORIGIN

Approximately 1530; from Old English, *cwealm*: death, destruction, plague; cognate with Old Saxon and Old High German, *qualm*: death, destruction, and related to Old English, *cwelan*: to die.

BONUS WORD Related

rue: to feel remorse for

IN ACTION

"All this family drama and trauma could drive a man crazy. And Jerrold Post, the GWU professor and former CIA psychiatrist, believes that the Dear Leader [Kim Jong Il] has a serious mental illness.

"'He has the core characteristics of the most dangerous personality disorder, malignant narcissism,' Post theorized in a recent psychological profile.

"The disorder is characterized by self-absorption, an inability to empathize, a lack of conscience, paranoia and 'unconstrained aggression.'

"The Dear Leader, Post concluded, 'will use whatever aggression is necessary, without **qualm** of conscience, be it to eliminate an individual or to strike out at a particular group.'"

Peter Carlson. "Sins of the Son: Kim Jong Il's North Korea Is in Ruins, but Why Should That Spoil His Fun?" Washington Post (May 11, 2003).

Audio pronunciations for the words in this pack can be found on our website: www.vocabvitamins.com/book/pack1.

Fill-in Frenzy!

These disastrous pickup lines need your help. Fill in the word that best fits each blank from the five words that precede each.

mawkish   qualms   fervid

jaunty   dudgeon

1. I wish to profess my _____ love for you as soon as you tell me your name.

2. I always look so _____ at the altar in my tuxedo.

3. It is so nice to meet you, but I am keeping my real thoughts to myself. I don't want you taking off in high _____.

4. I am looking for that special someone I can send _____ Hallmark cards to.

5. At first I had some _____ talking to you since you were sitting in the second stool down, with your drink in your left hand, I had just seen a red SUV, the wind was blowing from the south, and it is a Tuesday. But I am so glad I did!

simper   revelry   impetuous

contrition   acrimony

6. You are the kind of person who makes even people like me feel _____ enough to talk to strangers.

7. I don't need a partner in crime; I need a partner in _____.

8. I am looking for someone nonconfrontational since I am still reeling from the _____ of my last relationship. But I have resolved never to clean out a bank account again.

9. You look so cute when you _____ like that. I love women with an ambiguous self-image.

10. I just used a particularly potent laxative to spike the beer of the guy you were chatting with, and I am feeling a certain amount of _____ over this.

maudlin   copacetic   irascible

chagrin   irate

11. I come here in the evenings to hide from my _____ wife. How about you?

12. If I can just slip into that bar stool next to you, everything will be _____ for the next eight hours.

13. You know, I am the kind of girl to get _____ over just about the tiniest infraction.

14. For the record, I am not just sensitive, I am downright _____.

15. To my _____, I know I will never make enough money to keep you happy.

confection   apoplexy   compunction

precipitant   mollify

16. I am feeling _____; I just sold my stamp collection!

17. I used to _____ my pain with alcohol, food, and gambling. You look like a healthier alternative.

18. When I gaze into your eyes, I am not sure if it is love or _____ I feel.

19. And what _____ factory were you made in?

20. Your manicure is so flawless and your outfit so well accessorized that I had no _____ about marching straight up to you.

levity expiate saccharine

tempestuous ebullition

21. You have the most _____ eyes I have ever seen.

22. I can see that you are the kind of person to appreciate _____—want to read tomorrow's comics together?

23. I took one look at you and felt just like milk at _____.

24. Are you sure your _____ smile will not give me cavities? Well, no issue—I have a cute dentist.

25. Let me _____ my rudeness by buying you another drink.

[vo'·cab]
VITAMINS

PACK 2

AGAINST
AUTHORITY

THEME 1
Uniting and Conspiring

SIMILAR TO:

cabal	secret group, ring
collusion	cahoots, cooperation, conspiracy
complicity	conspiracy, agreement, partnership
coterie	group, company, alliance
phalanx	mass, throng, group

THEME 2
Resistance and Mutiny!

SIMILAR TO:

factious	divisive, hostile
recusant	dissenter, nonconformist
refractory	antagonistic, obstinate
restive	unruly, unyielding
sedition	rebellion, insurrection

THEME 3
Put Up Your Dukes!

SIMILAR TO:

bellicose	aggressive, combative, hostile
lambaste	attack, beat, denounce
petulant	irritable, ill-tempered
pugilism	boxing, fist-fighting
truculent	bad-tempered, violent, opposing

THEME 4
Surrender!

SIMILAR TO:

abdicate	give up, relinquish
acquiesce	agree, accept, accede
capitulate	give in, surrender, defer
kowtow	show deference, worship, grovel
succumb	surrender, yield, submit

THEME 5
Blistering Reprimands

SIMILAR TO:

upbraid	scold, reproach
berate	chew out, tongue-lash
castigate	punish, criticize harshly
rebuke	reprimand, repress
excoriate	chafe, censure, denounce

Uniting and Conspiring

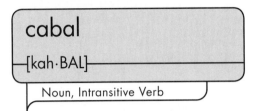

cabal
[kah·BAL]

Noun, Intransitive Verb

Noun
1. a small group of secret plotters united to promote their private views and interests by intrigue: "My initiatives were ultimately undermined by a cabal of naysayers."
2. the secret plots or schemes of such a group; a conspiracy

Intransitive Verb
3. to form a cabal; to plot; to conspire

ORIGIN
Approximately 1660; borrowed from French, *cabale*: secret group, intrigue; from Medieval Latin, *cabbala*; from postbiblical Hebrew, *qabbalah*: received teachings, tradition.

BONUS WORD   Synonym

camarilla: a secret clique that seeks power usually through intrigue

IN ACTION

"'There is no secret **cabal** of violent thugs in this movement,' she said in a voice quavering with emotion. 'There are people in this movement who are angry, and have a right to be, because the level of injustice in this world is so great.'"

Clyde Haberman. *"Even Grief Can't Stop This Protest,"*
New York Times (January 30, 2002).

"Slashdot's weekly polls give me even more opportunity for mischief. Like, a few weeks ago, they had people vote for Favorite Bot Weapon. I picked Pneumatic Jack Spikes, but they were beat out by Spinning Sledge/Armature and Backlash-style Saws. Furious that Pneumatic Jack Spikes lost, I suggested in IRC that the poll's voting was rigged, calling it 'the product of a vast conspiracy by a secret **cabal** of BeOS users.' You better believe that got a reaction!"

Nate Orenstam. "Who Says Java Programmers Don't Have a Sense of Humor?" Onion.com.

collusion

[kah·LOO·zhahn]

Noun

1. a secret agreement and cooperation for a fraudulent or deceitful purpose; deceit; fraud; conspiracy: "I began to suspect collusion when I noticed that my employees had been scheduling team meetings at times they knew I would not be available."
2. (as in law) an agreement between two or more persons to defraud another person of his or her rights or to obtain something illegally

ORIGIN
Approximately 1389; from Latin, *colludere*: to collude (*col*: together + *ludere*: to play, from *ludus*: game).

BONUS WORD Antonym

discord: lack of agreement or harmony

IN ACTION

"Of course, even if the game isn't the out-and-out destruction of Saudi Arabia, the existence of tacit U.S.-Russian cooperation can't be ruled out. If it suits the Russians to produce more oil at the moment, it also suits the recession-stricken United States to buy oil at lower prices. In the long term, the United States is quite keen, for political reasons, to reduce its dependency on Middle Eastern oil. Russia is equally keen, for political reasons, to make everyone more dependent on Russia. Those who believe that there is U.S.-Russian **collusion** to increase oil exports from Russia and other ex-Soviet nations to the West can also point to the Caspian Pipeline Consortium, the first successful Russian-Western-Kazakh pipeline venture, which just happens to kick in this month."

Anne Applebaum. *"Russia, Oil, and Conspiracy Theories,"* Slate.com *(November 27, 2001)*.

complicity

{kahm·PLIS·i·tee}

Noun

1. involvement as an accomplice in a crime or questionable act: "I swore that it wasn't my idea, and that much was true, but the uncertain tone of my voice betrayed my complicity."

ORIGIN

Approximately 1656; borrowed from French, *complicite*; from Late Latin, *complicem*, accusative of *complex*: partner; from Latin, *complicare*: to fold together.

BONUS WORD Origin

complacent: contented to a fault

IN ACTION

"Moments later, Lennon's name appeared fluidly amid the thorny Mediterranean babble. Our translator held up his hand, demanding full silence, listened a moment or two, then cocked his raised hand like a gun and said, simply, 'Shot.' No more details were forthcoming. The group, which regarded this as an unsatisfactory nugget of information, proceeded to elaborate a number of conspiracy theories that would have impressed Kennedy assassination investigator Jim Garrison. These all seemed strangely plausible to me at the time, including one involving the **complicity** of the recently elected Ronald Reagan."

Wayne Curtis. "Coping in the Absence of News," National Geographic Traveler (September/October 1994).

"Though dozens of arrests were made in the bombings, no one has been convicted of direct **complicity**. Moreover, the bombings laid the groundwork for the furious military campaign against Chechnya and for the political rise of Mr. Putin, then the prime minister, whose relentless prosecution of the war garnered a surge of popular support that propelled him into the presidency."

Patrick Tyler. "Russian Says Kremlin Faked 'Terror Attacks,'" New York Times (February 1, 2002).

coterie

[KO·tah·ree, ko'·tah·REE]

Noun

1. a circle of people who meet familiarly or who associate with one another closely; a clique: "It never looks good for any candidate when his coterie of supporters consists primarily of friends and family."

ORIGIN

Approximately 1738; borrowed from French, *coterie*: circle of acquaintances; from Middle French, *coterie*: an association of tenant-farmers; from Old French, *cotier*: cottager, from *cote*: hut, cottage.

BONUS WORD   Sound

causerie: light informal conversation for social occasions

IN ACTION

"Kerkorian, a self-made mogul with an estimated worth of $6.4 billion, argued in the court papers that the support requested by his ex-wife would benefit the mother not the child, who turns four in March.

"'It is quite reasonable to believe that Kira, would be far happier eating a Happy Meal at McDonald's . . . than she would be sitting at an upscale, adult restaurant with a **coterie** of nannies,' or going to Disneyland rather than 'taking a long, boring plane trip to Paris,' the court papers said."

"Kerkorian Says Not Girl's Dad in Megabucks Battle,"
CNN.com *(February 1, 2002).*

"President Bush delighted an intimate gathering of White House dinner guests Monday, regaling the **coterie** of dignitaries, artists, and friends with a spirited, off-the-cuff discussion of the Roman poet Virgil's lesser-known works."

"Bush Regales Dinner Guests with Impromptu Oratory on Virgil's Minor Works," Onion.com (April 18, 2001).

phalanx
[FAY·langks, FAL·angks]

Noun

1. a body of people formed in close array or distinguished for firmness of union: "The faculty presented itself as a united phalanx to win important budget changes that would bring their school's program into the modern age."
2. a body of heavily armed infantry formed in ranks and files close and deep, carrying overlapping shields and long spears

ORIGIN
Approximately 1553; borrowed from Latin, *phalanx*; from Greek, *phalanx* (from *phalangos*): battle formation, finger or toe bone, log, or wooden roller.

BONUS WORD   Sound

pharynx: the passage to the stomach and lungs

larynx: a cartilaginous structure at the top of the trachea

IN ACTION

"A party for participants at the New York Stock Exchange—the citadel of global capitalism—went into the early hours Sunday, with 2,000 forum participants attending the 'Gala-Soiree.'

"Most partygoers arrived by bus under police escort. A **phalanx** of police blocked the surrounding area to keep anti-globalization protesters away."

"World Forum Focuses on Trouble Spots,"
Associated Press (February 3, 2002).

"'We're doing everything we can to help it survive, but it's an uphill battle,' says Ewald Falk, the Swiss chef at Jakarta's Oasis Restaurant, one of the few in Indonesia still featuring the meal, which is typically served by up to 15 waitresses.

"In Indonesian restaurants in the Netherlands, South Africa and elsewhere, Rijstafel is still popular, but it is usually laid out as a buffet and without the **phalanx** of waiters."

"Few Seats Left: Indonesia's 'Rice Table':
A Dutch Colonial Showpiece, Now Hard to Find,"
CNN.com (January 27, 2002).

"Shortly after his announcement, Clinton served as Grand Marshal of an immense triumphal procession down Pennsylvania Avenue. The procession . . . featured a display of Exocet missiles; several Stealth bombers flying in formation; a **phalanx** of prominent military leaders, senators and bureaucrats; dancers, fire-eaters and contortionists; two rare Siberian white tigers, who pulled a gilded coach containing the current Miss America, Nicole Johnson; a battalion of bull elephants; and Barbra Streisand."

"Congress Approves $4 Billion for Bread, Circuses,"
Onion.com (August 18, 1999).

Resistance and Mutiny!

factious

recusant

refractory

restive

sedition

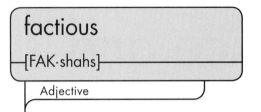

factious

[FAK·shahs]

Adjective

1. of, related to, caused by, or characterized by conflict within a group: "The power vacuum created by Kurt's departure led to factious quarrels among the employees."
2. given to or liable to cause conflict within a group; seditious

ORIGIN

Approximately 1532; from Latin, *factiosus*, from *factionem*: faction, literally, a doing, from *facere*: to do.

BONUS WORD   Sound

fictitious: formed or conceived by the imagination

IN ACTION

"'There hasn't been a day this year when someone from the media or another school district hasn't called wanting to talk about it,' sighs Durtan, who has headed the Colonial district, just outside Philadelphia, for more than 11 years. 'The pressure here has been tremendous.'

"But perhaps not surprising. When the Colonial school board voted earlier this year to pay individual teachers annual bonuses based upon their students' standardized student test scores, the prosperous suburban district became the first in the country to do so. It also became a real-life test case for an idea that has proven to be enormously **factious**."

Scott LaFee. "Linking Teacher to Student Scores,"
School Administrator *(October 2000).*

recusant

[REK·yah·zahnt, ri·KYOO·zahnt]

Noun

1. an English Roman Catholic who refused to attend services of the Church of England between the sixteenth and eighteenth centuries and in so doing committed a statutory offense
2. one who refuses to accept or obey established authority; a nonconformist: "Steve is an unabashed recusant with time on his hands, which means that our neighborhood can count on new, politically charged leaflets every two weeks."

ORIGIN

Approximately 1553; from Latin, *recusant-*, *recusans*, present participle of *recusare*: to refuse (*re-* + *causari*: to give a reason, from *causa*: cause, reason).

BONUS WORD   Synonym

recalcitrant: marked by stubborn resistance to and defiance of authority or guidance

IN ACTION

"Most important of all Charles liked the style of the Catholics who surrounded his wife. He was, for instance, especially fond of Father George Con, Panzani's successor as papal agent. The younger son of a Scots noble, Con was witty, a good conversationalist, and highly charming. He knew how to make himself agreeable. When he was presented to the queen on his arrival in England in 1636,

he gave her a cross, a present from the pope, that
she immediately hung about her neck. To the king
he gave paintings and sculptures, and would talk
intelligently about the works of leading European
artists for hours. . . . Yet Con's influence over the king
remained social rather than political or religious. He
might persuade Charles to free a **recusant** or two,
restore mass paraphernalia confiscated in Norwich, or
the patrimony of an heir who had gone over to Rome,
but Con never had a chance of achieving his chief
goal, the conversion of the king and his kingdom."

Charles Carlton. Charles I:
The Personal Monarch *(1995).*

"One such case is that of Dorothy Wadham, entrusted
by her husband Nicholas Wadham on his deathbed
in 1609 with carrying through his ill-formulated
design for the foundation of a college at Oxford. The
responsibility for the actual foundation fell entirely on
Dorothy, and both husband and wife were officially
designated as 'founders'.

". . . For the remaining five years of Dorothy's life
she had to withstand fierce lobbying for positions
at the college, approve amendments to the statutes
and witness continued legal battles about the
college estates. In all this she had to contend with
more disadvantages than that of gender. She was
seventy-four years old at the time of Nicholas's
death, unable to travel from her homes in Somerset
and Devon. All business had to be transacted by
letter, or, more commonly, through her agents. The
Catholic sympathies of the Wadhams were a further
complication; they came close to, although ultimately
escaping, conviction as **recusants**; yet inevitably
their college was a pillar of the established church,

and its foundation involved securing the active cooperation of ecclesiastical dignitaries including two successive Archbishops of Canterbury and the Calvinistically inclined Bishop of Bath and Wells."

C. S. L. Davies. "A Woman in the Public Sphere: Dorothy Wadham and the Foundation of Wadham College, Oxford," English Historical Review (September 2003). Reprinted by permission of Oxford University Press.

refractory

[ri·FRAK·tah·ree]

Adjective, Noun

Adjective
1. resistant to authority or control; stubborn; unmanageable: "Gilbert tried to appease his refractory children by patiently explaining all of his requests."
2. resistant to heat, and therefore difficult to melt or work
3. resistant to medical treatment: "a refractory case of acne"

Noun
4. a refractory person
5. material with a very high melting point—for example, the clay used to line furnaces

ORIGIN
Approximately 1606; alteration of *refractarie, refractary*; borrowed from Latin, *refractarius*: obstinate, from *refract-*, past participle stem of *refringere*: to break up.

BONUS WORD   Antonym

complaisant: showing a cheerful willingness to do favors

IN ACTION

"Miss Huskisson, like so many of the female denizens of the Middle West, was tall and blonde and constructed on substantial lines. She was a girl whose appearance suggested the old homestead and fried pancakes and pop coming home to dinner after the morning's ploughing. Even her bobbed hair did not altogether destroy this impression. She looked big and strong and healthy, and her lungs were obviously good. She attacked the verse of the song with something of the vigour and breadth of treatment with which in other days she had reasoned with **refractory** mules. Her diction was the diction of one trained to call the cattle home in the teeth of Western hurricanes. Whether you wanted to or not, you heard every word."

P. G. Wodehouse. English-American novelist and humorist. *From* The Indiscretions of Archie *(1921).*

restive

[RES·tiv]

Adjective

1. impatient under restriction, opposition, or delay: "While we were relaxing in Bermuda, our beagle was stuck at the kennel, where he was growing restive and contemplating his revenge."
2. stubbornly resisting control
3. refusing to move or be guided—usually said of an animal, such as a horse

ORIGIN

Approximately 1410; from Latin, *restare*: to keep back
(*re-* + *stare*: to stand).

BONUS WORD Origin

restless: unable to relax or be still

IN ACTION

"Saddam's capture is likely to prove a heavy blow to
any of his followers planning terrorist strikes. This
may well weaken the argument of those who oppose
SDF participation in Iraq reconstruction for reasons
of safety. However, so long as al-Qaida members
are at large and the Iraqi people remain **restive**
and unhappy because of safety concerns and high
unemployment, there will be no immediate end to
terrorist attacks. There may be times when the SDF
troops will not only be unable to carry out their
humanitarian relief work, but be forced to remain in
defensive positions for their own safety."

Masayuki Yamauchi. "Point of View: Japan
Should Lead Peace Coalition for Iraq,"
Asahi Shimbun (January 3, 2004).

"When reporters travel to the **restive** areas of the
so-called Sunni Triangle north and west of Baghdad,
a swath that formed the power base of the ousted
government, their cars are routinely chased by
gunmen and frequently fired upon. Reporters have
also been attacked by angry crowds when covering
suicide bombings."

Neela Banerjee. "Hazardous Assignments Killed 36
Journalists in '03," New York Times (January 3, 2004).

sedition

[si·DISH·ahn]

Noun

1. action or language inciting discontent or rebellion against government authority: "The newly formed opposition group was concerned that their actions would be perceived as sedition."
2. insurrection; rebellion; tumult

ORIGIN

Approximately 1350; borrowed directly from Latin, *seditionem*: civil disorder, literally, a going apart, from *sed-*, variant of *se-*: apart + *itio*: act of going, from *it-*, past participle of *ire*: to go.

BONUS WORD   Synonym

perfidy: an act of deliberate betrayal

IN ACTION

"Musharraf has won plaudits abroad for Pakistan's roundup of about 500 al Qaeda fugitives since Sept. 11, 2001, but his record at home—especially when it comes to restoring democracy—is less clear. More than four years after he seized power in a bloodless coup, pledging 'real democracy' in place of corrupt civilian rule, democratic freedoms in this volatile, nuclear-armed and mostly Muslim nation of 150 million remain tenuous and in some areas may even be in retreat, according to human rights monitors, opposition politicians and many ordinary Pakistanis.

"They cite the arrest on **sedition** charges this fall of a leading opposition lawmaker, Javed Hashmi, and note a recent uptick in arrests and harassment of journalists. They also point to Musharraf's continuing efforts to manipulate the country's constitution and parliament—elected last year in a contest that European Union observers described as having suffered from 'serious flaws'—to ensure that the army retains ultimate power."

John Lancaster. "Musharraf's 'Real Democracy' Still Elusive in Pakistan," Washington Post *(December 25, 2003).*

"A native Taiwanese, he had studied law in Japan and France. In the early 1960s he wrote a manifesto calling for the independence of Taiwan. In Peng's view, Taiwan should be independent of Chinese rule, and should establish a democratic state.

"Chiang's government charged him with **sedition** and put him under house arrest. In the late 1960s it appeared that he might be secretly executed."

Richard C. Kagan. "Human Rights Veteran Looks Back," Taipei Times *(January 2, 2004).*

Put Up Your Dukes!

THEME 3

bellicose

lambaste

petulant

pugilism

truculent

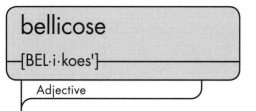

bellicose

[BEL·i·koes']

Adjective

1. having or showing a warlike disposition; pugnacious: "Many of the fringe political groups in Alan's area carried bellicose, antiestablishment agendas that he found alienating."

ORIGIN

Probably before 1425; borrowed, perhaps through influence of Italian, *bellicoso*, from Latin, *bellicosus*, from *bellicus*: of war, from *bellum*: war.

BONUS WORD   Origin

belligerent: characteristic of an enemy or one eager to fight

IN ACTION

"I put the question to Kerr: Why did [the GE] Work-Out keep its momentum while other [corporate] change programs were losing theirs?

"He offered a couple of explanations: Welch's insistence—the man has, we all know, a persuasive style—and the way Work-Outs energize people and identify really stupid organizational tics, which anyone can agree must go. Kerr talked mostly about two things that were banned from Work-Outs: blaming and complaining. At GE, a company of strong, sometimes arrogant bosses and big, sometimes **bellicose** unions, sticking a finger in your co-worker's eye had become almost a loved tradition. That was forbidden in a Work-Out. You could call a rule stupid, but not a ruler."

Thomas A. Stewart. "Making Change Stick," Business 2.0
(August 23, 2002), ©2002 Time Inc. All rights reserved.

"What happens now that fundamentalists have such a great deal of support in the Islamic world and many appear to tacitly support terrorist action?

"These are all bad religions. In a hostile world, they play down the compassionate ethos of religion and accelerate the more **bellicose** elements of religion. When you have bad religion, like bad art or bad sex, it can easily tip over into nihilism and tip into things like what happened on Sept. 11."

Max Garrone. "Fundamental Problems: Religious Writer Karen Armstrong Explains Why Muslim Nations Have Difficulty with Democracy and the Qualities That All Forms of Fundamentalism Share," Salon.com (October 22, 2001).

lambaste

[lam·BAYST, lam·BAST]

Transitive Verb

1. to beat, thrash, or assault
2. to scold or criticize severely; to censure; to berate: "I knew that I was leaving work a little early, but I wasn't expecting Carol to lambaste me for it."

ORIGIN
Approximately 1637; probably formed from English, *lam*: to beat soundly + *baste*: to thrash; *lam* probably Scandinavian in origin.

BONUS WORD   Sound

bombast: pompous or pretentious talk or writing

IN ACTION

"'Why aren't you enthusiastic?' he asked. 'I thought you were such dead nuts on marriage.'

"Birkin lifted his shoulders.

"'One might as well be dead nuts on noses. There are all sorts of noses, snub and otherwise—'

"Gerald laughed.

"'And all sorts of marriage, also snub and otherwise?' he said.

"'That's it.'

"'And you think if I marry, it will be snub?' asked Gerald quizzically, his head a little on one side.

"Birkin laughed quickly.

"'How do I know what it will be!' he said. 'Don't **lambaste** me with my own parallels—'

"Gerald pondered a while.

"'But I should like to know your opinion, exactly,' he said.

"'On your marriage?—or marrying? Why should you want my opinion? I've got no opinions. I'm not interested in legal marriage, one way or another. It's a mere question of convenience.'"

"Still Gerald watched him closely.

"'More than that, I think,' he said seriously. 'However you may be bored by the ethics of marriage, yet really to marry, in one's own personal case, is something critical, final—'

"'You mean there is something final in going to the registrar with a woman?'

"'If you're coming back with her, I do,' said Gerald. 'It is in some way irrevocable.'"

D. H. Lawrence (1885–1930). English author.
"Marriage or Not," Women in Love (1921).

petulant

[PECH·ah·lahnt]

Adjective

1. capriciously ill-tempered or peevish
2. insolent or contemptuous in speech or behavior: "We timidly approached the bus driver—a petulant man who had already shown a great mastery of four-letter words—to request our stop."

ORIGIN

Approximately 1599; borrowed from Middle French, *petulant*, or directly from Latin, *petulantem*: wanton, insolent (nominative *petulans*), from the root of *petere*: to rush at, to seek.

BONUS WORD   Synonym

querulous: habitually complaining

IN ACTION

"She's always singing about boys, although not very lustily. Her lyrics are full of chaste entreaties and **petulant** rebuffs: 'I like you the way you are.' 'Why'd you kiss me on the mouth?' 'If you're trying to turn me into someone else, it's easy to see I'm not down with that.'

"There are love songs even an 8-year-old could understand and appreciate. And that's precisely why they're good, and sometimes great."

> Kelefa Sanneh. "This Is for You, Mom and Dad"
> (music review: Avril Lavigne), New York Times
> (April 12, 2003)

"The parent who loves his child dearly but asks for nothing in return might qualify as a saint, but he will not qualify as a parent. For a child who can claim love without meeting any of the obligations of love will be a self-centered child and many such children have grown up in our time to become **petulant** lovers and sullen marriage partners because the promise of unconditional love has not been fulfilled."

Selma H. Fraiberg. Twentieth-century U.S. child psychoanalyst. The Magic Years (1959).

pugilism

[PYOO·jah·liz'·ahm]

Noun

1. the skill, practice, or sport of fighting with fists; boxing: "Several minutes into the debate the personal insults began to fly, and from then on, all contentions were going to be settled through pugilism."

ORIGIN

Approximately 1791; from Latin, *pugil*: boxer, related to *pugnus*: fist + English suffix *-ism*: action, practice.

BONUS WORD Origin

pugnacious: inclined to fight or be aggressive

IN ACTION

"An examination of the narratives of each workplace fatality provides insight into the activities that athletes were performing at the time of their fatal injury. Just over a third (37.4 percent) of the deceased were performing a task associated with automobile or motorcycle racing (such as driving or flagging) when they were killed. Decedents who were participating in water activities (diving, swimming, and boating) accounted for just less than one-quarter (23.3 percent) of the fatalities. In addition, 16 percent of the athletes were killed working with horses or bulls, and about 6 percent were killed in some form of **pugilism** such as boxing, kickboxing, or wrestling."

U.S. Bureau of Labor Statistics. "Fatalities Among Athletes," Monthly Labor Review (August 2004).

truculent

[TRUK·yah·lahnt]

Adjective

1. inclined to fight
2. expressing bitter or scathingly harsh opposition: "Though his overall frustration remained, Khalid regretted some of the things he had said to his little brother during the truculent monologue."
3. displaying, or inclined to display, great anger, aggression, or destructiveness; ruthless; fierce

ORIGIN

Approximately 1540; borrowed from Latin, *truculentus*: fierce, savage, from *trux*: fierce, savage, wild (genitive *trucis*); possibly akin to Middle Irish, *tru*: doomed person.

BONUS WORD Antonym

pacifistic: opposed to war

IN ACTION

"'We are changing everything,' Aeroflot's marketing director, Tatyana A. Zotova, said. . . .

"All well and good, veteran fliers might say, but for one thing: behind the paint and designer outfits and fancy silverware, there remains Aeroflot. This is, after all, the airline whose logo remains a winged hammer and sickle; the carrier whose late-1990's advertising slogan, a not so implicit apology for its **truculent** service, was 'We don't smile, because we're serious about making you happy.'"

Michael Wines. "Aeroflot Declares End to Its Cold
War on Fliers," New York Times (April 5, 2003).

"When writers meet they are **truculent**, indifferent, or over-polite. Then comes the inevitable moment. A shows B that he has read something of B's. Will B show A? If not, then A hates B, if yes, then all is well. The only other way for writers to meet is to share a quick pee over a common lamp-post."

Cyril Connolly (1903–74). British critic. "The Journal
of Cyril Connolly 1928–1937," Journal and Memoir,
by David Pryce-Jones (1983).

Earth's a howling wilderness,
Truculent with fraud and force.

Ralph Waldo Emerson (1803–82). U.S. essayist, poet,
and philosopher. "Berrying," Poems (1847).

Surrender!

THEME 4

abdicate

acquiesce

capitulate

kowtow

succumb

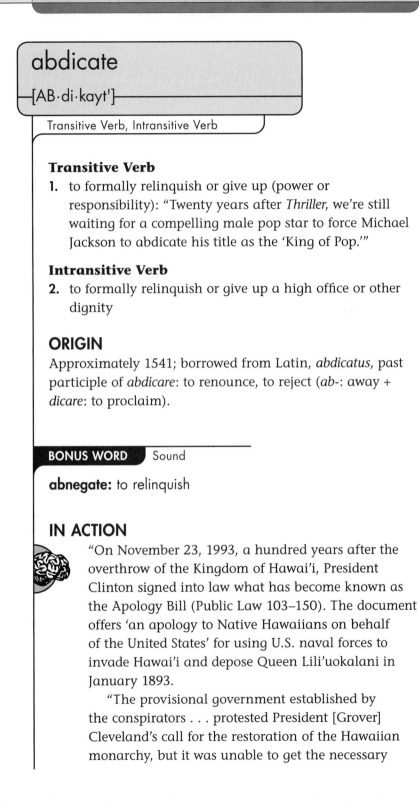

abdicate

[AB·di·kayt']

Transitive Verb, Intransitive Verb

Transitive Verb

1. to formally relinquish or give up (power or responsibility): "Twenty years after *Thriller*, we're still waiting for a compelling male pop star to force Michael Jackson to abdicate his title as the 'King of Pop.'"

Intransitive Verb

2. to formally relinquish or give up a high office or other dignity

ORIGIN

Approximately 1541; borrowed from Latin, *abdicatus*, past participle of *abdicare*: to renounce, to reject (*ab-*: away + *dicare*: to proclaim).

BONUS WORD   Sound

abnegate: to relinquish

IN ACTION

"On November 23, 1993, a hundred years after the overthrow of the Kingdom of Hawai'i, President Clinton signed into law what has become known as the Apology Bill (Public Law 103–150). The document offers 'an apology to Native Hawaiians on behalf of the United States' for using U.S. naval forces to invade Hawai'i and depose Queen Lili'uokalani in January 1893.

"The provisional government established by the conspirators . . . protested President [Grover] Cleveland's call for the restoration of the Hawaiian monarchy, but it was unable to get the necessary support from two-thirds of the Senate to ratify a treaty of annexation. On July 4, 1894, the new Hawaiian government declared itself the Republic of Hawai'i and in January of the following year forced Queen Lili'uokalani, who had been imprisoned in her palace, to officially **abdicate** her throne."

Cate Lineberry. "Hawaii: Did You Know?" National Geographic (December 2002).

"Belgian Cardinal Godfried Danneels suggested in a recent magazine interview that he thought ailing popes in the future would **abdicate**, because there are currently no provisions in church law to remove an incapacitated pontiff. He later stressed that such a decision must be the prerogative of the pope and not something imposed on him."

Nicole Winfield. "Pope Asks Cardinals to Pray for Him," Associated Press (October 18, 2003).

acquiesce

[ak'·wee·ES]

Intransitive Verb

1. to accept or comply passively or through lack of objection—usually followed by *in*: "I may be your boss, but I need your honest feedback, so please don't acquiesce in matters that you feel strongly about."

ORIGIN

Approximately 1620; borrowed from French, *acquiescer*; from Latin, *acquiescere*: to remain at rest (*ac-*: to + *quiescere*: to become quiet, to rest).

BONUS WORD Origin

quiescent: being quiet, still, or inactive

IN ACTION

"When a player as savvy as Bryant says he wants to test free agency, it's not an academic pursuit. He wants to see what other teams are interested and what he can cook up somewhere else. A lot of folks think that somewhere else is Memphis, where Jerry West, whom Bryant admires greatly, runs the show. But of course the field is going to expand. Who wouldn't move heaven and earth to try to get Bryant? Presuming he is free to play after his trial, Bryant can go anywhere he wants; maybe a new start will be exactly what he needs. He's got three championship rings, so it's not like he needs another right away to validate his career. Any team he's on is an instant contender, just the way Michael Jordan made any team an instant contender when he was 25 years old. And Kobe, just 25, can play someplace where he doesn't have to **acquiesce** to Shaq's wishes. What, Kobe couldn't go to Phoenix or Atlanta? Kobe couldn't go someplace and team up with the suddenly available Pat Riley?

"And then, Shaq and Kobe will have what each claims he wants, no matter that neither has won a championship without the other."

Michael Wilbon. "Ah, the Soap Opera That Is the Lakers," Washington Post (October 28, 2003).

"I make this direct statement to the American people that there is far less chance of the United States getting into war, if we do all we can now to support the nations defending themselves against attack by the Axis than if we **acquiesce** in their defeat, submit tamely to an Axis victory, and wait our turn to be the object of attack in another war later on."

Franklin D. Roosevelt (1882–1945). U.S. president.
[Quoted in] Franklin D. Roosevelt and American
Foreign Policy, 1932–1945, by Robert Dallek (1979).

capitulate

[kah·PICH·ah·layt']

Intransitive Verb

1. to surrender under agreed-upon conditions: "The court would have forgiven half of his parking tickets if Travis had agreed to drop his ridiculous disputes—but he wouldn't capitulate."
2. to cease resisting; to give in; to acquiesce

ORIGIN

Approximately 1580; back formation of *capitulation*; borrowed from Medieval Latin, *capitulatus*, past participle of *capitulare*: to arrange in chapters; from Latin, *capitulum*: chapter, section, diminutive of *caput*: head (genitive *capitis*).

BONUS WORD   Origin

capitation: a fixed amount per person tax

IN ACTION

"Powerful, yes, that is the word that I constantly rolled on my tongue, I dreamed of absolute power, the kind that forces others to kneel, that forces the enemy to **capitulate**, finally converting him, and the more the enemy is blind, cruel, sure of himself, buried in his conviction, the more his admission proclaims the royalty of he who has brought on his defeat."

Albert Camus (1913–60). French-Algerian novelist, dramatist, and philosopher. "The Renegade, or a Confused Spirit," Exile and the Kingdom (1957).

"Truman had served as an Artillery Officer in France during World War I and, prior to becoming President, was not aware of the 'Manhattan Project' and its Atom Bomb. His advisors estimated the war could be shortened by a year and that 1 million Allied casualties, 500,000 of them American lives, could be saved if the Atomic Bomb was used on Japan. He decided that enough American blood had been spilled in trying to reestablish the peace that Japan had shattered.

"At approximately 9:15 A.M. on August 6, 1945, after repeated warnings for Japan to surrender, the Atomic Bomb was dropped on Hiroshima. In spite of the horrific carnage and destruction that resulted Japan did not **capitulate**. On August 9, 1945, another Atomic Bomb was dropped on Nagasaki. Japan sued for peace the next day and the formal surrender papers were signed, on the deck of the Battleship U.S.S. Missouri, on September 2, 1945. Peace had been restored."

Gary Groman. Editorial, "Would Truman Apologize for Hiroshima and Nagasaki?" Branson Courier (November 7, 2003).

kowtow

[kou·TOU, KOU·tou']

Intransitive Verb, Noun

Intransitive Verb
1. to show respect, awe, or submission by kneeling and touching the forehead to the ground, as formerly done in China
2. to show submissive deference, usually to someone in a position of authority; to fawn: "We were all embarrassed at the Christmas party watching our CEO kowtow to the anchorwoman of channel seven's 'Breaking News from Your Backyard.'"

Noun
3. the act of kneeling and touching the forehead to the ground to show respect, awe, or submission
4. an extremely submissive or slavish act, usually directed toward someone in a position of authority

ORIGIN
Approximately 1804; borrowed from Chinese (Mandarin), *k'o-t'ou*: literally, knock the head (*k'o*: to knock + *t'ou*: head).

BONUS WORD   Synonym

prostrate: lying face down

IN ACTION

"Patriotism is an odd thing, no more than half of which dwells in the conscious mind. Chinese patriotism is a particularly knotty variety, all tangled up with racial pride and historical resentments. The very concept of a nation, as it has been understood in the West since the Middle Ages, did not take hold in China until well into the 20th century.

In imperial times, the common term used by the Chinese to refer to their country was tianxia—'all under heaven.' The imperial Chinese were of course aware of the existence of foreigners, but under the official ideology, all non-Chinese were mere savages, whose proper relationship to the Dragon Throne was one of subservient admiration. This applied to the British and French just as much as to Tibetans or Mongolians; that is why Lord Macartney, sent by Britain as an ambassador in 1793, was expected to **kowtow** to the Emperor. (He refused, and after much diplomatic wrangling, a compromise was struck.)"

John Derbyshire. "Wife to a Footnote:
The Passing of Madame Chiang Kaishek,"
National Review Online (October 28, 2003).

succumb

[sah·KUM]

Intransitive Verb

1. to yield to overpowering force or desire; to submit: "Stella knew she would eventually succumb to market forces and get a paying job, but in the meantime, she planned to spend her days painting."
2. to be fatally overwhelmed

ORIGIN

Approximately 1604; borrowed from Middle French, *succomber*, and directly from Latin, *succumbere*: to submit, to lie under (*sub-*: down + *-cumbere*: to lie down, related to *cubare*: to lie down).

BONUS WORD   Antonym

oppugn: to challenge, oppose, or fight

IN ACTION

"'I think best when I'm drawing,' [film director Tim] Burton said as he folded himself into a large red velvet sofa. 'I always loved drawing, but that's true of all kids. When children draw, they all draw the same. There's a certain kind of passion that all kids share. And then it gets beaten out of them. At that point, most people stop drawing. I almost **succumbed** to the idea that I couldn't draw. I wasn't that good at life drawing, and I almost gave up. But I thought, I don't care if I can't draw in this traditional way. To punch through, that was what saved me. It was a catharsis. I realized that a kind of dark, dramatic, depressed, sad, moody thing was kind of healthy.'"

Lynn Hirschberg. "Drawn to Narrative,"
New York Times (November 9, 2003).

"I do not blame you if you are angry with me. After all, my torrid affair with Miss Bernadette Fiske was highly publicized, and after my wife passed away in 1937, I had pledged my eternal love to you and only you. So why, you must be asking in your tearful anguish, did I **succumb** to the charms of another woman?"

T. Herman Zweibel. [From the deathbed of T. Herman
Zweibel, the Zweibel Estate, to Miss Lillian Gish,
Hollywood, California.] "Do Not Be Cross with Me,
Sweet Lillian," Onion (June 8, 2000).

Blistering Reprimands

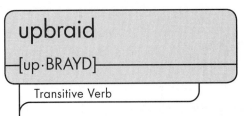

upbraid

[up·BRAYD]

Transitive Verb

1. to reproach or scold severely; to rebuke: "My crazy uncle took several hours every day to water, fertilize, trim, and upbraid any house plant not growing perfectly."

ORIGIN

Approximately 1150; from Old English, *upbregdan*: to bring forward as a ground for censure (*up-*: up + *bregdan*: to move quickly, to snatch, to intertwine, to braid).

BONUS WORD Related

echelon: level in hierarchy

IN ACTION

"He felt that it would be dull times in Dublin, when they should have no usurping government to abuse, no Saxon Parliament to **upbraid**, no English laws to ridicule, and no Established Church to curse."

Anthony Trollope (1815–82). English novelist.
The Kellys and the O'Kellys (1848)

"The case of Khidhir Hamza, however, illuminates how information can become propaganda. Hamza is a nuclear scientist who served as a senior administrator in Saddam's nuclear-weapons program during the nineteen-eighties. He defected from Iraq in 1994. He was at first spurned by the C.I.A., which thought he knew little of interest. In 1997, he was asked to join the Institute for Science and International Security, an organization in Washington run by David Albright, a former nuclear-weapons inspector. When Hamza first started working with him, Albright told me, his information seemed reliable. In 1998, Hamza even helped debunk an inflated story offered by another defector, just as Chalabi was trying to drum up support for the Iraq Liberation Act. 'We saw the claws of Chalabi then,' Albright said. Someone from the I.N.C., he said, called to **upbraid** Hamza, telling him that he had undercut the cause of liberating Iraq. 'Hamza was shaken, and said he'd never do that again,' Albright told me."

Jane Mayer. "The Manipulator: Ahmad Chalabi Pushed a Tainted Case for War. Can He Survive the Occupation?" New Yorker (June 7, 2004)..

berate

[bi·RAYT]

Transitive Verb

1. to scold vehemently and at length: "If we didn't hold on to the bat after every swing, coach would berate us in the dugout until we couldn't think of anything else."

ORIGIN
Approximately 1548; formed in English from *be-*: thoroughly + *rate*: to scold.

BONUS WORD Antonym

adulate: to flatter excessively

IN ACTION

"Dr. Laura writes of the 'avalanche of expressed pain' that she hears from male listeners saddled with 'hostile, dismissive or undermining' wives who nag, **berate** and ignore them, and who top it all off by dressing, as one henpecked husband puts it in her book, 'like Eskimos.'"

> Judith Warner. "Unhappily Married: Post-Boomer Do-It-All Dads," New York Times (June 21, 2004).

"I was between 10 and 12 years old. We always cleaned on Saturday morning. My job was to dust. While dusting my parents' bedroom, I found some change on my Dad's bedside table. No one was around, so I put it in my pocket. A short while later, my mother told my older sister to get the change from Dad's bedside table and go to the store with her. . . . The money wasn't there and, though I tried to deny it, my mother soon knew that not only had I taken the money, but tried to lie about it.

"When Dad came home they talked a few minutes and, then, he walked into the living room, sat down, and called me over to him. He didn't spank me; he didn't harangue me or **berate** me. He sat me on his lap and, with a quiet voice, he told me how awful he felt that I had taken something that wasn't mine and, even worse, lied about it. . . . To this day (I am now 65), I remember him looking me straight in the eye, telling me how sad he was about what I had done, and all the while tears kept running down his face."

> William R. Wineke. [Excerpt by Margaret Hollenberger.] "Dad Always Said . . .," Wisconsin State Journal (June 19, 2004).

castigate

[KAS·ti·gayt']

Transitive Verb

1. to punish severely: "The company policy does not allow a manager to castigate an employee for infractions that are accidental or well-intended."
2. to criticize severely; to chastise

ORIGIN

Approximately 1607; borrowed from Latin, *castigatus*, past participle of *castigare*: to correct, to chastise (*castus*: pure, chaste + *-ate*: to cause to be).

BONUS WORD   Antonym

exalt: to raise in rank, character, or status

IN ACTION

"'We are pleading with the American people to, please, not to **castigate** the entire community for the act of a few,' said Assaf."

Catherine Jun. "N.J. Muslims, Arabs Condemn Beheading," New Jersey Star-Ledger (June 20, 2004).

"The head of the Senate Committee on Homeland Security and Governmental Affairs, Republican Senator Susan Collins, called the homeland security department's performance 'late, uncertain and ineffective'.

"The top Democrat on the committee, Senator Joseph Lieberman, **castigated** [U.S. Homeland Security chief] Mr Chertoff for his decision to attend a bird flu conference in Atlanta the day after the

hurricane hit—instead of heading straight to
New Orleans."

"Chertoff Castigated *over Katrina,"* BBC News online
(February 15, 2006).

rebuke
[ri·BYOOK]

Transitive Verb, Noun

Transitive Verb
1. to criticize sharply and summarily; to reprove; to
   reprimand: "Leonard was quick to rebuke his daughter's
   proposal, but only because it hadn't been his idea."
2. to check, silence, or put down

Noun
3. a direct and pointed reproof; a reprimand

ORIGIN
Approximately 1330; borrowed from Anglo-French, *rebuker*;
from Old French, *rebuchier* (*re-*: back + *buschier*: to strike, to
chop wood, from *buche, busche*: wood, log).

BONUS WORD   Continuum

LESS EXTREME . . .   **. . . MORE EXTREME**
rebuke   ⟶   rebuff

rebuff: to reject outright and bluntly

IN ACTION

"In April 1998, Hawthorne tried to remove that
shadow by writing a letter to People for the Ethical
Treatment of Animals. ('To whom it may concern: I'm
coordinating a multimillion-dollar canine-cloning

project.') Each Missyplicity surgery carries the risk of death. Still, he wanted the animal-rights group to understand that he was 'designing this project to a very high bioethical standard, involving not just the physical well-being of all animals involved, but also their psychological well-being.' PETA responded two weeks later: It hoped his letter was a joke.

"Selling PETA on a lab dog-based clone project was a losing proposition, but the **rebuke** still stung. Hawthorne is an animal lover—in the late '80s he even volunteered for PETA. He considers himself spiritual and, his new biotech business notwithstanding, philosophically opposed to vivisection. To balance his business with his Buddhist conscience, Hawthorne has come up with a kind of karmic spreadsheet, a ledger tallying Missyplicity's ethical red and black."

Charles Graeber. "How Much Is That Doggy in the Vitro? [Move Over, Dolly. Here Comes Fido Forever]," Wired *magazine (March 2000).*

"But current international inspections have uncovered equipment that Iran did not disclose in what it described as a comprehensive report on its nuclear program. Among the equipment was a P-2 gas centrifuge, which is better than other similar devices at producing bomb-grade nuclear material. The governments of France, Britain and Germany urged the International Atomic Energy Agency to **rebuke** Iran, citing information previously undisclosed by Iran, as well as contradictory explanations and the slow pace of cooperation.

"Khatami sent a letter to the three countries this week saying that Iran felt betrayed."

Karl Vick. "Iran Threatens to Resume Nuclear Activity [Khatami Says He Has 'No Moral Commitment' to Suspend Uranium Enrichment]," Washington Post *(June 17, 2004).*

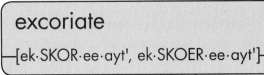

excoriate

[ek·SKOR·ee·ayt', ek·SKOER·ee·ayt']

Transitive Verb

1. to wear off the skin of, as a person or animal; to abrade
2. to censure or denounce very strongly: "When Kendra decided to excoriate the administration's policies in an editorial for the local paper, she acquired some powerful enemies."

ORIGIN

Approximately 1425; borrowed from Late Latin, *excoriatus*, past participle of *excoriare*: to strip off the hide; from Latin, *ex-*: off + *corium*: hide, skin.

BONUS WORD   Synonym

vituperate: to criticize in a harsh or abusive manner

IN ACTION

"Mr. Clinton confesses that his affair with Monica Lewinsky was 'immoral and foolish,' but he spends far more space **excoriating** his nemesis, independent counsel Kenneth W. Starr, and the press. He writes at length about his awareness that terrorism was a growing threat, but does not grapple with the unintended consequences of his administration's decisions to pressure Sudan to expel Osama bin Laden in 1996 (driving the al Qaeda leader to Afghanistan, where he was harder to track) or to launch cruise missile attacks against targets in Sudan and Afghanistan in retaliation for the embassy bombings in 1998 (an act that some terrorism experts believe fueled terrorists' conviction that the United States was an ineffectual giant that relied on low-risk high technology)."

Michiko Kakutani. "The Pastiche of a Presidency, Imitating a Life, in 957 Pages" (book review of My Life, by Bill Clinton), New York Times (June 20, 2004).

"Yes, it's that time of year again, when well-meaning baseball writers **excoriate** Major League Baseball for failing to turn the June draft into a media circus. Yes, it would be a lot of fun to see who your favorite team considers a big part of their future. And of course the NFL and the NBA both garner a great deal of valuable publicity with their televised drafts."

Rob Neyer. "Don't Televise Draft," ESPN.com (June 2, 2004).

Audio pronunciations for the words in this pack can be found on our website: www.vocabvitamins.com/book/pack2.

Heads or Tails

Don't you ever wish that we were one of those creatures that could regrow any body part? These odd verbal creatures lost either their head or their tail, and they need your help to regrow them. Using the short definitions intended to facilitate regrowth, fill in the missing letters for each word.

1. recus__ __ __: dissenter, nonconformist

2. __ __alanx: mass, throng, group

3. complic__ __ __: conspiracy, agreement, partnership

4. __ __ __culent: bad-tempered, violent, opposing

5. __ __llicose: aggressive, combative, hostile

6. succ__ __ __: surrender, yield, submit

7. capitu__ __ __ __: give in, surrender, defer

8. __ __ __tigate: punish, criticize harshly

9. rest__ __ __: unruly, unyielding

10. cab__ __: secret group, ring

11. __ __tulant: irritable, ill-tempered

12. abdi__ __ __ __: give up, relinquish

13. bera__ __: chew out, tongue-lash

14. __ __ __oriate: chafe, censure, denounce

15. __ __ __uiesce: agree, accept, accede

16. __ __ __ lusion: cahoots, cooperation, conspiracy

17. __ __ terie: group, company, alliance

18. __ __ dition: rebellion, insurrection

19. __ __ gilism: boxing, fist-fighting

20. __ __ __ tious: divisive, hostile

21. lamba__ __ __ : attack, beat, denounce

22. __ __ __ tow: show deference, worship, grovel

23. reb__ __ __ : reprimand, repress

24. __ __ fractory: antagonistic, obstinate

25. __ __ __ raid: scold, reproach

SEALED FOR PROTECTION

[voˈcab]
VITAMINS

PACK 3

TALK,
TALK, TALK

THEME 1
Ramble On

	SIMILAR TO:
circumlocution	circular speech, wordiness
verbose	wordy, long-winded, talkative
loquacious	chattering, wordy
garrulous	talkative, babbling
tautology	redundancy, repetition

THEME 2
Slander and Scandal

	SIMILAR TO:
aspersion	damaging statement, slander
calumny	slander, lie
defamation	reputation damage
libel	malign, slander, bad-mouth
vilify	denounce, defame

THEME 3
Talking About It

	SIMILAR TO:
allocution	speech, formal address
effusion	outpouring, gushing
ineffable	inexpressible, beyond words, heavenly
inquest	investigation, probe
prattle	chatter, babble

THEME 4
Talking the Talk

	SIMILAR TO:
argot	dialect, lingo
lexicon	glossary, vocabulary
neologism	new word, coinage
patois	slang, dialect
vernacular	local, colloquial

THEME 5
Verbal Combat

	SIMILAR TO:
diatribe	bitter denouncement
invective	accusation, condemnation
filibuster	lengthy and irrelevant speech
perorate	recap, summarize, lecture
repartee	comeback, retort, banter

Ramble On

THEME 1

circumlocution

verbose

loquacious

garrulous

tautology

circumlocution

[sur'·kahm·loe·KYOO·shahn]

Noun

1. the use of many more words than are necessary to express something, especially to avoid direct language: "I asked him if he loved me, and I was terribly disappointed to hear his wandering circumlocution, full of kind words that fell just short."
2. the use of evasion in writing or speech
3. indirect or roundabout language

ORIGIN

Before 1401; borrowed from Latin, *circumlocutionem* (*circum-*: around + *locutionem*, nominative *locutio*: a speaking, from stem of *loqui*: to speak, which is related to the root *tolkw*: to speak).

BONUS WORD   Synonym

pleonasm: redundancy of language, use of more words than are necessary

IN ACTION

"John Gadsby, 'Youth's champion,' is the hero of Ernest Vincent Wright's 1939 'Gadsby', fearlessly subtitled 'A Novel of Over 50,000 Words Without Using the Letter E.' Like the paragraph above, the book eschews our tongue's bedrock letter. The absence creates a tone alternately lofty ('It is an odd kink of humanity which cannot find any valuation in spots of natural glory') and rambunctious ('Books!! Pooh! Maps! BAH!!'), and demands comical **circumlocutions** for the simplest things—a turkey dubbed the 'Thanksgiving National Bird,' a wedding cake rechristened 'an astonishing loaf of culinary art.'"

Ed Park. "Egadsby!" Village Voice
(Education Supplement, August 7–13, 2002).

"The maxim that should be drummed into users is brevity before verbosity: **circumlocution** is akin to a sin in e-mail terms."

Karl Cushing. "Should We Ban E-mail?"
Computer Weekly (May 9, 2002).

verbose

[vahr·BOES]

Adjective

1. using or containing an excessive number of words, producing language that is unnecessarily complicated or tedious; wordy: "On our commencement day, Dean Tiseo took the stage and held it for forty-five excruciating minutes, delivering a hopelessly verbose speech, as if he was being held hostage by his own indomitable mouth."

ORIGIN

Approximately 1672; borrowed from Latin, *verbosus*: full of words, wordy, from *verbum*: word.

BONUS WORD   Antonym

compendious: succinct, concise, condensed

IN ACTION

"I'm a student of nudity laws, which never fail to be entertaining and vocabulary-building. We've been lucky here in Palm Beach County to be treated to some gems. The town of Palm Beach fought in vain for seven years to keep an ordinance that prohibited men from jogging topless. And a legal case over a topless doughnut shop in West Palm Beach led to some groundbreaking discussions of the doughnut as entertainment.

"Nudity laws are wonderfully **verbose**—you might even say, 'discernibly turgid' with words. Palm Beach County's ordinance defines the limits of breast exposure in a sentence that carries on for a dizzying 79 words."

> Frank Cerabino. *"I Can Barely Understand Nudity Laws,"* Palm Beach Post (October 11, 2002).

"As a legally blind photographer, she beat out nearly 50 other amateur and professional photographers to win an annual photo competition at a Calgary camera store. Austin's vision is limited to reading large print and taking close-up photos.

"'Unfortunately, I don't see in focus, so I have to have a camera that can focus on its own. I always want to get close. I am a real zoom person. The camera, at least, does tell me when I get too close.'

"She says she couldn't believe it when she was told her photo had won first place. 'I'm usually pretty **verbose** and I sort of just stood there and didn't know what to say.'"

> CP. *"Blind Shutterbug Wins: Beats Field of 50 Pros, Amateurs,"* Winnipeg Sun (October 13, 2002).

loquacious

[loe·KWAY·shahs]

Adjective

1. tending to talk a great deal; talkative: "Audrey was loquacious and opinionated, providing reams of material in our short interview and making my article incredibly easy to write."

ORIGIN

Approximately 1667; from the stem of Latin *loquax*: talkative (genitive *loquacis*), from *loqui*: to speak.

BONUS WORD Origin

obloquy: defamation, censure, severely critical language

IN ACTION

 "Claudia is one of my more frank, **loquacious** and downright refreshing female friends. She eschews the false posturing and tut-tutting. . . . She also has a profound streak of showmanship, which dovetails nicely with my chosen profession. We try to meet weekly at Starbuck's—a deliberately reactionary choice of venue. Claudia hates bowing to political correctness."

Courtney Weaver. "Unzipped,"
Salon.com (January 1997).

garrulous

—[GAR·ah·lahs, GAR·yah·lahs]—

Adjective

1. prone to talk excessively, especially about trivial things; talkative: "My neighbor transformed before my eyes, from an antisocial recluse to a garrulous braggart, just because I complimented his lawn."
2. wordy or rambling: "a garrulous lecture"

ORIGIN

Approximately 1611; borrowed from Latin, *garrulus*: talkative, from *garrire*: to chatter. May be a back formation from *garrulity*.

BONUS WORD   Continuum

LESS EXTREME . . .   **. . . MORE EXTREME**
voluble   ⟶   garrulous

voluble: fluent, glib

IN ACTION

"Asked by the Guardian Weekend magazine's Q&A column recently how he would like to die, Simon Armitage replied: 'I'm still young enough to think that death is something that happens to other people.' The response was characteristic: blunt, self-deprecating, humorous, evasive. It is belied by 'The Universal Home Doctor,' which is fully conscious of the skull beneath the grin.

"Armitage's poetic strategy is **garrulous** evasion. His poems are amusing and charming—effortlessly winning over an audience when read out loud—yet essentially serious, substantial enough to repay reconsidering. They achieve this because their preferred method is allegory, 'mouthing off' about one thing while thinking about another."

> Jeremy Noel-Tod. "Allegory and a Low-Key Intimacy"
> (book review of The Universal Home Doctor, by
> Simon Armitage), Guardian (October 12, 2002).

"Nature is **garrulous** to the point of confusion, let the artist be truly taciturn."

> Paul Klee (1879–1940). Swiss artist.
> [From his diaries.] (1909).

tautology

[taw'·TOL·ah·jee]

Noun

1. (a) unnecessary, useless repetition of the same meaning in different words or phrases: "He yelled 'I win, and you lose!' with a huge, giddy smile, leaving me to ponder the absurdness of his schoolyard tautology."
   (b) an instance of such repetition

ORIGIN
Approximately 1579; borrowed from Late Latin, *tautologia*: repetition of the same thing + *-logy*: discourse, expression; from Greek *tautologia*, from *tautologos*: repeating what has been said, redundant (*tauto*: the same + *-logos*: saying, related to *legein*: to say).

BONUS WORD Related

alliteration: the repetition of similar consonants for poetic effect, as "around the rock the ragged rascal ran"

IN ACTION

"To create man was a quaint and original idea, but to add the sheep was **tautology**."

Mark Twain [Samuel Langhorne Clemens] (1835–1910). U.S. author. "More Maxims of Mark," Mark Twain: Collected Tales, Sketches, Speeches, & Essays, 1891–1910 (1992).

"As a former intelligence officer, I have had some personal experience with what goes right and sometimes wrong in what the Russians used to call 'certain of the organs of state security.' The 9/11 debacle is simply an astounding reminder of how little has changed, how the unpredictable is the only predictable thing, and, when the unpredictable actually happens, how the same lame excuses get trotted out for public consumption. Just look at what happened when the USS Cole was bombed in 1998. The same anonymous officials complained of 'ambient noise' in the system that did not allow for specific warnings that might have saved the ship and her crew. In the characteristic **tautology** of the usual Pentagon spokesman: 'We did not have warning of a specific attack against U.S. interests in Yemen . . . and these . . . reports did not constitute a specific warning.' Well dammit, does anyone think that it might just be a good idea if we had an intelligence community that could provide specific warnings, actually predicting and preventing such attacks?"

Kenneth Allard. "Lessons of History," MSNBC.com (September 20, 2002).

"'Yes or no?' said Murphy. The eternal **tautology**."

Samuel Beckett (1906–89). Irish dramatist and novelist. Murphy (1938).

Slander and Scandal

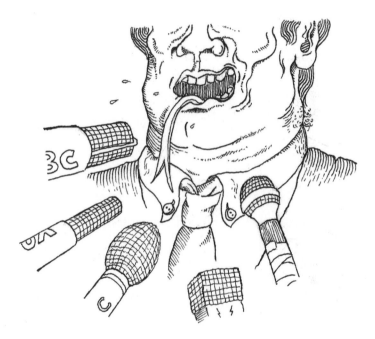

THEME 2

aspersion

calumny

defamation

libel

vilify

aspersion

[ah·SPUR·zhahn, ah·SPUR·shahn]

Noun

1. (a) a damaging or derogatory remark; slander: "Sandy had little regard for the opinions of her classmates, but any aspersion from a teacher affected her deeply."
    (b) the act of slandering or defaming
2. the act of sprinkling, especially with water, as in baptism

ORIGIN

Approximately 1448; borrowed from Latin, *aspersionem*, from *aspers*, stem of *aspergere*, *adspergere*: to sprinkle (*ad*: on + *spargere*: to scatter).

BONUS WORD　Related

Schadenfreude: delight in another's misfortune

IN ACTION

"In suggesting that the United States review its own foreign policy rather than casting **aspersions**, Mr. Khatami specifically cited what he depicted as the plight of Palestinians denied human rights because of American support for Israel.

"The threats expressed by Mr. Bush and other administration officials over the last two weeks surprised many in Iran. In some ways they have united the reformists and the old guard here in criticism of the United States; in others they have strengthened the hand of the conservatives."

> Neil MacFarquhar. "Chants of 'Death to America!'
> Mark March by Millions in Iran,"
> New York Times (February 11, 2002).

"'As for my language, I had no intention of casting **aspersions** on anyone of another race,' he said. 'In my attempt to articulate strongly held feelings, I may have offended people.'"

"Top Senate Democrat Apologizes for Slur,"
CNN.com *(March 4, 2001).*

calumny
[KAL·ahm·nee]
Noun

1. a false statement made maliciously to injure the reputation of another: "As their conversation began to deteriorate in front of their friends, Inga's words became sloppy and vindictive, and she concluded with a calumny that left everyone in stunned silence."
2. the act of uttering maliciously false statements; slander; defamation

ORIGIN
Approximately 1447; borrowed from Middle French, *calomnie*; from Latin, *calumnia*: trickery, false accusation, from *calvi*: to trick or deceive.

BONUS WORD Sound

calamity: a disastrous event

IN ACTION

"What she won't have is immunity from the usual impediments for female candidates in New York State: coverage dripping with **calumny** indirectly related to her gender (consider the numerous cartoons of Hillary as a harridan or dominatrix); subtle accusations that she's an unnatural woman in a fake marriage (why don't these charges ever stick to Donna-less Rudy?); and a righteous rage betraying deep-seated and unacknowledged fear. She will be accused of being too tough, too cold, too corrupt, and just plain oogly. These may or may not be traits that apply to Hillary Clinton, but isn't it interesting that they have also been applied to every other woman who dared to storm the state's political gates?"

Richard Goldstein. "Hillary's Big Problem: No Woman Has Ever Won Higher Office in New York State," Village Voice (July 14–20, 1999).

"'This surplus is not the government's money,' [Bush] said in a characteristic line yesterday in Council Bluffs, Iowa. 'It's the people's money. . . .'

"Democrats are having some trouble coming up with a snappy comeback to this bit of demagoguery. They don't want to argue with Bush too directly lest they lend credence to the Republican **calumny** that they think all money belongs to the government. Liberals are desperately afraid to offer an answer that smacks of the view that Bush claims they hold, which is that the surplus is really the government's money."

Jacob Weisberg. "Bush and the People's Money," Slate.com (March 1, 2001).

Calumny will sear
Virtue itself.

William Shakespeare (1564–1616). English dramatist and poet. [Leontes, in] The Winter's Tale (1611).

defamation

[def'·ah·MAY·shahn]

Noun

1. the act of defaming, injuring another's reputation by slanderous communication; aspersion, calumny, slander: "Our CEO did not take kindly to the defamation of her character in a recent trade journal, and she resolved to defend herself with an assertive editorial in the next issue."

ORIGIN

Approximately 1303; from Latin, *diffamare*: to spread abroad by ill report (*dif* a variant of *dis* + *famare*, a variant of *fama*: news, report, rumor).

BONUS WORD Related

renown: having honor and acclaim

IN ACTION

"Indeed, in the case of the student whose Web site featured a photograph of his teacher's face morphing into Hitler, the criminal charges were dismissed, but a jury later awarded the teacher $200,000 in damages after a **defamation** suit in civil court."

Amy Benfer. "Cyber Slammed: Kids Are Getting Arrested for Raunchy Online Bullying. It's Definitely Offensive, but Is It Against the Law?" Salon.com (July 3, 2001).

"This is the only major sport in which death and serious injury are not considered an aberration. Earnhardt's death reinforced that reality, which is clearly a major selling point. Yet it took that almost mythical death to create an official climate in which drivers finally did not feel unmanly wearing advanced safety equipment. Since Nascar did not mandate helmets, no wonder that a year ago only 20 percent of drivers wore the head and neck restraints that might have saved Earnhardt. Now most wear them.

"Not only has Nascar been overly deliberate in its precautionary measures, but it also has yet to clarify an early statement that made a torn seat belt a factor in Earnhardt's death. Bill Simpson, former owner of the company that manufactured that belt, the highly respected Simpson Performance Products, filed a **defamation** of character suit last week against Nascar. Simpson has said that he would not have filed it if Nascar had apologized."

Robert Lipsyte. "One Year Later, Nascar's Discovery Rolls On," New York Times (February 17, 2002).

libel
[LIE·bahl]

Noun, Transitive Verb

Noun
1. (as in law) (a) a false and malicious publication in writing or print, or in pictures or other signs, tending to damage a person's reputation or expose him or her to public condemnation or ridicule
    (b) the act or crime of presenting such a statement to the public
2. anything that is defamatory or that maliciously misrepresents, especially in writing; a lampoon: "My father was infuriated by how the local press represented his efforts to open a deli shop on parkland, but there was more fact to their commentary than libel."

Transitive Verb

3. to publish or communicate a defamatory statement about in writing or pictures, signs, and so on

ORIGIN

Approximately 1300; borrowed from Old French, *libel, libelle*; from Latin, *libellus*: a little book or petition, diminutive of *liber*: book.

BONUS WORD Synonym

canard: a deliberately misleading fabrication

IN ACTION

"The lawsuit, filed in Delaware state court, amplifies an already contentious dispute over how far public health advocates can go to dissuade teenagers from smoking without violating the settlement or **libel** laws, especially through radio and television commercials that depict tobacco companies as underhanded while mentioning them by name."

> Greg Winter. "Antismoking Group Sues to
> Preserve an Ad Campaign's Tone,"
> New York Times (February 14, 2002).

"This is not a book. This is **libel**, slander, defamation of character. This is not a book, in the ordinary sense of the word. No, this is a prolonged insult, a gob of spit in the face of Art, a kick in the pants to God, Man, Destiny, Time, Love, Beauty . . . what you will. I am going to sing for you, a little off key perhaps, but I will sing."

> Henry Miller (1891–1980). U.S. author. Tropic
> of Cancer (1934). [Tropic of Cancer was banned
> on grounds of obscenity in the United States
> until 1961, when it became a bestseller.]

Nor do they trust their tongue alone,
But speak a language of their own;
Can read a nod, a shrug, a look,
Far better than a printed book;
Convey a **libel** in a frown,
And wink a reputation down.

Jonathan Swift (1667–1745). Anglo-Irish satirist.
The Journal of a Modern Lady (1729).

vilify
[VIL·ah·fie']

Transitive Verb

1. to make defamatory statements about; to slander: "Shoji stood by, appalled that his sister would vilify him in front of their parents, despite her own share of the guilt."

ORIGIN
Approximately 1425; borrowed from Late Latin, *vilificare*: to make cheap, from *vilificus* (from Latin, *vilis*: cheap or worthless + root of *facere*: to make).

BONUS WORD　　Antonym

extol: praise, glorify, honor

IN ACTION

"Official newspapers on Friday quoted the CCDI [Central Commission for Discipline Inspection] as saying in a statement that cadres who 'fabricate and broadcast political rumors and who circulate views that **vilify** the image of the party and state' would be punished."

Willy Wo-lap Lam. *"China's Dissenting Cadres to Face Crackdown,"* CNN.com *(September 28, 2001).*

"Some reviews **vilify** the film, others exalt it, and a few do both."

Eliza Truitt. *"Björk's Bathos"* (review of Dancer in the Dark), Salon.com *(September 22, 2000).*

"To **vilify** a great man is the readiest way in which a little man can himself attain greatness."

Edgar Allan Poe (1809–49). U.S. poet, critic, and short-story writer. *"Marginalia,"* Southern Literary Messenger *(July 1849).*

Talking About It

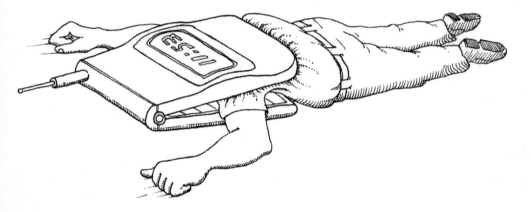

allocution

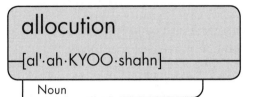

[al'·ah·KYOO·shahn]

Noun

1. a formal and authoritative address or speech: "With last week's strong allocution to the American people and the rest of the world, it seems that our president has finally come into his own in the public eye."
2. a hortatory or authoritative address delivered by the pope to his clergy, especially on a matter of policy

ORIGIN

Approximately 1610; from Latin, *allocutio* or *allocution-*, from *allocutus*, past participle of *alloqui*: to speak to (*al* + *loqui*: to speak).

BONUS WORD　Sound

elocution: the art of effective public speaking

IN ACTION

"The impression made by his words was immediate but shortlived. It was effaced as easily as it had been evoked by an **allocution** from Mr Candidate Mulligan in that vein of pleasantry which none better than he knew how to affect, postulating as the supremest object of desire a nice clean old man."

James Joyce (1882–1941). Irish novelist and poet. Ulysses (1921).

"Less than six months after the President-Dictator's visit, Sulaco learned with stupefaction of the military revolt in the name of national honour. The Minister of War, in a barrack-square **allocution** to the officers

of the artillery regiment he had been inspecting, had
declared the national honour sold to foreigners."

Joseph Conrad (1857–1924). English novelist of
Polish descent. Nostromo *(1904).*

effusion

[i·FYOO·zhahn]

Noun

1. (a) the act of pouring out or effusing, as with water,
   blood, words, and so on
   (b) that which is poured out: "As a student of literature
   and an aspiring writer, Gila was constantly scribbling
   away in her journal, and the poor thing looked as
   if it was bursting at the seams from her unrelenting
   effusions."
2. an unrestrained expression of emotion, especially in
   speech or writing; an outpouring of feeling; an outburst:
   "The most brilliant musicians are those that can exhibit
   a technical coherence in the midst of passionate effusion,
   allowing for the full force of their musical thoughts to be
   accurately communicated to the people around them."

ORIGIN
Approximately 1402; from Latin, *effusionem* (nominative of
effusio), from *effud*, stem of *effundere*: to pour forth (*ef*: out +
fundere: to pour).

BONUS WORD   Related

profusion: lavish expenditure or extravagance

IN ACTION

"You could hear Mahler laboring with all his considerable intellectual and technical resources to hold his huge canvas together—and even more excitingly, simply brazening his way through the most difficult junctures with glorious **effusions** of sound and reckless bravado."

> Joshua Kosman. *"Mahler's First Symphony Played to Vibrant Perfection,"* San Francisco Chronicle (September 21, 2001).

"Liberty is a blessing so inestimable, that, wherever there appears any probability of recovering it, a nation may willingly run many hazards, and ought not even to repine at the greatest **effusion** of blood or dissipation of treasure."

> David Hume (1711–76). Scottish philosopher. *"Of the Coalition of Parties,"* Essays, Moral, Political, and Literary (1741).

"*Beloved* by Toni Morrison: The baby murdered by her mother to spare her from slavery returns as a ghost. Ignore the **effusions** that academics have spent on this book and you still have a beautiful and harrowing parable. The second half consists largely of figurative language and is pretty slow going, but the first half, which lushly recounts the appearance of the ghost and the relations between a living man and woman in the years directly following emancipation, helped win Morrison the Nobel Prize."

> Jonathan Franzen. *"Chained: The Author of 'The 27th City' Picks Five Great American Novels About Slavery,"* Salon.com (August 18, 2000).

ineffable

[in·EF·ah·bahl]

Adjective

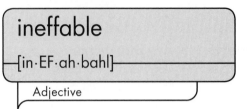

1. incapable of being expressed in words; defying description; unspeakable: "Sandy never talked much about her sea kayaking tours along the Washington coastline, but every trip gave her an ineffable sense of peace and a smile that lasted for days."
2. too sacred or taboo to be uttered: "John, please don't use the ineffable name of God in vain."

ORIGIN

Approximately 1398; from Old French, *ineffable*: unspeakable; from Latin, *ineffabilis* (*in*: not + *effabilis*: speakable, from *effari*: utter, from *ef*: out + *fari*: to speak).

BONUS WORD   Related

reticent: untalkative, cool and formal in manner

IN ACTION

"I ordered the buffalo mozzarella with fresh and roasted tomatoes with apprehension, but the mozzarella was first rate, with that **ineffable** texture, simultaneously creamy and fluffy, that makes this cheese a high-risk proposition. When it's not there, your heart sinks."

William Grimes. "An Alliance of Sun-Dappled Cuisines," New York Times (September 19, 2001).

"'We are saved! We are saved!' she murmured; 'to return to the arms of our dear, dear father, and his heart will not be broken with grief. And you, too, Cora, my sister, my more than sister, my mother; you, too, are spared. And Duncan,' she added, looking round upon the youth with a smile of **ineffable** innocence, 'even our own brave and noble Duncan has escaped without a hurt.'"

James Fenimore Cooper (1789–1851). American novelist. The Last of the Mohicans (1826).

inquest

[IN·kwest]

Noun

1. (as in law) (a) a judicial inquiry or official examination, especially before a jury, often made by a coroner to resolve the cause of a death
   (b) a body of people assembled under authority of law to hold such an inquiry, especially a coroner's jury
   (c) the decision or finding upon such an inquiry
2. an investigation, inquiry, or search: "I am leading a journalistic inquest for the school paper on this matter."

ORIGIN

Approximately 1300; from Old French, *enqueste*: inquiry; from *inquirere*: to inquire into.

BONUS WORD Sound

bequest: a gift of personal property via a will

IN ACTION

"The Ulster Unionists, however, have emphasized they want an open-ended suspension, then a lengthy **inquest** into why parts of the 1998 accord have failed."

Shawn Pogatchnik. "IRA Disarmament Pledge 'Not Enough' as Northern Ireland Government Again Faces Suspension," Associated Press (September 20, 2001).

"To be fair, she does seem genuinely concerned. She has noticed that certain books, magazines, TV shows and Web sites portray women in an unflattering light and that the advertisers who prop up these media appear to want nothing more than these women's money. A sad and ugly cycle to be sure. But, dare I say it? Duh. This is birds-and-bees stuff. Someone needs to sit down and talk with [Francine] Prose, maybe one of the women 'staging these expensive **inquests** into the natures and buying patterns of their newly affluent sisters.' Turncoats though they may be, these advertising gals have their eyes wide open."

Jennifer Foote Sweeney. "Beware of 'Women's Culture,'" Salon.com (February 15, 2000).

"But Kentridge hardly grew up divorced from the politics of apartheid. His father, Sir Sydney Kentridge, was one of the most important attorneys in the antiapartheid movement, representing Nelson Mandela at the infamous treason trial in 1956 and the family of Steve Biko at the 1977 **inquest** hearing into the activist's death."

Barbara Pollack. "Art of Resistance: William Kentridge Animates the Soul of South Africa," Village Voice (May 30–June 5, 2001).

prattle

[PRAT·l]

Intransitive Verb, Transitive Verb, Noun

Intransitive Verb

1. to speak about unimportant matters incessantly; to chatter idly; to babble: "In stressful times, Jane would keep herself occupied by prattling like an overcaffeinated parrot."

Transitive Verb

2. to utter by babbling or otherwise speaking foolishly: "The principal will try to catch you off guard when you go into her office, but be careful not to prattle our secrets away, or we'll all get busted."

Noun

3. idle or foolish talk; babble: "Maria tried to be casual about asking Tom if he had a girlfriend, but her roundabout prattle gave the suave cover away."
4. a sound suggestive of such babbling or chattering: "Nothing is more relaxing than the gentle prattle of water rushing over stones."

ORIGIN

Approximately 1532; a frequentative (expressing repeated action) of English *prate*; from Middle Low German, *pratelen*: to chatter or grumble, frequentative of *praten*: to prate.

BONUS WORD   Antonym

incisive: penetrating, clear, and sharp

IN ACTION

"But no one speaks as passionately about the fabulosity of becoming a brownhead than Gwyneth Paltrow, who claims to 'feel sexier and cooler as a brunette.'

"'The director of *Bounce* was very tired of the blonde Gwyneth Paltrow person. And I was too. I'm tired of her,' the brunette Gwyneth Paltrow person **prattled** to Scotland's *Daily Record*. 'So there's a new Gwyneth Paltrow person. I like it because nobody knows who I am.'"

Amy Reiter. "Wardrobe Is Hell," Salon.com
(December 22, 1999).

"Anyone who's read the papers over the past 10 days—or for that matter, the past 20 years—knows about the pre-super bowl media blitz. With two weeks between the conference championship games and the big one, football writers are as much involved in making the news—through pronouncements, predictions, and maudlin **prattle**—as covering it."

Brian P. Dunleavy. "Making Sense of the
Pre-Super Bowl Media Blitz," Village Voice
(January 24–30, 2001).

Talking
the Talk

THEME 4

argot

lexicon

neologism

patois

vernacular

argot

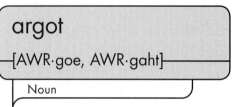

[AWR·goe, AWR·gaht]

Noun

1. a specialized language or vocabulary used by a particular group; dialect; jargon: "Using typically indirect singles argot, Suzanne informed her date that they 'would work better as friends.'"

ORIGIN

Approximately 1860; borrowed from French, *argot*; from Middle French, *argot*: group of beggars; of unknown origin.

BONUS WORD   Synonym

localism: a phrase, an idiom, or a custom specific to a certain area

IN ACTION

"Nemo, a squeaky-voiced youngster who was born with one fin smaller than the other, disappears on his first day of school after defying his father with a daredevil stunt. Leaving the security of the Great Barrier Reef where he and his dad live comfortably inside a sea anemone, he swims out to inspect a distant boat and is scooped up in a scuba diver's net.

"Although Marlin swims to the rescue, he is repelled by the blast of the boat's propeller. The boy eventually lands inside the aquarium of a dentist in Sydney, Australia, where his tank companions are so bored they have picked up the technical **argot** of dentistry from observing their keeper. In setting out to find Nemo, Marlin has only a single clue as to his whereabouts: the address of the fishing boat."

Stephen Holden. "Vast Sea, Tiny Fish, Big Crisis" (movie review
of Finding Nemo), New York Times (May 30, 2003).

"Grizzlies are long-serving superstars of the environmental movement.

"Since they came under the protection of the Endangered Species Act in 1975, the hirsute, meat-eating beasts—'charismatic megafauna' in the activist **argot**—have helped raise money and motivate voters for environmental causes.

"'They are our big guns for mobilizing people and protecting places,' said Tracy Stone-Manning, executive director of the Clark Fork Coalition, a conservation group in western Montana's bear country. 'They represent all that is wild. You know, they can eat you.'"

Blaine Harden. "Bush Shows No Fear in Grizzly Territory: White House Takes on Popular Icon with Mining Plan," Washington Post (May 18, 2003).

lexicon

[LEK·si·kon']

Noun

1. a reference book containing an alphabetical list of words with the definition of each; a dictionary
2. the stock of words or terms belonging to a branch of knowledge or style; a vocabulary: "After signing up, Laura had to follow the mailing list for several months just to acclimate herself to the highly technical lexicon of its participants."

ORIGIN

Approximately 1603; borrowed from Middle French, *lexicon*; from Greek, *lexikon*: wordbook (*biblion*), from neuter of *lexikos*: pertaining to words, from *lexis*: word, from *legein*: to say.

BONUS WORD   Origin

lexis: all of the words in a language

IN ACTION

"It has been, for Israel's settlers, a most unsettling week. First the Israeli government endorsed the idea of eventually creating a Palestinian state, giving qualified backing to an American-backed peace plan. Then Mr. Sharon criticized what he called Israel's 'occupation' in the territories of the West Bank and Gaza Strip, captured in the 1967 war.

"This is a right-wing Israeli government, and Mr. Sharon is a visionary and engineer of the settlement movement, which since the war has moved more than 200,000 Israelis into the West Bank and Gaza. Yet in a conflict in which every word can be inspected for political freight, in which names for everything from the city streets to the violence itself are contested, Mr. Sharon has adopted a term—'occupation'— that is central to the **lexicon** of Israeli doves and Palestinians."

> James Bennet. "Sharon Laments 'Occupation' and Israeli Settlers Shudder," New York Times (June 1, 2003).

"She didn't have symptoms of SARS at the time— something the medical establishment would suggest means she couldn't have been contagious.

"But Dr. Tweeddale isn't so sure the medical establishment is always right in its assumptions about this disease that wasn't even in the **lexicon** four months ago."

> Gloria Galloway. "Oncologist battles SARS, assumptions," Globe and Mail (May 31, 2003).

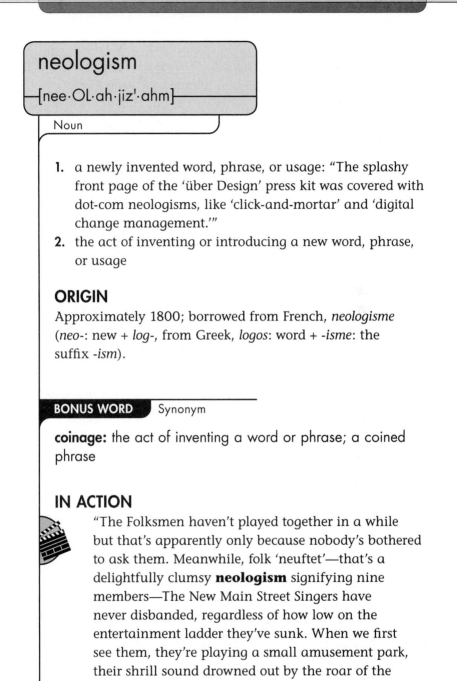

neologism

[nee·OL·ah·jiz'·ahm]

Noun

1. a newly invented word, phrase, or usage: "The splashy front page of the 'über Design' press kit was covered with dot-com neologisms, like 'click-and-mortar' and 'digital change management.'"
2. the act of inventing or introducing a new word, phrase, or usage

ORIGIN

Approximately 1800; borrowed from French, *neologisme* (*neo-*: new + *log-*, from Greek, *logos*: word + *-isme*: the suffix *-ism*).

BONUS WORD Synonym

coinage: the act of inventing a word or phrase; a coined phrase

IN ACTION

"The Folksmen haven't played together in a while but that's apparently only because nobody's bothered to ask them. Meanwhile, folk 'neuftet'—that's a delightfully clumsy **neologism** signifying nine members—The New Main Street Singers have never disbanded, regardless of how low on the entertainment ladder they've sunk. When we first see them, they're playing a small amusement park, their shrill sound drowned out by the roar of the rollercoaster directly behind them."

John Boonstra. "The Answer Is Blowing in
Your Face" (movie review of A Mighty Wind),
Westchester County Weekly (May 15, 2003).

"The worst culprit was also the one with the most 'embedded' reporters and the most exciting live footage, and so it was, sadly, the one that I watched most of the time: CNN, the voice of Centcom. CNN was more irritating than the gleefully patriotic Fox News channel because CNN has a pretense of objectivity. It pretends to be run by journalists. And yet it dutifully uses all the language chosen by people in charge of 'media relations' at the Pentagon. It describes the exploding of Iraqi soldiers in their bunkers as 'softening up'; it describes slaughtered Iraqi units as being 'degraded'; some announcers have even repeated the egregious Pentagon **neologism** 'attrited' (to mean 'we are slowly killing as many of them as we can'). I don't know if I'm more offended by the insidiousness of this euphemism or by the absurdity of its grammar."

Russell Smith. "The New Newsspeak,"
New York Review of Books (May 29, 2003).

patois

[PAT·waw', pa·TWAW]

Noun

1. a regional form of a language, often with nonstandard elements and usually without a literary tradition: "The southern rim of the country had its own patois, and I had difficulty picking up on its nuances, despite my fluency in the language."
2. an uneducated or provincial form of speech
3. a creole
4. the jargon used by a particular group; dialect

ORIGIN

Approximately 1643; borrowed from French, *patois*: a
native or local speech; from Old French, *patoier*: to handle
clumsily, from *pate*: paw; from Vulgar Latin, *patta*, perhaps
of imitative origin.

BONUS WORD   Sound

pâté: a paste made from meat or liver; meat-filled pastry

IN ACTION

"The Jstar principals think Effen can succeed for
several reasons. First and foremost, there is the
product name. 'We spent more time thinking about
what to call our vodka than we did anything else,'
Trayser said. More than 500 names were seriously
considered. 'Effen' means 'smooth' in the Netherlands,
where the vodka is actually made.

"The name, of course, reflects the premium
quality of the product, but it's also a fun word in the
American **patois** and an inducement for drinkers to
tell bartenders or waiters to 'give me an Effen vodka.'
The unusual bottle, sheathed in white rubber, also
was designed to stand out on the back bar and make
a fashion statement."

> Lewis Lazare. "Trio Toasts Success of Effen Vodka,"
> Chicago Sun-Times *(May 19, 2003)*.

"The only thing he hates more than a cheater is
a cheater-coder (or 'hax0r' as they are known in
gaming **patois**). Hax0rs are almost universally
maligned. Most are young kids, around 12 to 14 years
old, although some are as young as nine. Ruinously
bright, they hunger for the pure intellectual buzz they
get from hacking a protection system. They know they

are bringing online gaming to its knees, but don't seem to care."

David McCandless. "Make Cheats, Not War:
The US Army's Foray into Violent PC Games Has
Been Hailed a Success. But, Says David McCandless,
It Didn't Allow for One Thing—Cheaters,"
Guardian (May 22, 2003).

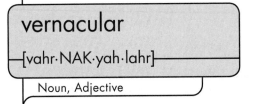

vernacular

[vahr·NAK·yah·lahr]

Noun, Adjective

Noun
1. the everyday or native language of a country or region
2. the common spoken language (as opposed to the literary language) of a people: "Just summarize the important points in vernacular, and let our attorney generate a contract with the proper legal language."
3. the distinctive vocabulary or idiom of a particular trade, profession, or group: "legal vernacular"
4. an idiomatic word or phrase

Adjective
5. native to or commonly spoken by people in a particular country or region
6. using the native or common spoken language (as opposed to the literary language) of a people: "a vernacular poet"
7. relating to or spoken in the native or commonly spoken language

ORIGIN
Approximately 1601; formed from Latin, *vernaculus*: native, from *verna*: a slave born in the master's house, native + English suffix -*ar*: relating to, resembling.

BONUS WORD Related

endemic: native or present in a certain region

IN ACTION

"'I see that Mr. Cook has been as punctual as usual,'
he says, extending a hand in greeting. Persinger, 54,
blends a crisp, scientific demeanor with a mischievous
smile, but overall he's a very serious man. His erect
posture is enhanced by a dark, pin-striped, three-
piece suit with a gold chain swag at the bottom of
the vest. His sentences are clipped and stripped of
any **vernacular**—so painstakingly scientific that
they can be coy. For example, he tells me that he
is actually an American who 'moved to Canada in
July of 1969, because I had a rather major ethical
disagreement with my government.' It takes me a
follow-up or two before I realize he had dodged the
draft."

> Jack Hitt. "This Is Your Brain on God: Michael Persinger
> Has a Vision—the Almighty Isn't Dead, He's an Energy
> Field. And Your Mind Is an Electromagnetic Map to Your
> Soul," Wired magazine (November 1999).

"Would you convey my compliments to the purist who
reads your proofs and tell him or her that I write in
a sort of broken-down patois which is something like
the way a Swiss waiter talks, and that when I split an
infinitive, God damn it, I split it so it will stay split,
and when I interrupt the velvety smoothness of my
more or less literate syntax with a few sudden words
of bar-room **vernacular**, that is done with the eyes
wide open and the mind relaxed but attentive."

> Raymond Chandler (1888–1959). U.S. author.
> Letter to Atlantic Monthly editor Edward Weeks
> (January 18, 1948).

Verbal Combat

diatribe

[DIE·ah·tribe']

Noun

1. bitter or invective language denouncing somebody or something: "Mary had difficulty speaking with people on the other side of such emotional issues without launching into diatribe."

ORIGIN

Approximately 1643; borrowed from French, *diatribe*, and directly from Latin, *diatriba*: learned discourse; from Greek, *diatribe*: discourse, pastime, literally, a wearing away of time (*dia-*: away + *tribein*: to rub).

BONUS WORD Related

acrid: unpleasantly strong and sharp; corrosive

IN ACTION

"On his Web site, veteran rocker John Mellencamp served up 'To Washington,' an anti-Bush **diatribe** that praises 'eight years of peace under Bill Clinton.' Jonatha Brooke, George Michael, Chuck D, Yo La Tengo and the Neptunes are also taking musical stances against the war."

Teresa Wiltz. *"From Rap to Country, Musicians Record Opposing Views on War,"* Washington Post (March 22, 2003).

"But then there was the recent review by J. Hoberman, film critic of *The Village Voice* (counterbalancing the rave by that paper's art critic, Jerry Saltz). Mr. Hoberman systematically blasted each film, although he had grudging praise for '3.' Passing phrases in his

diatribe included 'glib homage,' 'narcotized self-satisfaction,' 'migraine-inducing,' 'lugubrious,' 'gives ridiculous a bad name' and 'never afraid to distend his ideas beyond ostentation.'

"Well. Other than that he liked it. And so, it seems, do the hordes of mostly young people coursing around the Guggenheim, although how many of them sit through the films is another matter."

John Rockwell. "Movies: Man vs. 'Cremaster': The 10-Hour Test," New York Times (March 23, 2003).

invective

[in·VEK·tiv]

Noun, Adjective

Noun
1. severe or violent denunciatory language: "I'm sure that some of these young musical stars have a lot to offer, but sometimes I have difficulty getting beyond the invective of their songs."
2. a harsh or reproachful accusation
3. a severe or violent expression or discourse: "Michael had the kind of aggressive, overbearing personality that would regularly turn conversations about the most menial subjects into unpleasant invective."

Adjective
4. characterized by or relating to severe or violent denunciatory language

ORIGIN
Approximately 1523; borrowed from Middle French, *invectif*; from Late Latin, *invectivus*: abusive or reproachful; from Latin, *invectus*, past participle of *invehi*: to attack with words.

BONUS WORD Antonym

dulcet: gently pleasant to the ear, soothing, agreeable

IN ACTION

"The art of **invective** resembles the art of boxing. Very few fights are won with the straight left. It is too obvious, and it can be too easily countered. The best punches, like the best pieces of invective in this style, are either short-arm jabs, unexpectedly rapid and deadly; or else one-two blows, where you prepare your opponent with the first hit, and then, as his face comes forward, connect with your other fist: one, two. Both are effective; but they can be administered only by a real artist, with a real wish to knock his enemy out."

Gilbert Highet (1906–78). Scottish-born
U.S. biographer, critic, and educator.
"The Art of Invective," A Clerk of Oxenford:
Essays on Literature and Life (1954).

filibuster

—[FIL·ah·bus'·tahr]——————

Noun, Intransitive Verb, Transitive Verb

Noun

1. a tactic for delaying or obstructing legislative action using long and often irrelevant speechmaking
2. an instance of this tactic in use: "Senator Karasik's absurd filibuster included wishing Natalie Madenberg a happy birthday and naming all fifty states in alphabetical and size order."
3. a military adventurer or mercenary who engages in action in a foreign country

Intransitive Verb

4. to use long speechmaking as a delaying or obstructionist tactic in the legislature
5. to serve as a military adventurer or mercenary in a foreign country

Transitive Verb

6. to use long speechmaking as a delaying or obstructionist tactic against something (a legislative measure, for example)

ORIGIN

Approximately 1851; borrowed from Spanish, *filibustero*: a freebooter, and from French, *flibustier*, possibly from English, *flibutor*: pirate, adventurer; borrowed from Dutch, *vrijbuiter*: pirate, freebooter.

BONUS WORD   Related

buccaneer: pirate

IN ACTION

"With all the surgical skill and the vital rays lavished on him he should talk like a—like a congressman at a **filibuster**."

Movie written by Kenneth Langtry, directed by Herbert L. Strock. [Professor. Frankenstein, to his assistant (who is trying to figure out why the monster won't speak), in] I Was a Teenage Frankenstein (1957).

"In 1957 he staged the longest **filibuster** in Senate history, speaking for over 24 hours against a civil-rights bill. Thurmond switched from the Democratic to the Republican party in 1964. In 1996 he became the oldest sitting, in 1997 the longest serving, U.S. senator in history."

"James Strom Thurmond," The Columbia Encyclopedia, *sixth edition (2001).*

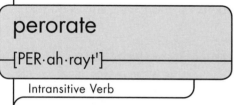

perorate

[PER·ah·rayt']

Intransitive Verb

1. to finish a speech with a concise restatement of its main points
2. to speak or orate at length, especially in a pompous or bombastic manner: "Tim noted her mistake and began to perorate about the sanctity of proper English, as if it were a moral virtue Amrita did not possess."

ORIGIN

Approximately 1603; probably a back formation from *peroration*; borrowed from Latin, *perorationem*: the ending of a speech or argument, from *perorare*: to argue a case to the end (*per-*: to the end + *orare*: to speak).

BONUS WORD   Origin

orate: talk pompously

IN ACTION

"The characters in 'The Biographer's Tale' are an eclectic bunch: blaseé professors, a reclusive and melancholic radiographer, a flamboyant Swedish ecologist, eccentric travel agents, a pornocrat. All are instrumental in Nanson's investigation. These people don't talk, they **perorate**, pontificate, bombast. They use words as weapons, smoke screens, instruments of seduction, just like writers do. Ditto for Nanson, the novel's narrator, who says things like, 'I had decided to put a new punctilious formality into my dealings with him.'"

> Jean Charbonneau. "Biographer's Quest Becomes Self-Searching Journey" (book review of The Biographer's Tale, by A. S. Byatt), Denver Post (January 28, 2001).

"The illusion of deeper and more meaningful themes that [film director Peter] Jackson managed to preserve in *The Lord of the Rings* is entirely absent from *King Kong*. . . .

"Jackson [allows] himself a pretentious little gesture towards significance when he shows a sailor on the ship heading for Kong's island reading *Heart of Darkness*, which gives rise to a portentous **peroration** from another (black) crew-man. Joseph Conrad's novel is, famously, about a trip up the Congo river at the darkest times of Belgian colonialism, to find a man who has 'gone native' and become a tribal despot. *Heart of Darkness* was criticised by Chinua Achebe, among others, for using Africans to represent the savage shadow of white civilisation; others have found in it a sense of the evils of colonialism and the darkness at the heart of humanity (and/or civilisation) itself."

> *Shaun de Waal. "Spank the Monkey: Peter Jackson's King Kong Is the Ultimate Creature Feature" (movie review of* King Kong*), Mail & Guardian (South Africa) (December 15, 2005).*

repartee
[rep'·ahr·TEE, rep'·ahr·TAY, rep'·awr·TAY]

Noun

1. a smart, witty, and swift remark or reply; a retort: "Ian shot back at his opponent with a repartee that sent snickers throughout the audience."
2. conversation marked by the exchange of swift and witty remarks

ORIGIN
Approximately 1645; borrowed from French, *repartie*; noun use of the feminine past participle of Old French, *repartir*: to retort, to reply promptly (*re-*: back + *partir*: to part).

BONUS WORD Continuum

LESS HOSTILE . . .   **. . . MORE HOSTILE**
repartee   ⟶   riposte

riposte: a quick and effective retort or retaliatory action

IN ACTION

"Rodeo evolved from displays of the skills developed to trail cattle, to catch them for branding, and to break and ride horses. At events sanctioned by the Professional Rodeo Cowboys Association (PRCA), like

Belt's, the contests of these skills have been refined into seven main events for men—saddle bronc riding, bareback riding, bull riding, calf roping, steer roping, team roping, and steer wrestling—and one event for women, barrel racing. The show is held together by continuous patter from an announcer who conducts a raunchy **repartee** with a clown who tells jokes like this:

"Clown: 'I got beat up by my wife last night.'"

"Announcer: 'I thought your wife was out of town last night.'"

"Clown: 'So did I.'"

> Michael Parfit. "Rodeos—Behind the Chutes,"
> National Geographic (September 1999).

"Previews, that is, embody the great promise of modern consumerist entertainment: that there will always be more. They are like the still-wrapped packages under a Christmas tree: the one you are about to tear into might turn out to be a pair of wool socks or a cheap knockoff of the toy you really wanted, but there is still all this other stuff yet to be opened up.

". . . Whatever disappointments the movies themselves might bring are safely in the future, as you feel the rush of all their expensive promise—the fights, the explosions, the computer-generated imagery, the macho **repartee**—in compact, thrill-packed doses. Big, commercial movies may rarely be surprising these days, but the possibility that they might be is always there."

> A. O. Scott. "Tease, Thrill or Scare 'Em, You Have to
> Snare 'Em," New York Times (March 21, 2003).

Audio pronunciations for the words in this pack can be found on our website: www.vocabvitamins.com/book/pack3.

Friend or Foe?

Ever feel like you are not going to get anything done on a day jam-packed with meetings? Ever settle down with a good book, just to hear the phone ring? Has it ever dawned on you that you will never get any sleep in that crowded hostel without earplugs and an eye patch? Well, in this world, some situations or items are just not conducive, or friendly to something else. Happiness is knowing this distinction. Here, you must choose the friend to each word. For example, sunbathing: eighty-five degrees (friend), williwaw (foe). Circle the friend, and cross out the foe. Friends are listed in the Answer Key.

1. defamation   a. anonymous   b. truth serum
                        phone call

2. allocution   a. podium   b. riot-ready mob

3. argot   a. tin ear   b. babel fish

4. invective   a. ample   b. mouth full of food
                        vocabulary

5. loquacious   a. crazy busy boss b. hour-long cab ride

6. circumlocution   a. five-minute   b. three-hour meeting
                        speech

7. vernacular   a. *My Fair Lady*   b. computer-
                                            synthesized speech

8. ineffable   a. vow of silence   b. magnetic poetry

9. aspersion   a. political   b. karma
                        competition

10. perorate   a. the giggles   b. a suit

11. prattle

a. coffee and dessert

b. sprinting

12. tautology

a. telegram

b. Grandpa's bad ear

13. patois

a. cosmopolitan trade port

b. isolated island

14. repartee

a. gift of gab

b. bad toothache

15. filibuster

a. dry mouth

b. comfortable shoes

16. vilify

a. jealousy

b. Zen

17. verbose

a. patent application

b. audience of five-year-olds

18. neologism

a. hipsters

b. outdated dictionaries

19. diatribe

a. meditation

b. alcohol

20. calumny

a. mentorship

b. bad divorce

21. garrulous

a. unlimited cell phone minutes

b. international phone call

22. libel

a. fact checking

b. tabloids

23. effusion

a. open

b. closed

24. lexicon

a. index cards

b. lack of interest

25. inquest

a. ticket out of the country

b. cooperation

[vo'·cab]
VITAMINS

PACK 4

GROW YOUR ROOTS

THEME 1
Indo-European Root *ak*: sharp

SIMILAR TO:

acerbic	sour, sharp, tart, biting
acuity	savvy, sharpness, capacity
acumen	astuteness, sharpness, insightfulness
mediocre	ordinary, average, common
paroxysm	outburst, eruption

THEME 2
Indo-European Root *ger*:
to gather

SIMILAR TO:

agoraphobia	fear of open space
allegory	symbolic, figurative
egregious	outrageously bad, horrendous
gregarious	outgoing, extroverted, social
panegyric	praise, eulogy

THEME 3
Indo-European Root *nek*: death

SIMILAR TO:

innocuous	inoffensive, flat, bland
necromancy	witchcraft, black magic
necrosis	loss, death
noxious	harmful, poisonous
pernicious	devastating, ruinous

THEME 4
Indo-European Root *pau*:
few, little

SIMILAR TO:

paucity	poverty, insufficiency
pusillanimous	timid, lacking courage
puerile	childish, immature
pullet	young chicken
poltroon	coward

THEME 5
Easy as 1-2-3

SIMILAR TO:

bifurcate	fork, split into two
quadruped	four-legged
quintessence	epitome, pure essence
trialogue	three-way conversation
univocal	unambiguous, one meaning

Indo-European Root *ak*: sharp

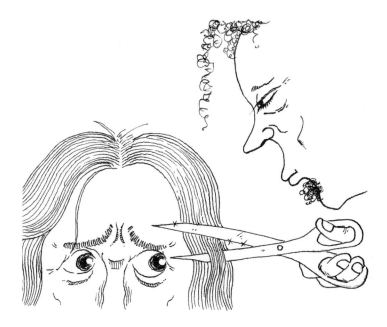

145

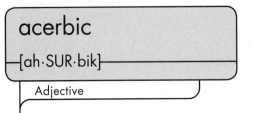

acerbic

—[ah·SUR·bik]—

Adjective

1. sour or bitter in taste
2. bitter, sharp, or severe in tone or character: "Victor was a notoriously acerbic critic, and I wasn't eager to show him my work."

ORIGIN

Approximately 1865; from Latin, *acerbus:* bitter, related to *acer*: sharp, related to the root *ak*: sharp + English suffix *-ic*.

BONUS WORD   Sound

aesthetic: concerning an appreciation of beauty or good taste

IN ACTION

"The tenor of 'SpongeBob SquarePants' is distinctly sweet and silly. It lacks most of the blatant scatology of recent crossover hits like 'Ren & Stimpy,' and avoids the **acerbic** social commentary of adults-only cartoons like 'The Simpsons' and 'South Park.' SpongeBob, in contrast, 'lives in a pineapple under the sea' (were you singing along?) with his pet snail, Gary. He is a relentlessly optimistic naif with a sound work ethic and an affinity for tighty-whitey underwear who basically has fun and plays nice."

Tom Zeller. *"How to Succeed Without Attitude,"*
New York Times *(July 21, 2002).*

"In other words, Quorn is a kind of fungus, and it's not at all a kind of mushroom. That doesn't mean there's anything wrong with it. Indeed, the FDA thought well enough of the fungus to approve late last year, admitting it into a class of foods 'generally recognized as safe.'

". . . For about an hour on Thursday, the office went a bit Quorn crazy, with 10 or so people popping into the coffee bar to taste this advanced food. The feedback was mostly positive. Everyone liked it, and some people said they loved it. Several said that the nuggets were indistinguishable from chicken, and others said that while they could taste a difference, they thought Quorn was very similar to meat.

"But Wired News's **acerbic** copy chief, a man who seems to know his way around a slab of steak, said that the nuggets weren't 'chicken-y' at all—bizarrely and cryptically, he said that they tasted like 'some sort of hors d'oeuvres.'"

Farhad Manjoo. "A Mushrooming Quorn Controversy," Wired.com (April 16, 2002).

acuity

—[ah·KYOO·i·tee]—

Noun

1. sharpness or acuteness of sight, perception, or intellect: "He had the acuity to gauge the precise mood of his audience on the spot and to adjust his message accordingly."

ORIGIN

Approximately 1543; from Latin, *acutus*: sharp, related to *acus*: needle, related to the root *ak*: sharp.

BONUS WORD   Sound

fatuity: smug, complacent stupidity

IN ACTION

"The legend of a Churchill debilitated by heart ailments and exhaustion, woozy with liquor and showing the signs of early senility still persists, although the truth seems to be that he survived the stresses of the war in far better physical condition and with greater mental **acuity** than younger political leaders and general officers."

> *Eliot A. Cohen. "Churchill Asks a Question,"*
> Supreme Command: Soldiers, Statesmen,
> and Leadership in Wartime *(2002).*

"The information links are like nerves that pervade and help to animate the human organism. The sensors and monitors are analogous to the human senses that put us in touch with the world. Databases correspond to memory; the information processors perform the function of human reasoning and comprehension. Once the postmodern infrastructure is reasonably integrated, it will greatly exceed human intelligence in reach, **acuity**, capacity, and precision."

> *Albert Borgman.* Crossing the
> Postmodern Divide *(1992).*

acumen

[AK·yah·mahn, ah·KYOO·mahn]

Noun

1. speed and shrewdness of discernment or insight: "Tyra didn't have much faith in her mother's romantic acumen, but she eventually broke down and accepted her matchmaking services."

ORIGIN

Approximately 1531; borrowed from Latin, *acumen*: sharpness, from *acuere*: to sharpen to a point, related to *acus*: needle, related to the root *ak*: sharp.

BONUS WORD   Synonym

perspicacity: shrewdness, astuteness, intelligence

IN ACTION

"Mr. Ford's independence has been known to manifest itself off screen as well, and he has a reputation, which he does not deny, as an actor who sometimes second-guesses his directors. 'Generally speaking,' he said, 'I don't consider what I read to be finished scripts, but a work in progress. There may be further development and I generally enjoy being part of that process. It's been that way for a long time. And I haven't worked with anybody who wasn't comfortable working that way with me.'

"Kathryn Bigelow confirms Mr. Ford's close involvement: 'I was surprised and impressed by his story **acumen**—it's like speaking to a writer. And it's not as if he's looking at the story solely from the standpoint of his character. He sees the whole piece.'"

Dave Kehr. "Harrison Ford: An American Face, Rough Edges and All," New York Times (July 21, 2002).

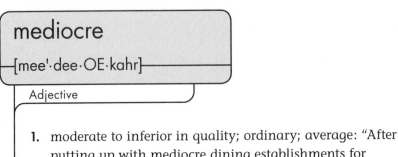

mediocre

[mee'·dee·OE·kahr]

Adjective

1. moderate to inferior in quality; ordinary; average: "After putting up with mediocre dining establishments for years, Lester used the extra bounty from his promotion to treat himself to a new fancy restaurant every week."

ORIGIN

Approximately 1586; from Latin, *mediocris*: of moderate quality, or originally, halfway up a mountain (*medius*: middle + *ocris*: a jagged or rugged mountain, related to *acer*: sharp, related to the root *ak*: sharp).

BONUS WORD Continuum

LOW QUALITY . . .   **. . . HIGH QUALITY**

flagrant   ⟶   mediocre   ⟶   stellar

flagrant: conspicuously and outrageously bad or reprehensible

stellar: leading, outstanding; related to stars

IN ACTION

"'I have made so far 32 records, some of them quite marvelous, some of them **mediocre**, but all necessary,' he wired Washington from Harlan, Kentucky, in September 1937.

"Collecting was only half of the Lomax hourglass. The sand flowed through to the bottom when he went home and assumed his role as popularizer.

"A ubiquitous part of the New York City folk scene of the early 1940s, Lomax passed the songs he had collected to the musicians who would later become cornerstones of the Folk Revival. Among those who adopted Lomax finds: Lead Belly, whom Lomax's father had 'discovered' in a Louisiana prison, Woody Guthrie and the young Pete Seeger."

Associated Press. "Alan Lomax: The Most
Important Musical Figure You Never Heard Of,"
CNN.com (July 20, 2002).

"Well, it's been two weeks now since my fatal heart attack, and all I can say is, thanks, guys. Thanks so much for honoring my 56 years of life on this planet by dedicating that episode of *Veronica's Closet* to me."

Bill Unseld. "Thanks For Dedicating That
Mediocre Sitcom Episode to My Memory,"
Onion.com (February 2, 2000).

"The British came relatively late to sushi, but there are lots of sushi restaurants now. You can even get **mediocre** prepackaged sushi in some supermarkets, although you'll see warning signs posted in the refrigerated cabinets reading, 'Sushi may contain raw fish,' so they're not quite there yet."

Ben Greenman. "Q & A with Rebecca Mead:
More Than London Broil," New Yorker Online
(August 6, 2001).

paroxysm

[PAR·ahk·siz'·ahm]

Noun

1. a sudden, violent fit of emotion or action: "Drew was not one to giggle easily, but his younger brother aped around in circles relentlessly until he submitted in a paroxysm of laughter."

2. (as in medicine) an attack, fit, or recurrence of a disease, especially a disease that surfaces at intervals

ORIGIN

Probably before 1500; from Medieval Latin, *paroxysmus*: fit of a disease; from Greek, *paroxysmos*, from *paroxynein*: to irritate or stimulate (*para*: beyond + *oxynein*: sharpen or provoke, from *oxys*: sharp, related to the root *ak*: sharp).

BONUS WORD   Related

febrile: feverish; related to fever

IN ACTION

"While watching the pained looks on the runners' faces at mile 23, it struck me: These people are not happy. They're driven not by pleasure, but rather by pain. Indeed, the only happy people were the spectators, and they were not as I would have imagined. I had assumed the marathon crowd would consist of fat people watching thin runners. But it turned out to be average people watching average runners. Many runners were obese or out of shape—the marathon may have been their only serious physical activity of the year (and, according to the latest AMA study, people who embark on massive exercise programs with little pre-training have a heightened risk of heart attacks). Many of the female spectators were beautiful, healthy and rosy-cheeked, like cheerleaders in sweaters. Most of the female runners were anorexic and unappealing. And I saw the guy with one sleeve, now just ahead of my wife and well on his way to a respectable 4:20 finish, although by now he was missing both sleeves. When I saw Ellen, I was so elated that she had made it to mile 23 that, in an inexplicable **paroxysm** of poor judgment, I started to run parallel to her along a nearby footpath. After four blocks running and cheering, I was exhausted (in my defense, I was carrying a bag of clothes and snacks)."

Steven A. Shaw. "A Tale of Two Marathons: The Fat Guy Snacks His Way Through the New York City Marathon," Salon.com (November 24, 1999).

"Before my eyes could adjust to the stage, there was a **paroxysm** of bleating like a broken car alarm. Female singer Yasuko O bolted upright with a flurry of barely decipherable lyrics, squeezing her eyes shut through each volley of machine-gun-fire verse. . . .

"The blistering song ended abruptly after a minute and O squeaked a mouselike 'Thank you,' as she did after every aural cluster bomb that night."

Brent Baldwin. "Recalling the Mayhem of Melt Banana," Style Weekly (June 8, 2005).

Indo-European Root *ger*: to gather

agoraphobia

[ag'·ahr·ah·FOE·bee·ah]

Noun

1. an irrational fear of open or public spaces: "We knew our neighborhood could be rough, but we had no idea our son was being affected until he began exhibiting signs of agoraphobia."

ORIGIN

Approximately 1873; coined by German psychiatrist Carl Westphal as German, *Agoraphobie*; formed from Greek, *agora*: marketplace, related to the root *ger*: to gather + *phobia*: fear.

BONUS WORD Related

acrophobia: a morbid fear of great heights

IN ACTION

"I went to therapy. I went to the doctor. I had an abortion. Twenty minutes before my appointment, the phone rang. A faraway sister. She wanted me to reconsider. How did she know? He had tracked her down. He, who had never met my family, who spoke to my sister just once before, had contacted her. He knew that everyone in my family is adamantly pro-life. This was a low blow. I took it as a message that he would do what he could to maintain a presence in my life.

"I found a new neighborhood, a new apartment, a new school. More therapy. I was diagnosed as clinically depressed and suffering from post-traumatic stress disorder. I hardly left the house—borderline

agoraphobia induced by fear. Anti-depressants only fed my insomnia."

Spike Gillespie. *"Life of Restraint: I Have a Restraining Order on My Ex. But He Has a Grip on My Life,"* Salon.com *(October 25, 1999).*

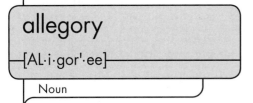

"So, where were you, anyway? No, wait, never mind that. True, without knowing what took you out of the game for seven years—prison, **agoraphobia**, 'Star Trek' reruns—it's difficult for us to devise a specific plan. Almost impossible, even. But on the other hand, when has that sort of thing ever stopped us?!

"You are right, the subject will come up eventually, so you should have a general idea of what you're going to say when it does. But unless you feel you have a moral obligation to explain your recent past (you're worried, for instance, that you might show up any day on 'America's Most Wanted'), then ambiguity is a fine course of action. . . . Because—and here's your Male Call Tip o' the Week—guys are suckers for a little mystery. It plays into our rich and varied fantasy lives. So don't ruin it for us!"

"Male Call: Advice from a Guy," San Jose Mercury News *(August 2, 2005).*

allegory

—[AL·i·gor'·ee]

Noun

1. the symbolic expression of a deeper or more abstract concept through characters or figures in a story, picture, or dramatic work: "Roger was fond of lacing his creative writing pieces with subversive allegory, which never pleased his professors."

2. a work employing such symbolic expression, often with a spiritual, moral, or political meaning

3. a symbolic representation of something

ORIGIN

Approximately 1384; borrowed from Latin, *allegoria*; from Greek, *allegoria*, from *allegorein*: to speak otherwise than one seems to speak, to interpret allegorically (*allos*: another, other + *agoreuein*: to speak publicly, from *agora*: public place, marketplace, related to the root *ger*: to gather).

BONUS WORD   Related

hyperbole: an exaggerated statement, as in "I could eat a horse"

IN ACTION

"In 'Chromophobia,' a short film made in 1966 by the great Belgian animator Raoul Servais, a squad of grim, antlike soldiers sets out to drain the world of color. They turn a child's red balloon into an iron ball and chain, a brightly hued rooster-shaped weathervane into a crow and trees into hangman's gibbets. Their gray tyranny is opposed by a spindly jester, who wages an aesthetic guerrilla war, causing flowers to sprout from the barrels of rifles and prison-camp searchlights to refract into rainbows.

"This whimsical little **allegory** will be shown, along with a selection of Mr. Servais's other work, next Saturday and Nov. 26 as part of a series on Belgian cinema at Lincoln Center's Walter Reade Theater that began last week and continues until Nov. 27."

A. O. Scott. "Redeeming Life's Pain with a Bit of Beauty," New York Times (November 15, 2002).

"The coyote is a living, breathing **allegory** of Want. He is always hungry. He is always poor, out of luck and friendless. The meanest creatures despise him, and even the fleas would desert him for a velocipede."

Mark Twain [Samuel Langhorne Clemens]
(1835–1910). U.S. author. Roughing It (1871).

egregious

[i·GREE·jahs, i·GREE·jee·ahs]

Adjective

1. conspicuously and outrageously bad or offensive: "Jackie's egregious behavior at dinner last night may have cost her several friends."

ORIGIN

Approximately 1534; borrowed from Latin, *egregius*, from *e grege*: standing out from the flock (*e*: out of + *grege*: ablative of *grex*: herd, flock [genitive *gregis*], related to the root *ger*: to gather).

BONUS WORD   Antonym

decorous: proper, dignified

IN ACTION

"As for the more **egregious** cases of Internet plagiarism—those in which students can have no doubt they are breaking the rules—many teachers say that as the Internet giveth, so the Internet taketh away.

"Ballou noted that the Internet allows teachers to confirm suspected cases of plagiarism, whereas in the past they might have been reluctant to punish students based only on a strong hunch.

"In addition to sites like 'Turnitin,' which analyze papers for likely plagiarism, Ballou said she can usually enter key phrases from an essay into a search engine to find the source from which they were copied."

Dustin Goot. "Thin Line Splits Cheating, Smarts,"
Wired.com (September 10, 2002).

"Lest anyone believe I am astride my high horse—or acting as though I am better than anyone else—I will now disclose the following personal information:

- "I am a recovered alcoholic. The last time I had a drink, the only wines the American middle class drank were Italian Chianti with raffia wrapped around the bottle. . . .
- "I was once fired by a newspaper for the most **egregious** sin the press can commit; I made up parts of a news story, because in the midst of a several-year-long drunk, I was too lazy to call a news source.
- "I served several years in Purgatory working for a Catholic weekly newspaper.
- "I got sober. I cleaned up my act. I worked long and hard to regain respectability."

Connie Coyne. "Reader Advocate: Credibility Demands
That Journalists Avoid Even Appearance of Conflict of
Interest," Salt Lake Tribune (November 16, 2002).

gregarious

[gri·GARE·ee·ahs]

Adjective

1. seeking and enjoying the company of others; sociable; friendly: "We moved to the city at the same time, but Ian

was so naturally gregarious that his social circle seemed to grow several times faster than mine."

2. tending to form a group with others of the same kind and living or moving in such a group: "Elephants are gregarious animals."

ORIGIN

Approximately 1668; borrowed from Latin, *gregarius*: belonging to a flock or herd, from *grex*: flock, herd (genitive *gregis*), related to the root *ger*: to gather.

BONUS WORD   Continuum

LESS FRIENDLY, LIKABLE . . .   **. . . MORE FRIENDLY, LIKABLE**

cordial ⟶ affable ⟶ gregarious

cordial: sincere; warm and friendly

affable: easy and pleasant; approachable; gracious

IN ACTION

"The Sanders family does its quintessentially embarrassing American thing, which is to come into a closed, 'foreign' community and just hang out, trying by dint of earnestness and good humor to fit right in. But isolated rural French peasants aren't the most **gregarious** folks around, and the author and his wife spend long days and nights inside their house, reading, or outside, walking, while their daughter negotiates the deep waters of preschool conducted in French."

Carolyn See. "Garden of Eatin'" (book review of
From Here, You Can't See Paris: Seasons of a French
Village and Its Restaurant, by Michael S. Sanders),
Washington Post (November 14, 2002).

"They were dangerous times for earth's largest land mammals. From the 60s through the 80s, soaring ivory demand led to dramatic declines in elephant populations throughout most of Africa. Fully eighty percent of the ivory traded was from illegally killed elephants. Much needed salvation finally came with the 1990 'ivory ban'. But recently, easing of the trade ban is leading more of these **gregarious**, sociable animals to early graves."

"Elephants Walk One Step Closer to Twilight: Easing of CITES Trade Ban Will Mean More Illegal Elephant Kills in Africa," Greenpeace.org (November 15, 2002).

panegyric
[pan'·ah·JIR·ik, pan'·ah·JIE·rik]

Noun

1. a formal oration or eulogy in praise of a person or an achievement: "We arranged a homecoming for our local celebrity, complete with music from the high school band and a panegyric from the mayor."
2. extravagant praise; an encomium

ORIGIN
Approximately 1603; from Latin, *panegyricus*; from Greek, *panegyrikos (logos)*: a speech at a public assembly, from *panegyris*: public assembly (*pan-*: all + *agyris*: place of assembly, marketplace, related to the root *ger*: to gather).

BONUS WORD   Related

eulogize: praise formally and eloquently, often at a funeral

IN ACTION

"Last Monday Mr. Palmieri went to Yale for a class discussion, a banquet and a concert with La Perfecta. At the banquet Mr. Thompson delivered a **panegyric**. 'You remind me of Aeneas,' he intoned rapturously, 'who lost Troy but found Rome. You closed the Palladium in 1966. And though we lost the Palladium, you found salsa. You teach us how to slice, drag, tease and release the beat, in the name of sabor. You teach us how to triumph over time.' Mr. Palmieri beamed."

Ben Ratliff. "Latin-Music Patriarch Stays Hungry; Eddie Palmieri Dusts Off, and Polishes, His 1960's Sound," New York Times (April 30, 2002).

Indo-European Root *nek*: death

THEME 3

innocuous

necromancy

necrosis

noxious

pernicious

innocuous

[i·NOK·yoo·ahs]

Adjective

1. producing no ill effect; harmless
2. not likely to offend or arouse strong feelings; inoffensive; insipid: "Alex evaded contentious subjects during his father-in-law's visit by replying to even the most pointed questions with innocuous generalities."

ORIGIN

Approximately 1598; from Latin, *innocuus* (*in-*: not + *nocuus*: harmful, hurtful, from *nocere*: to harm, from the root *nek*: death) + English suffix *-ous*.

BONUS WORD Origin

inoculate: vaccinate; introduce an idea or attitude into the mind of

IN ACTION

"It's a cute picture. If it's 1983 and you're Blair Warner's tarty new best friend on 'The Facts of Life.'

"Probably not the look Jennifer Aniston was going for. And not the one the budding *Picture Perfect* movie star wanted to see on the cover of a national fashion magazine.

"So, justlikethat, *Allure* has withdrawn the cover of its March issue at the behest of Aniston's camp—swapping the full-body, MTV-babe shot of the 'Friends' friend with an **innocuous** head shot."

Joal Ryan. "Jennifer Aniston Not Allured," E! Online
(March 12, 1998).

"There seems to be no stopping drug frenzy once it takes hold of a nation. What starts with an **innocuous** HUGS, NOT DRUGS bumper sticker soon leads to wild talk of shooting dealers and making urine tests a condition for employment—anywhere."

Barbara Ehrenreich. U.S. author and columnist.
"Drug Frenzy," The Worst Years
of Our Lives (1988).

necromancy

[NEK·rah·man'·see]

Noun

1. the practice of attempting to communicate with spirits of the dead to reveal or influence the course of future events: "Tina puts psychology in the same category as necromancy, so seeing a therapist is out of the question."
2. witchcraft; sorcery; black magic

ORIGIN

Approximately 1550; from Greek, *nekromanteia* (*nekros*: dead body, corpse, from the root *nek*: death + *manteia*: divination, from *manteuesthai*: to prophesy, from *mantis*: prophet).

BONUS WORD   Related

incantation: a ritual recitation of words or sounds for magical effect

IN ACTION

"'Sinatra: His Voice, His World, His Way,' a two-hour multimedia extravaganza, arrived at the 5,800-seat theatre promising to resurrect the singer. 'Frank Sinatra, in his prime, will be brought to life via

breakthrough technology,' trumpeted the show's press releases. 'He's back!'

"Pop **necromancy** is nothing new. Who can forget the wheezy-voiced John Lennon on Free As a Bird, or Nat King Cole, 25 years dead, 'dueting' with his daughter Natalie? But the creators of this show aimed for a new level of verisimilitude. It was to star a hologram Sinatra: images excerpted from old footage projected on to huge panels to create the illusion of a walking, talking, 3D crooner. Would Virtual Frank stalk the stage, highball in hand, threatening to 'kick Sinead O'Connor's ass' like the late-model Actual Frank?"

Jody Rosen. "Ol' Blue Eyes Is Back from the Dead," Guardian (October 22, 2003).

"The Monterey County Sheriff's Office requires a permit for fortune telling and related businesses that open in unincorporated areas. The county code applies to practitioners of 'clairvoyance, clairaudience, cartomancy, phrenology, spirits, tea leaves or other such reading, mediumship, seership, prophecy, augury, astrology, palmistry, **necromancy**, mind-reading, telepathy, or other craft, art cards, talisman, charm, potion, magnetism, magnetized article or substance, crystal gazing, or magic of any kind or nature.'"

Dan Laidman. "Ethical Issues in Fortune Telling," Monterey Herald (October 19, 2003).

necrosis

[nah·KROE·sis, ne·KROE·sis]

Noun

1. death, through disease or injury, of living tissue in a localized area of the body: "The necrosis of my ankle after the injury prompted the end of my rugby days—and the beginning of my love affair with golf."

ORIGIN

Approximately 1665; from Late Latin, *necrosis*: killing; probably borrowed from Greek, *nekrosis*: death, from *nekroun*: to make dead, from *nekros*: dead body, corpse, from the root *nek*: death.

BONUS WORD   Related

contusion: an injury that doesn't break the skin but results in discoloration

IN ACTION

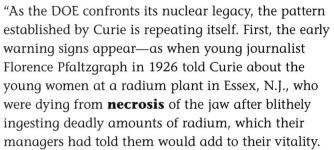

"As the DOE confronts its nuclear legacy, the pattern established by Curie is repeating itself. First, the early warning signs appear—as when young journalist Florence Pfaltzgraph in 1926 told Curie about the young women at a radium plant in Essex, N.J., who were dying from **necrosis** of the jaw after blithely ingesting deadly amounts of radium, which their managers had told them would add to their vitality.

"Today, the signs are still either ignored or attacked as not being credible. . . . By the time officials acknowledge the problem, it's too late."

Robert Alvarez. "America's Cold War Casualties: A Former Energy Department Official Dissects President Clinton's New Plan to Help the Sick Workers Who Built the Country's Nuclear Arsenal," Salon.com (May 6, 2000).

"By 1989, [Bo] Jackson was a baseball all-star. His mammoth homer to centerfield in Anaheim off Rick Reuschel leading off for the American League made him the All-Star Game MVP.

"In 1990, the 698 yards he gained in 10 games with the Raiders earned him a selection to the Pro Bowl, though he would never play in the game. That's because on Jan. 13, 1991, he suffered a hip injury while being tackled during the Raiders' playoff victory over the Cincinnati Bengals. No one knew at the time, but the resulting condition, known as avascular **necrosis**, would lead to the deterioration of the cartilage and bone around his left hip joint.

"When Jackson's hip did not respond to treatment, the Royals released him in spring training. Picked up by the White Sox two weeks later, Jackson only played 23 games. By 1992, his left hip had deteriorated so much, doctors replaced it with an artificial one."

Ron Flatter. "Bo Knows Stardom and Disappointment," ESPN.com.

noxious

—[NOK·shahs]————————————

Adjective

1. physically harmful or destructive to living things, especially by being poisonous: "The noxious air in our freshly painted apartment was too much to bear, so we ended up spending the weekend on our neighbor's couch."
2. corrupting to the mind or morals: "noxious practices," "noxious ideas"

ORIGIN

Fifteenth century; from Latin *noxius*: hurtful, injurious, from *noxa*: damage, harm, related to *nocere*: to harm, related to the root *nek*: death.

BONUS WORD Related

conflagration: a powerful and damaging fire

IN ACTION

"What makes this hangover remedy unique is that it may actually work. When alcohol enters the bloodstream, the liver quickly converts it to acetaldehyde, a **noxious** chemical that causes headaches and other hangover symptoms, and then slowly turns the acetaldehyde into harmless acetic acid. Antipokhmelin helps by slowing the production of acetaldehyde. Mayevsky's 1972 trials were effective in four of five drinkers. In 2000 the Russian Ministry of Health confirmed that the pill worked on both rats and humans. Soldiers who took Antipokhmelin after consuming a half liter of vodka in an hour reported milder hangovers than those who had not. The pill is sold in the United States as a food supplement, which doesn't require testing."

Frank Brown. "A Drunk's Best Friend: A Russian Firm Is Marketing a Pill That Is Supposed to Alleviate the Worst Symptoms of the Dreaded Hangover. Bottom's Up!" Newsweek (November 3, 2003).

"As a result, the iron-jawed goat has found its niche in a South that's looking for a hero to fight the creeping, tenacious, broad-leafed invader.

"'Goats have gotten a bad rap over centuries,' says Jean-Marie Luginbuhl, a North Carolina State agronomist who sponsored this summer's 'Goat

Invasion 2003' on campus. 'But if you understand the way goats browse, you can really use them in a very positive way.'

"Employing goats to clear woodlands is not the newest trick in the book. But thanks to emerging research on their browsing habits—as well as vastly improved portable fences to hold them in—goats are slowly gaining acceptance as environmentally friendly 'bio-agents' that fight **noxious** vines at their root."

Patrik Jonsson. "In Curbing Kudzu, Goats May Be Man's Best Friend," Christian Science Monitor *(October 21, 2003).*

pernicious

[pahr·NISH·ahs]

Adjective

1. tending to cause great harm, injury, or death: "The pernicious rumors circulating among Kelli's staff and peers were undermining her ability to function as a leader in the organization."

ORIGIN
Approximately 1425; borrowed from Middle French, *pernicios*, and directly from Latin, *perniciosus*: destructive, from *pernicies*: destruction (*per-*: completely + *necare*: to kill, *nec-*: violent death, from the root *nek*: death).

BONUS WORD   Antonym

benign: pleasant and beneficial in nature or influence; not dangerous

IN ACTION

"Clearly, the practice of determining the sex of the unborn child and eliminating it if the foetus is found to be female is behind the adverse child sex ratio. Neglect of the girl child resulting in higher mortality between 0–6 years of age is another.

"The widespread preference for sons is held responsible for this **pernicious** trend. Sushma Swaraj, Union health and parliamentary affairs minister, told this newspaper that the hurdle to even population control 'is society's preference for a son'."

N. Chandra Mohan. "Op-Ed: Adverse Child Sex
Ratio in India," Financial Express (October 27, 2003).

"More than 2,200 firefighters battled the **pernicious** blaze, which officials suspect started Tuesday as the result of arson. Officials reported 10 injuries, none serious, mostly to firefighters.

"More than 14,000 acres had burned as of Saturday afternoon, and the fire threatened electrical lines that provide power for up to 1 million customers in the Los Angeles basin."

"Thousands of Residents East of L.A. Evacuate as Fire
Approaches," Bay 9 News.com (October 25, 2003).

Indo-European Root *pau*: few, little

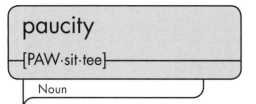

paucity
[PAW·sit·tee]

Noun

1. smallness of number; fewness
2. smallness or insufficiency of quantity; scarcity: "Despite my noble intentions, my first bonsai quickly wilted under the paucity of my experience."

ORIGIN
Fifteenth century; originally from Latin, *paucus*: few, from the root *pau*: few, little.

BONUS WORD   Antonym

opulence: wealth, abundance, profusion

IN ACTION

"My son was born in Paris at the Hôpital Pierre Rouques. Originally made for steelworkers in the 1800s and only partially renovated, the hospital still bears the mark of its age: a **paucity** of bathrooms (two in a maternity ward for 20 women), nurse assistants with the grim, forbidding air of characters in a Balzac novel and long, vaulting windows that look onto squalid courtyards, from which the sky is a tiny pinhole of blue above a rise of sooty concrete.

"But never mind. Having a French husband qualified me for the breathtaking generosity of socialized health care: nine months of all-expense-paid medical, including the standard one week post-delivery stay at the hospital and subsequent free trips to the physiotherapist. I took the bathrooms in stride."

Debra Ollivier. "Bringing up Bebe," Salon.com
(November 7, 1997).

"For my part I distrust all generalizations about women, favourable and unfavourable, masculine and feminine, ancient and modern; all alike, I should say, result from **paucity** of experience."

> Bertrand Russell (1872–1970). British philosopher and mathematician. "An Outline of Intellectual Rubbish," Unpopular Essays (1950).

"It is very strange, and very melancholy, that the **paucity** of human pleasures should persuade us ever to call hunting one of them."

> Samuel Johnson (1709–84). British author. Anecdotes of Samuel Johnson (1786).

pusillanimous

[pyoo'·sah·LAN·ah·mahs]

Adjective

1. utterly lacking in courage, strength, and determination; cowardly: "He talked a good game, but he became a pusillanimous leader at the faintest hint of confrontation."

ORIGIN

Approximately 1586; from Latin, *pusillus*: little, weak, diminutive of *pullus*: young animal, related to the root *pau*: few, little + *animus*: spirit, courage, mind.

BONUS WORD Continuum

LESS EXTREME . . .   . . . MORE EXTREME

irresolute ⟶ pusillanimous ⟶ craven

irresolute: not resolute, wavering

craven: characterized by abject cowardice, spiritless

IN ACTION

"**Pusillanimous** legislators have allowed abortion politics to compromise women's access to complete health services. They are being counterbalanced by increasingly female medical school enrollments. Women doctors-in-training founded MSFC and are the force behind the wave of curriculum reforms. Who better to emerge as welcomed champions of women's health and providers of safe and legal abortion services?"

B. Meredith Burke. "Women Docs Counter Abortion Politics," San Francisco Chronicle (June 28, 2002).

"Fujioka says that he was brought to the cause of textbook reform by the 1991 Gulf War. After seeing Japan appear weak and **pusillanimous** during the affair, he concluded that a flawed history-education system had failed to produce bold, self-confident leaders."

Sangwon Suh and Murakami Mutsuko. "The War at Home: It's Japanese Versus Japanese Over How to Portray Their Militaristic Past," Asiaweek (August 31, 1999).

puerile
[PYOO·ahr·ahl, PYOOR·ahl, PYOOR·ile']

Adjective

1. pertaining to or characteristic of childhood
2. showing or suggesting a lack of maturity; silly; childish: "John's sense of humor was puerile and occasionally offensive, but he was still the funniest man I had ever met."

ORIGIN
Approximately 1661; from Latin, *puerilis*: childish, from *puer*: child, boy, related to the root *pau*: few, little.

BONUS WORD　Continuum

LESS EXTREME . . .　　**. . . MORE EXTREME**
sophomoric　——▶　puerile

sophomoric: immature, naïve

IN ACTION

"For all the fun it conjures, 'Goldmember,' the third episode of the Austin Powers series, is also a bloated (and dare I say?) decadent mess. Overstuffed with **puerile** humor, it cannibalizes its own running gags and grovels to plant icky wet kisses on the feet of Hollywood royalty. As if to certify the series' importance, everyone from Tom Cruise to Steven Spielberg to Gwyneth Paltrow pops in for a cameo appearance, and although these celebrities are cleverly used, the shameless star worship leaves you feeling a little queasy."

Stephen Holden. "Got Lots of Mojo, Needs a Little Love," New York Times (July 26, 2002).

"Women are told from their infancy, and taught by the example of their mothers, that a little knowledge of human weakness, justly termed cunning, softness of temper, outward obedience, and a scrupulous attention to a **puerile** kind of propriety, will obtain for them the protection of man; and should they be beautiful, every thing else is needless, for, at least, twenty years of their lives."

Mary Wollstonecraft (1759–97). British feminist. A Vindication of the Rights of Woman (1792).

"The idea that leisure is of value in itself is only conditionally true. . . . The average man simply spends his leisure as a dog spends it. His recreations are all **puerile**, and the time supposed to benefit him really only stupefies him."

H. L. Mencken (1880–1956). U.S. journalist. Minority Report: H. L. Mencken's Notebooks, no. 87 (1956).

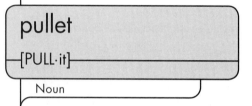

pullet

[PULL·it]

Noun

1. a young hen usually less than a year old: "A real, live pullet clucked blithely atop a New York City penthouse."

ORIGIN

Approximately 1362; from Old French, *poulette*, diminutive of *poule*: hen; from Latin, *pullus*: young animal, young fowl.

BONUS WORD Origin

pullulate: to sprout, breed, teem

IN ACTION

"I will say that when Thornton was a week old, sprouting brown feathers on his wings, he struck me as being very alone in the fowl world. I brought the two incubators out of storage and started heating a new clutch of four eggs—three of which hatched without incident. When Thornton met his younger reflections of himself, he was the only one with feathers, which he puffed up and in which he allowed the infants to snuggle. This supported Cathy's hunch, stated at the outside, that Thornton was a female, and that dubbing her a male, with no evidence whatsoever, was mere gender chauvinism.

"Thornton is now fully grown and very henlike indeed, a beautiful rust-toned Rhode Island Red **pullet** with a golden head—an eagle among chickens."

Steven Leigh Morris. "Chicken-Hearted: The Hatching of Memory," LA Weekly (June 29–July 5, 2001).

"I never complained of the vicissitudes of fortune, nor suffered my face to be overcast at the revolution of the heavens, except once, when my feet were bare, and I had not the means of obtaining shoes. I came to the chief of Kfah in a state of much dejection, and saw there a man who had no feet. I returned thanks to God and acknowledged his mercies, and endured my want of shoes with patience, and exclaimed,

"'Roast fowl to him that's sated will seem less
"Upon the board than leaves of garden cress.
"While, in the sight of helpless poverty,
"Boiled turnip will a roasted **pullet** be.'"

Sadi (1184–1291). Persian poet. The Gulistn [or Rose Garden, translated by Edward B. Eastwick] (1880).

"Amber is a pretty strawberry blonde, on this Saturday night sitting on a planter at the corner of Broadway and Pine in Long Beach. A spray bottle, comb and small scissors (with the dangerous points ground down to rounded tips) were tied to her belt with twine. A sandwich board to her left read, 'Free haircuts. It's free! For reals!'

"But the passersby weren't going to receive the free haircuts; they were going to give them. . . . It took 36 minutes to bald her almost completely. At the end, she looked like a newborn **pullet**. Her soft hair stuck to

her shoulders in itchy wisps, and she looked like she
might cry while she smiled."

Rebecca Schoenkopf. "Running with Scissors: Long
Beach's Dangerous but Gentle Performance Art,"
OC Weekly (September 22–28, 2001).

poltroon

[pol·TROON]

Noun

1. an abject coward; a dastard: "I knew they agreed with
    me, but instead of speaking up, the poltroons sat around
    the table silently while our team leader ridiculed my
    ideas."

ORIGIN

Probably before 1529; borrowed from Middle French, *poltron*:
rascal, coward; from Italian, *poltrone*: lazy fellow, from
poltro: a colt, or a sluggard (from the skittishness of an
unbroken colt); from Latin, *pullus*: young animal, related to
the root *pau*: few, little.

BONUS WORD Sound

dragoon: to coerce or subjugate; a cavalryman

IN ACTION

"No, this fellow citizen—who probably has a self-image as an upstanding American—became a sleazy, chicken-hearted, gutless, dastardly, invertebrate, punk **poltroon** . . . a cur who just banged into the back of my modest yet lovable little car and took off."

Chris Curle. *"The Marcophile: My Car, the Target,"*
Marco Island Eagle *(January 7, 2004)*.

"The editorial . . . was an attack made upon the printers of the Union. It was replied to by a Union printer, and a representative of the printers, who in a communication denounced the writer of that article as a liar, a **poltroon** and a puppy."

James L. Laird. *[Reprinted in]* Mark Twain
of the Enterprise *(1957)*.

Easy as 1-2-3

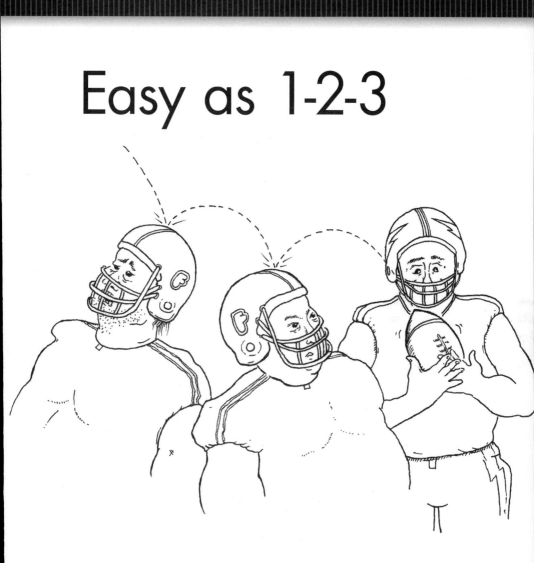

THEME 5

bifurcate

quadruped

quintessence

trialogue

univocal

bifurcate

[BIE·fahr·kate', bie·FUR·kate']

Transitive Verb, Intransitive Verb, Adjective

Transitive Verb

1. to split or divide into two branches or parts: "With a wall of reinforced concrete, the town was able to bifurcate the river."

Intransitive Verb

2. to separate or fork into two branches or parts: "Why did the American political system bifurcate into two succinct parties, and what has prevented a legitimate third contender?"

Adjective

(Adjective also pronounced BIE·fahr·kit', bie·FUR·kit')

3. divided or separated into two branches; forked

ORIGIN

Approximately 1615; from Medieval Latin, *bifurcare*: to divide; from Latin, *bifurcus*: two pronged (*bi*: two + *furc(us)*: fork). Both the *bi-* and *di-* prefixes mean two.

BONUS WORD   Origin

bilateral: having two sides, often symmetrical

dichromatic: exhibiting two colors

bicoastal: relating to or coexisting on two coasts

biannual: twice a year

IN ACTION

"But still the main thing that affects those rhythms is the system of trading itself, and no one has any idea what will happen to various trading systems. Will the specialist system survive all the criticism just as it survived the crashes of 1929 and 1987? Will it be scrapped for a whole other form of centralization? Will the market **bifurcate** into two kinds of trading systems—one that's centralized and one that's direct?"

Amanda Griscom. "Tools of the Trader: Could the NYSE Hold the Key to the Future of Electronic Trading?" Village Voice (September 8–14, 1999).

quadruped
[KWOD·rah·ped']

Noun, Adjective

Noun

1. an animal having four limbs specialized for walking, especially a mammal: "The alley cats in the Bowery are the scariest looking quadrupeds I've ever seen, and I'm convinced they have no genetic relationship to my cat at home."

Adjective

2. having four feet

ORIGIN

Approximately 1646; from French, *quadrupede*; borrowed from Latin, *quadrupes* (*quadru*: four + *pes*: foot).

BONUS WORD   Origin

quadruple: four times as much

quadrant: one of four equal sections

quadriceps: four-part muscle at the front of the thigh

IN ACTION

"We thus learn that man is descended from a hairy **quadruped**, furnished with a tail and pointed ears, probably arboreal in its habits. . . . The main conclusion arrived at in this work . . . will, I regret to think, be highly distasteful to many persons. . . . But we are not here concerned with hopes and fears, only with the truth as far as our reason allows us to discover it."

Charles Darwin (1809–82). English naturalist.
The Descent of Man (1871).

quintessence

—[kwin·TES·ahns]——

Noun

1. the purest and most concentrated essence of something
2. the most representative or pure example of a type: "My uncle Declan was the quintessence of a free spirit in my eyes, and I always aspired to live a similar lifestyle."

ORIGIN

Approximately 1435; borrowed from Middle French, *quinte*: essence; from Medieval Latin, *Quinta essentia*: fifth essence. The concept traces to Aristotle, who spoke of a fifth element that permeated all things.

BONUS WORD   Origin

quintet: group of five

quintuplet: one of five from the same birth

IN ACTION

"The mayor is also doing his best to gin up his decency panel to screen out offensive works of art. . . . Eager-to-please urban attractions, like the Chelsea Piers, hustle to offer suburban pleasures like driving ranges. And there is Times Square, once the **quintessence** of urban sin, now a suburb of Orlando."

> Peter Applebome. "Those Little Town Blues, in Old
> New York?" New York Times (April 29, 2001).

"It seems not to have been written. It is the **quintessence** of life. It is the basic truth."

> Justin Brooks Atkinson (1894–1984).
> American journalist and drama critic. [Writing
> of Tennessee Williams's Cat on a Hot Tin Roof in]
> New York Times (March 25, 1955).

trialogue

[TRY·ah·log']

Noun

1. a conversation or discussion between three people or groups: "The trialogue that ensued between the three partners was laced with as much delicate political maneuvering as a congressional hearing."

ORIGIN

Approximately 1535; from Latin, *tri*: three + a mistaken formation of English *(di)alogue*. The English *dialogue* has its roots in Greek *dialogos* and *dialegesthai*: converse (*dia*: across + *legein*: speak), not in the Latin *di*: two.

BONUS WORD Origin

trident: three pronged

triarchy: government of three people

triathlon: athletic event consisting of swimming, biking, and running

tricycle: human-powered vehicle with three wheels

IN ACTION

"The programming environment facilitated Ellie's conducting her own investigation. It provided a language, a different notation in which Ellie could express her mathematical ideas. It provided a signing environment, a place-holder for these ideas to exist outside of Ellie. Moreover, because this language is dynamic—it can be 'run'—it provided feedback to Ellie's ideas. This **trialogue** between Ellie's mental model, the expression of her mental model in encapsulated code and the running of that code, allowed Ellie to successively refine the creative structure of her thought."

From Constructionism in Practice: Designing, Thinking, and Learning in a Digital World *(1996).*

univocal

[yoo·NIV·ah·kahl]

Adjective, Noun

Adjective

1. having only one meaning or interpretation; unambiguous: "Niall insisted on trying to distill the complex novels we were reading into univocal messages and themes, which never seemed to work."

Noun

2. a word or term having only one meaning

ORIGIN

Approximately 1545; from Late Latin, *univocus* (*uni*: one + *vocus* [derived from *voc*: voice]).

BONUS WORD Origin

united: existing as a single entity

unify: consolidate, connect

unisex: for both men and women

uniform: the same, unvarying; a school outfit

IN ACTION

"Hypertext does not permit a tyrannical, **univocal** voice. Rather the voice is always that distilled from the combined experience of the momentary focus, the lexia one presently reads, and the continually forming narrative of one's reading path."

> *George P. Landow. U.S.-based author and professor of English and digital culture. Hypertext: The Convergence of Contemporary Critical Theory & Technology (1992).*

ROOT	MEANING	WORD EXAMPLES
nek	death	nectar, pernicious, innocuous
ak	sharp	acute, mediocre, acerbic
pau	few, little	pauper, puerile, paucity
ger	to gather	segregate, gregarious, agoraphobia
uni, bi, tri, quad, quint	one, two, three, four, five	univocal, bifurcate, trialogue, quadruped, quintessence

Audio pronunciations for the words in this pack can be found on our website: www.vocabvitamins.com/book/pack4.

Antidote!

Find the right word from the pack that will neutralize the situation, or "poison," listed on the left-hand side. All the words in this pack will be used just once. Hurry and administer the antidote before it is too late!

allegory   quintessence   innocuous   acerbic
quadruped   acuity   bifurcate   panegyric
necromancy   paucity   univocal   gregarious
pullet   trialogue   acumen   paroxysm

POISON   **ANTIDOTE**

1. grouchy and much too serious   _____

2. her closet is completely
   overflowing   _____

3. hunger   _____

4. way too dangerous   _____

5. dumb as a door knob   _____

6. saccharine   _____

7. much too literal   _____

8. stoic and unemotional   _____

9. indecisive Papa, Mama,
   and Baby Bear   _____

10. one not enough   _____

11. approval ratings suffering   _____

12. can't see past my own nose   _____

13. need to talk to dead uncle   _____

14. need speed on land   _____

15. confusion   _____

16. diluted scent   _____

Now find the right word from the pack that describes the
"poison" for which the cure is listed in the right-hand column.

necrosis	pusillanimous	agoraphobia
poltroon	pernicious	noxious
egregious	mediocre	puerile

DISCOVER THE POISON   **WE HAVE THE ANTIDOTE**

17. _____   big and brave potion #7

18. _____   diligent hard work

19. _____   deep breaths

20. _____   etiquette school

21. _____   stem cell research or elvish
                             healing

22. _____   many, many trees

23. _____   growing up

24. _____   healing and rebuilding

25. _____   courage from Oz himself

[vo·cab]
VITAMINS

PACK 5

LIVING IN
THE PAST

THEME 1
Down Memory Lane

SIMILAR TO:

auld lang syne	the past, good-old days
lethe	forgetfulness, amnesia
annals	archives
mnemonic	memory aid, clue
eidetic	photographic, exact

THEME 2
Bygones and Has-Beens

SIMILAR TO:

antiquity	ancient times
quondam	former, once
antediluvian	ancient, before the Flood
obsolete	dated, useless
antebellum	before the war

THEME 3
Here to Stay!

SIMILAR TO:

perennial	continual, enduring
amaranthine	undying, constant, endless
inveterate	established, enduring
perdurable	permanent
immemorial	age-old, before memory

THEME 4
In the Past

SIMILAR TO:

erstwhile	former, bygone
archaic	ancient, outdated
hoary	gray, aged
primordial	prehistoric, original
superannuated	out-of-date

THEME 5
Telling the Story

SIMILAR TO:

raconteur	storyteller, narrator
fabulist	teller of tall tales
apologue	fable, parable
anecdote	short story, incident
recapitulate	summarize, paraphrase, repeat

Down Memory Lane

auld lang syne

[oald'·lang·ZINE, oald'·lang·SINE]

Noun

1. good days now past, especially those fondly remembered
2. long-standing friendship or camaraderie: "I won't miss the work much, or the commute, but the auld lang syne I've shared with you good people will be sorely missed."

ORIGIN

Date unknown; from Scots, *auld*: old + *lang*: long + *syne*: since.

BONUS WORD   Related

bibulous: given to the consumption of alcohol

IN ACTION

[Although "auld lang syne" may not be a common conversational phrase, we thought we would give you a jump on New Year's Eve. Now is the time to study the Western world's most nostalgic, feel-good song. Yes, there are words!]

Auld Lang Syne
Should auld acquaintance be forgot,
And never brought to mind?
Should auld acquaintance be forgot,
And auld lang syne!

CHORUS
For auld lang syne, my dear,
For auld lang syne.
We'll tak a cup o' kindness yet,
For auld lang syne.

And surely ye'll be your pint stowp!
And surely I'll be mine!
And we'll tak a cup o' kindness yet
For auld lang syne.
For auld lang syne.

We twa hae run about the braes,
And pou'd the gowans fine;
But we've wander'd mony a weary fit,
Sin' auld lang syne.
For auld lang syne.

We twa hae paidl'd in the burn,
Frae morning sun till dine;
But seas between us braid hae roar'd
Sin' auld lang syne.
For auld lang syne.

And there's a hand, my trusty fere!
And gie's a hand o' thine!
And we'll tak a right gude-willie waught,
For auld lang syne.
For auld lang syne.

Robert Burns (1759–96). Scottish poet.

lethe

[LEE·thee]

Noun

1. (as in Greek mythology) the river of forgetfulness in Hades (the souls of the dead were required to drink from it, causing them to forget the pleasures and concerns they had known when they were alive)
2. a state of forgetfulness or oblivion: "My husband seems to live in a perpetual lethe, and if he doesn't improve his

retention capabilities, I'm going to start tattooing notes onto his palm."

ORIGIN

Date unknown; from Greek, *lethe*: forgetfulness; related to *lanthanesthai*: to forget.

BONUS WORD   Origin

lethal: deadly or causing great destruction

IN ACTION

"I saw the Count sprinkle drops from a phial on to his handkerchief and give it to the little lady. I saw her fall back softly on the couch. . . .

"I thought that I called out, but heard no sound. There was a weight of lead upon my eyes—the air was thick with fog. I fought with might and main to get to her. I could not stir a step. I could not even see her now.

"Making one last effort to move, I missed my footing and fell—fell, as it seemed, into a yawning gulf that opened suddenly before me—fell down and down and down into the fathomless depths of that slumber wherein we spend the half of existence.

"But **Lethe** had been meted out unevenly; to her the sleep that knew no earthly morrow—to me the sleep that ended in a few hours, leaving the rest of life a dream."

Mary Coleridge (1861–1907). "The Friendly Foe."

annals

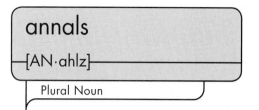

[AN·ahlz]

Plural Noun

1. a chronological record of events in successive years
2. a historical record or descriptive account, especially of an event, a series of events, or a period: "Many boom and bust periods have been documented throughout the annals of the American economy, but it was difficult to clearly identify them until they were over."
3. a periodic report or journal of the work of a society or learned body

ORIGIN

Approximately 1563; most likely borrowed from Latin, *annales libri*: annual books or records, plural of *annalis*: annual, from *annus*: year.

BONUS WORD   Origin

per annum: every year, annually

IN ACTION

"The **annals** of sport are littered with the names of athletes who fail to graduate from college and end up lost when a professional sports career fails to materialize or ends prematurely. . . . But Vince Carter, the Toronto Raptors basketball star, made a powerful symbolic statement last weekend when he attended his college graduation ceremony at the University of North Carolina on the morning of a crucial game. He was right to shrug off criticism from those who accused him of not taking seriously his role in the N.B.A. playoffs."

"Vince Carter Got It Right," New York Times (May 22, 2001).

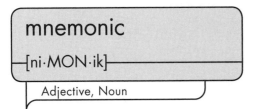

mnemonic

[ni·MON·ik]

Adjective, Noun

Adjective

1. intended to aid or assist the memory: "a mnemonic rhyme"

Noun

2. something intended to aid the memory, usually a rhyme or formula: "Nolan walked in to take his SATs with his head so packed full of mnemonics that any distraction would have caused them to tumble out of his head like clutter through a trap door in the attic."

ORIGIN

Approximately 1753; from Greek, *mnemonikos*: of or relating to memory; from *mnemon* (genitive of *mnemonos*): mindful, remembering, from *mnasthai*: remember.

BONUS WORD   Origin

Mnemosyne: Greek goddess of memory

IN ACTION

"Don't use **mnemonic** devices unless you're sure what you're doing. Remember the case of the guy who addressed a lady as 'Ms. Butt,' and she informed him, 'That's Ms. Bottomslee.'"

Ann Humphries. "Don't Wipe the Shrimp Juice on Your Clothes: Survive the Party with Your Career Intact," CNN.com (December 7, 2000).

eidetic

[ie·DET·ik]

Adjective

1. of visual imagery of almost photographic accuracy

ORIGIN

Approximately 1924; from German, *eidetisch*, coined by psychologist Erich Jaensch (1883–1940); from Greek, *eidetikos*: pertaining to images, from *eidesis*: knowledge, from *eidos*: form, shape.

BONUS WORD   Related

Doppelganger: a ghostly double of a living person

IN ACTION

"Pop cultural crazes come and go. Most people of a certain age, excluding VH1 commentators with weirdly **eidetic** memories, don't remember what they were doing in 1977 much less that year's biggest movies (hint, they include: *Saturday Night Fever, Annie Hall* & *Close Encounters of the Third Kind*). *Stars Wars* came out nearly thirty years ago and fans today, ranging from middle-aged men (who could recite every line from *Empire Strikes Back* verbatim) and college students to kids whose parents hadn't yet met in 1977, are still mesmerized. Then again, the *Star Wars* series isn't your average cinematic fad; it's the blockbuster of all blockbusters and is as relevant today as it was decades ago."

*Anhoni Patel. "The End of the Beginning"
(movie review of Star Wars Episode III: The Revenge
of the Sith), SFStation.com (June 2005).*

"But once you know that Tesla spoke eight languages, had **eidetic** memory and impressed his elementary school teachers with calculus, you have the luxury of accessing the play's depth. Once you realize that the man was simply one of those gift boxes that arrive periodically on the planet's doorstep, the play asks, what do we do with the gift? The sad revelation that comes out of *Brilliant!* is not that a man ahead of his time is a lonely thing, but that the world moves so slowly it can never take full advantage of such exceptional people."

Marianne Messina. "A Current Story" (theater review of Brilliant, the high-energy tale of inventor Nikola Tesla), *Metro Silicon Valley (June 8, 2005).*

Bygones and Has-Beens

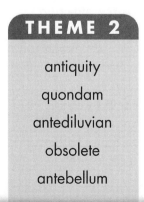

THEME 2

antiquity

quondam

antediluvian

obsolete

antebellum

antiquity

[an·TIK·wi·tee]

Noun

1. ancient times, or ancient history, especially the period preceding the Middle Ages: "Annie had difficulty identifying with the philosophers of antiquity her professors had focused on for much of her freshman year."
2. the people of ancient times
3. the quality of being very old or ancient; great age; considerable age
4. a relic or an artifact surviving from ancient times, especially something valuable, interesting, or collectible, as a coin, statue, monument, and so on

ORIGIN

Approximately 1280; from Latin, from *antiquus*: former, ancient, from *ante*: before.

BONUS WORD   Origin

propinquity: the property of being close together

IN ACTION

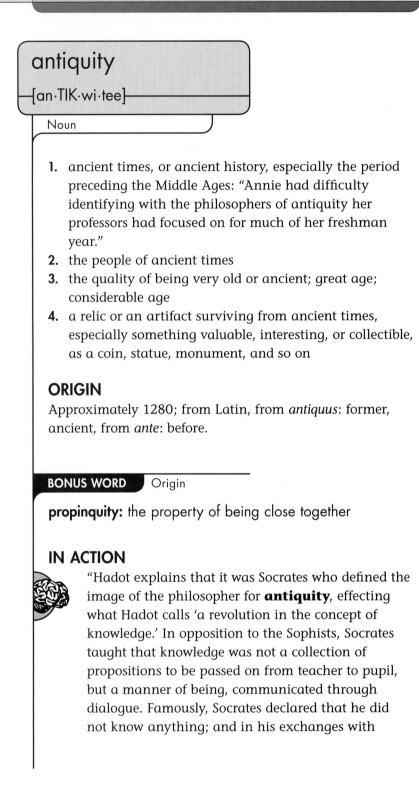

"Hadot explains that it was Socrates who defined the image of the philosopher for **antiquity**, effecting what Hadot calls 'a revolution in the concept of knowledge.' In opposition to the Sophists, Socrates taught that knowledge was not a collection of propositions to be passed on from teacher to pupil, but a manner of being, communicated through dialogue. Famously, Socrates declared that he did not know anything; and in his exchanges with his interlocutors, he brought them to a state of befuddlement by showing that they did not know anything either."

Barry Gewen. "Looking to the Ancients, Pierre Hadot Says Philosophy Should Be a Way of Life" (discussion of What Is Ancient Philosophy?, by Pierre Hadot), New York Times (August 18, 2002).

"It was an act of cultural desecration that shocked the world. The age-old Buddhas at Bamiyan in northern Afghanistan, which had withstood the ravages of Genghis Khan and centuries of invasions and wars, proved powerless against the destructive zealotry of the Taliban regime. . . .

"Other specialists also remain unconvinced that rebuilding the Buddhas is, in fact, the most appropriate response to their destruction.

"'What you're really talking about is building a new statue without the traditional background or struggle or purpose behind it. Once something is gone, it's difficult to change that,' said Tim Schadla-Hall of the Institute of Archaeology in London.

"Edmund Capon, the director of the Art Gallery of New South Wales in Sydney, Australia, was also critical of the plan: 'I think any kind of re-imaging, rekindling in the direct and physical way of something like that, whose true sensitivity and value and presence was embodied in its very **antiquity**, is just pure theater, it's circus,' he said."

Dermot McGrath. "Rebirth of the Afghan Buddhas," Wired.com (May 22, 2002).

quondam

[KWON·dahm, KWON·dam']

Adjective

1. having been formerly; former: "If I had known that Luther was your quondam lover, I wouldn't have been as comfortable with you spending so much time together."

ORIGIN

Approximately 1539; from Latin, *quondam*: formerly, from *quom*: when.

BONUS WORD   Continuum

LESS CONSTANT . . .   **. . . MORE CONSTANT**

quondam ⟶ intermittent ⟶ equable

intermittent: stopping and starting at intervals

equable: not varying

IN ACTION

"In less than a week Miss Mary had forgotten this episode, except that her afternoon walks took thereafter, almost unconsciously, another direction. She noticed, however, that every morning a fresh cluster of azalea-blossoms appeared among the flowers on her desk. This was not strange, as her little flock were aware of her fondness for flowers, and invariably kept her desk bright with anemones, syringas, and lupines; but, on questioning them, they, one and all, professed ignorance of the azaleas. A few days later, Master Johnny Stidger, whose desk was nearest to the window, was suddenly taken with spasms of apparently gratuitous laughter, that threatened the discipline of the school. All that Miss Mary could get from him was, that some one had been 'looking in the winder.' Irate and indignant, she sallied from her hive to do battle with the intruder. As she turned the corner of the school-house she came plump upon the **quondam** drunkard,—now perfectly sober, and inexpressibly sheepish and guilty-looking."

Francis Bret Harte (1836–1902). American short-story writer. "The Idyll of Red Gulch."

And therefore will come.
The god of love,
That sits above,
And knows me, and knows me,
How pitiful I deserve,—

"[I mean, in singing; but in loving, Leander the good swimmer, Troilus the first employer of pandars, and a whole book full of these **quondam** carpet-mongers, whose names yet run smoothly in the even road of a blank verse, why, they were never so truly turned over and over as my poor self, in love. Marry, I cannot show it in rime; I have tried: I can find out no rime to 'lady' but 'baby,' an innocent rime; for 'scorn,' 'horn,' a hard rime; for 'school,' 'fool,' a babbling rime; very ominous endings: no, I was not born under a riming planet, nor I cannot woo in festival terms.]"

William Shakespeare (1564–1616). English dramatist and poet. [Benedick in] Much Ado About Nothing (approximately 1598).

antediluvian

[an'·ti·dah·LOO·vee·ahn]

Adjective

1. extremely old or out-of-date, as if belonging to an earlier period; antiquated: "My father came sputtering up the road in the same antediluvian automobile, its body peppered with rust spots and its fender secured by a thickly coiled rope."
2. of or relating to the era before the biblical Flood

ORIGIN

Approximately 1646; formed in English from the prefix *ante-*: before + Latin *diluvium*: deluge, flood.

BONUS WORD Related

alluvion: the movement of sea against shore

IN ACTION

"[It is time to end] **antediluvian** assumptions concerning the role and status of women in marriage."

> *Massachusetts Supreme Judicial Court. [Ruling that wives have a right to sue their husbands] (July 30, 1980).*

"Founded in 323 BCE, the Great Library of Alexandria was the world's premier study center, an **antediluvian** Internet, a repository for every book in the Western world, and a laboratory for creative minds to debate politics or test the latest inventions. Then, after standing for seven centuries, it fell victim to two hideous episodes of intolerance that erased it from the world map."

> *Brian Trent. "A Greatness Reborn," Humanist (September–October 2004).*

obsolete

[ob'·sah·LEET, OB·sah·leet']

Adjective, Transitive Verb

Adjective
1. no longer in use (usually applied to words or writings)
2. of a kind or style that has been superseded by something newer or more fashionable; old-fashioned: "Despite its now obsolete hardware configuration, Robin's laptop had earned a special place in her heart with over three years of faithful service, and she was in no hurry to replace it."

Transitive Verb
3. to cause to become obsolete

ORIGIN
Approximately 1579; borrowed from Latin, *obsoletus*, past participle of *obsolescere*: to fall into disuse (probably from the prefix *ob*-: away + -*so-lescere*, from *solere*: to be accustomed to).

BONUS WORD   Antonym

avant-garde: radically new or original

IN ACTION

"Some airport managers say the government is installing **obsolete** equipment. They say the two systems licensed for use at U.S. airports are slow and often mistake ordinary substances for explosives. . . . With the current bomb-detection machines, which detect only density and shape, 'you can't tell the difference between chocolate and plastique explosives,' he said."

"Airports Wary of Baggage Deadline,"
Associated Press (August 18, 2002).

antebellum

[an'·tee·BEL·ahm, an'·ti·BEL·ahm]

Adjective

1. belonging to a period that precedes a war, especially the American Civil War: "Todd had moved into a beautiful antebellum building in rural Vicksburg to escape the manic pace of city life and to provide some extra inspiration for his writing."

ORIGIN

Approximately 1847; from Latin, *ante bellum* (*ante*: before, in front of + *bellum*: war).

BONUS WORD   Origin

anteroom: an entry room

IN ACTION

"From **antebellum** Kentucky to 20th-century Washington, [Malvina Harlan] observes customs, manners, clothing, people, places and events with the skills of a gifted storyteller. She offers, too, the only private glimpse of Justice Harlan's youth in a slaveholding family, an interesting historical context for his courageous later opposition to segregation in his lonely dissent in Plessy v. Ferguson (1896), the case that enshrined the doctrine of separate but equal in American law. His wife suggests that his dedication to the 'black man's claim to equal civil rights' arose from the traditions of racial paternalism he learned in **antebellum** Kentucky. What Malvina Harlan identifies as a 'close sympathy . . . between the slaves and their Master' in the Harlan household imbued John Marshall Harlan with a lifelong concern for those he had from his earliest days regarded as dependents. 'Obligations of Christian justice to the Negro race' learned in the days of slavery formed the foundation of Justice Harlan's progressive late-19th-century racial views."

Drew Gilpin Faust. *"Being There"* (book review of Some Memories of a Long Life, *by Malvina Shanklin Harlan*), New York Times *(August 4, 2002)*.

Here to Stay!

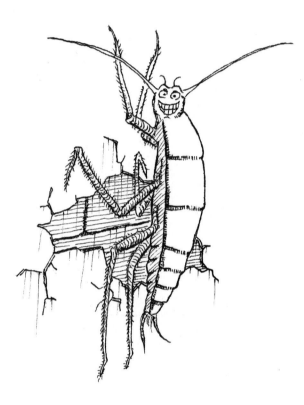

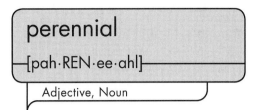

perennial

[pah·REN·ee·ahl]

Adjective, Noun

Adjective

1. continuing through the year: "perennial fountains"
2. continuing without cessation or intermission; perpetual; unceasing: "Recent efforts in Jason's perennial struggle with lateness have given us all reason for hope."
3. (as in botany) continuing more than two years: "perennial root," "perennial plant"

Noun

4. (as in botany) a plant that lives or continues more than two years, whether it retains its leaves in winter or not
5. something that continues or seems to continue without cessation

ORIGIN

Approximately 1644; formed in English from Latin, *perennis*: lasting through the year (*per-*: through + *annus*: year) + English suffix *-al*.

BONUS WORD   Origin

vicennial: occurring once every twenty years

IN ACTION

"The strategists call the Gen-X homebody mentality a 'backlash.' As a source of generational tension, child-rearing has been a hardy American **perennial**—and there's certainly lots of fodder for a family feud issuing from marketing analysts, intent on 'Capturing the Gen-X Mom' (the topic of a recent toy-industry seminar). You may remember all the hard-bitten qualities that once gave young Gen X'ers a bad name:

their disillusioned pragmatism and underachieving fatalism. The tables have turned. Those traits have now metamorphosed into a welcome antidote to the boomers' competitive, perfectionist brand of 'hyperparenting.'"

Ann Hulbert. "Look Who's Parenting,"
New York Times Magazine (July 4, 2004).

"The plant or plants chosen must be able to thrive in the specific climate, require minimal or no irrigation if there's a dry spell, and have few additional needs, such as fertilizers or regular mowing.

"If possible, the plant chosen should be a **perennial**, so the roof doesn't have to be replanted each year. The City of Portland has found that sedums, hardy, durable plants that are native to the region, work best."

Donald Dawson. "Plant-Covered Roofs
Ease Urban Heat," National Geographic News
(November 15, 2002).

amaranthine

[am'·ah·RAN·thin, am'·ah·RAN·thien]

Adjective

1. of or pertaining to an amaranth
2. undying and unfading, like the amaranth (an imaginary flower): "The amaranthine beauty of the park is protected by the National Park Service."
3. having a color inclining to purple

ORIGIN

Date uncertain; from *amaranth* (1616); from Latin, *amarantus*; from Greek, *amarantos*: literally, everlasting (*a-*: not + *marainesthai*: to wither, to decay, related to *marnasthai*: to fight).

BONUS WORD   Antonym

transient: enduring a very short time

IN ACTION

"'[T]he critic William Hazlitt wrote that, 'If Mr Coleridge had not been the most impressive talker of his age, he would probably have been the finest writer,' though he did concede that for all Coleridge had failed at gathering the promised 'immortal fruits and **amaranthine** flowers,' he had not gone Establishment-rotten, like Wordsworth and Southey."

"Today in Literary History: Literary Daybook, July 25 [Real and Imaginary Events of Interest to Readers]," Salon.com (July 25, 2002).

'T is hers to pluck the **amaranthine** flower
Of faith, and round the sufferer's temples bind
Wreaths that endure affliction's heaviest shower,
And do not shrink from sorrow's keenest wind.

*William Wordsworth (1770–1850).
English poet. "Weak Is the Will of Man,"
The Complete Poetical Works (1888).*

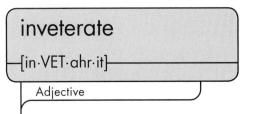

inveterate

[in·VET·ahr·it]

Adjective

1. firmly established by long continuance; obstinate; deep-rooted; of long standing: "an inveterate disease," "an inveterate abuse"
2. having habits fixed by long continuance; confirmed; habitual: "an inveterate idler"; "I don't know how my stomach will survive a weekend with those inveterate overeaters."

ORIGIN

Approximately 1392; from Latin, *inveteratus*: of long standing, chronic, from past participle of *inveterare*: to become old, to endure (*in-*: in, into + *vetus*, genitive *veteris*: old).

BONUS WORD Sound

invertebrate: lacking a spinal column

IN ACTION

"I wish that my side, the yuppie soccer fans, were blameless victims in these culture wars, but I've been around enough of America's soccer cognoscenti to know that they invite abuse. They are **inveterate** snobs, so snobbish, in fact, that they think nothing of turning against their comrades. According to their sneering critique, their fellow fans are dilettantes without any real understanding of the game; they are yuppies who admire soccer like a fine slab of imported goat cheese; they come from neighborhoods with spectacularly high Starbucks-per-capita, so they lack any semblance of burning working-class passion."

Franklin Foer. How Soccer Explains the World *(2004).*

perdurable

[pahr·DOOR·ah·bahl, pahr·DYOOR·ah·bahl]

Adjective

1. very durable; lasting; continuing long: "The perdurable
   statues in the town square have remained virtually
   unchanged, even as the buildings around them have
   been renovated, rebuilt, and refaced."

ORIGIN

Thirteenth century; from Late Latin, *perdurabilis*; from Latin,
perdurare: to endure (*per-*: throughout + *durare*: to last).

BONUS WORD   Origin

obdurate: stubborn or unfeeling

IN ACTION

"Writer-director Ronald Maxwell's epic new film *Gods
and Generals* is an act of public courage. Based on the
Jeff Shaara novel, *Gods and Generals* examines key
battles in Virginia during the early part of the Civil
War, chiefly through the eyes of Confederate generals
Lee and Jackson. The film dwells on the personal
motivations, particularly the religious concerns,
driving these men into battle. What we see foremost
is tragedy: Lee and Jackson opposed secession and
wanted slavery ended, but believed they had an
overriding duty to defend their Virginia homeland.
Though the film invites understanding instead of
judgment, it is by no means a romantic apologia for
the Lost Cause; rather, it is a reminder that history is
rarely a Manichean struggle between pure good and
uncut evil, but more often a drama played by actors
with noble ideals, perhaps, but blind to their flaws. It
is an indictment of the hubris of our politically correct

age that a film asserting this **perdurable** truth about mankind's affairs will strike many as offensive. But truth it is, and conservatives should be grateful to Maxwell, and Ted Turner, the film's financier (yes, that Ted Turner), for daring to tell it."

"The Week—Duct Tape, Civil Defense,
Anti-Americanism, Other Current Issues,"
National Review *(March 10, 2003).*

"The current installation at the Field Museum in Chicago—after previous appearances at venues in Rome and London—of a large-scale exhibition of ancient art centered upon the personality and historical role of the last Macedonian queen of Egypt testifies to the **perdurable** hold of Cleopatra upon the public imagination more than 20 centuries after her death."

Sheldon Nodelman. "Who Was Cleopatra?"
Art in America *(February 2002).*

"I have professed me thy friend, and I confess me knit to thy deserving with cables of **perdurable** toughness; I could never better stead thee than now."

William Shakespeare (1564–1616).
English dramatist and poet. [Iago in]
Othello, the Moor of Venice *(1603).*

immemorial

[im'·ah·MOR·ee·ahl, im'·ah·MOER·ee·ahl]

Adjective

1. extending beyond the reach of memory, record, or tradition; indefinitely ancient: "immemorial elms"

(Alfred, Lord Tennyson), "immemorial usage or custom" (Sir Matthew Hale), "existing from time immemorial"; "Alex considers barbecues to be an extension of the immemorial tradition of cooking meat over an open fire."

ORIGIN

Approximately 1602; probably from French, *immemorial*: old beyond memory or record; from Medieval Latin, *immemorialis*: literally, not belonging to memory; from Latin *in-*: not + *memorialis*: memorial.

BONUS WORD   Related

immutable: not subject or susceptible to change

IN ACTION

"Mexico—which boasts 120 varieties of chili ranging from small green Serranos to sweat-inducing orange Habaneros and has been spicing up its food with them since time **immemorial**—now ranks just fourth in the world market.

"With the once-exotic condiment now a kitchen staple in many countries and dried chili exports booming, China is fighting India for the lead position."

Catherine Bremer. "Protect Our Peppers,
Say Mexican Chili Farmers," Reuters (July 2, 2004).

"God is the **immemorial** refuge of the incompetent, the helpless, the miserable. They find not only sanctuary in His arms, but also a kind of superiority, soothing to their macerated egos: He will set them above their betters."

H. L. Mencken (1880–1956). U.S. journalist. Minority
Report: H. L. Mencken's Notebooks, no. 35 (1956)

In the Past

THEME 4

erstwhile

archaic

hoary

primordial

superannuated

erstwhile

[URST·hwiel', URST·wiel']

Adverb, Adjective

Adverb

1. at a previous time; formerly: "her erstwhile writing"

Adjective

2. former; previous: "She has been ostracized by her erstwhile colleagues since leaving the bank and opening a bar."

ORIGIN

Approximately 1569; from obsolete English, *erst*: before, from Middle English, *erest*: earliest, former, from Old English, *aerest*: earliest + while.

BONUS WORD Sound

ersatz: artificial and inferior.

IN ACTION

"Spitzer first came to the university as a resident and student at the Columbia Center for Psychoanalytic Training and Research, after graduating from N.Y.U. School of Medicine in 1957. He had had a brilliant medical-school career, publishing in professional journals a series of well-received papers about childhood schizophrenia and reading disabilities. He had also established himself outside the academy, by helping to discredit his **erstwhile** hero Reich. In addition to his weekly sessions on the Lower East Side, the teen-age Spitzer had persuaded another Reichian doctor to give him free access to an orgone accumulator, and he spent many hours sitting hopefully on the booth's tiny stool, absorbing healing orgone energy, to no obvious avail. In time, he became disillusioned, and in college he wrote a paper critical of the therapy, which was consulted by the Food and Drug Administration when they later prosecuted Reich for fraud."

Alix Spiegel. "The Dictionary of Disorder: How One Man Revolutionized Psychiatry," New Yorker (December 27, 2004).

archaic

[awr·KAY·ik]

Adjective

1. little evolved from or characteristic of an earlier ancestral type: "archaic forms of life"
2. so extremely old as seeming to belong to an earlier period; antiquated: "You would not believe the archaic laws still on the books in this town."
3. a word or phrase that is no longer in general use

ORIGIN

Approximately 1832; perhaps from earlier English, *archaical*; from Greek, *archaikos*: old-fashioned, from *archaios*: ancient, from *arkhe*: beginning, from *arkhein*: to begin.

BONUS WORD   Antonym

newfangled: of a new (often outrageous) kind

IN ACTION

"The Church of England has done its best to hasten its own demise. Desperate to be 'relevant', church leaders have stripped services of ancient ritual in favor of bland committee-speak. The playwright Alan Bennett summed up the results in one of his wonderfully

Eeyore-ish diary entries 20 years ago: 'In the new form of service God is throughout referred to as You; only one Thou left in the world, and the fools have abolished it. Of course, they can't do away with the vocative, which is every bit as **archaic**, so we still say 'O God'. It's a good job God doesn't have a name or we'd probably be calling him Dave.'"

Clive Davis. "Gauging How the 'Christmas Wars' Are Faring in Britain," Washington Times (December 26, 2004).

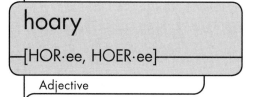

"Lo Spirito di Stella and its crew of 10, including Stella and his bride, Lara, left Genoa on Oct. 14. The boat made stops in Lanzarote, Canary Islands, Antigua and finally Miami Beach this week. The boat will remain here for several weeks. The public can see it at the marina at 300 Alton Rd.

"Stella, who comes from a prominent family, made the voyage in part to be an example to others with paralysis. He also hopes to bring change in Italy, where disabled-access is so **archaic** that people with disabilities recently have staged street demonstrations for recognition."

Luisa Yanez. "Paralyzed Man Sails Ocean, Grateful for Life Nearly Lost," Miami Herald (December 23, 2004)

hoary
[HOR·ee, HOER·ee]
Adjective

1. showing characteristics of age, especially having gray or white hair: "Holly patted the hoary head of her beloved sheep dog."
2. covered with fine whitish hairs or down: "hoary leaves"
3. ancient: "hoary jokes"

ORIGIN

Approximately 1530; from English, *hoar*: gray with age, grayish white, from Old English, *har*: gray, venerable.

BONUS WORD   Related

achromatic: having no hue

IN ACTION

"When Islamic countries met in Rabat, Morocco, last week, they were supposed to talk about how they could begin reforming themselves. Instead, they talked about why they couldn't. Every **hoary** excuse under the Saharan sun came out, from the cultural excuse ('Western' democracy doesn't fit with Islamic values) to the economic excuse (we can't bother with democracy while our people are poor) to the stability excuse (we want peace, not politics)."

> Marcus Gee. "Still in a Rut in Rabat,"
> Globe and Mail (December 22, 2004).

"Elizabeth Taylor is pre-feminist woman. This is the source of her continuing greatness and relevance. She wields the sexual power that feminism cannot explain and has tried to destroy. Through stars like Taylor, we sense the world-disordering impact of legendary women like Delilah, Salome, and Helen of Troy. Feminism has tried to dismiss the femme fatale as a misogynist libel, a **hoary** cliché. But the femme fatale expresses women's ancient and eternal control of the sexual realm. The specter of the femme fatale stalks all men's relations with women."

> Camille Paglia (b. 1947). U.S. author, critic, and
> educator. "Elizabeth Taylor: Hollywood's
> Pagan Queen," Penthouse (March 1992).

"The **hoary** head is a crown of glory, if it be found in the way of righteousness."

Bible: Hebrew Proverbs 16:31.

primordial

[prie·MOR·dee·ahl]

Adjective

1. having existed from the beginning: "Colin and Julie are primordial, and I can't imagine them not being together."
2. basic; essential; fundamental
3. (as in biology) in an earliest or original stage or state: "primordial cells"

ORIGIN

Approximately 1398; borrowed from Late Latin, *primordialis*; from Latin, *primordium*: the beginning, origin (*primus*: first + the stem of *ordiri*: to begin).

BONUS WORD Sound

primal: original or serving as an essential component

IN ACTION

"It is from this **primordial** vegetable matter [the virgin forest], celestially sanctified and unspoiled as yet by the touch of man, that America was born, so the writers and painters of the first native generation proclaim. In so doing, they self-consciously turned their back both on the classical contempt for the woodland barbarism and the long Puritan legacy that equated the forest with pagan darkness and profanity."

Simon Schama. Landscape and Memory (1995).

"The contemporary sports world was reflected in
having women compete for the first time in the
hallowed arena where the Olympics began 2,780
years ago. It also was the first time the shot put had
been contested in Olympia, but could any event be
more fittingly **primordial** than heaving an iron ball
as far as possible?"

Philip Hersh. "Their Mettle Medal-Worthy
[El Guerrouj, Phelps, Greek Organizer Help
Save Athens Games from Doubts, Doping],"
Chicago Tribune (December 26, 2004).

superannuated

[soo'·pahr·AN·yoo·ay'·tid]

Adjective

1. discharged as too old for use or work, especially with a
   pension: "a superannuated civil servant"
2. no longer in use or valid or fashionable; obsolete:
   "Shelly collects superannuated computers and adds their
   processing power to a growing supercomputer in her
   garage."

ORIGIN

Approximately 1633; from Medieval Latin, *superannuatus*:
(of cattle) over one year old; from Latin, *super*: beyond +
annus: year.

BONUS WORD   Origin

supercilious: showing arrogant superiority to

IN ACTION

"Because flu shots save lives, it is surprising that the vaccine supply is so fragile. A **superannuated** technology, combined with the Food and Drug Administration's entrenched conservatism and reluctance to accelerate the development of new production methods, has annually forced flu vaccine experts to rely on imperfect technology to create imperfect vaccines, risking contamination and shortage."

Wendy Orent. *"They're Sticking It to Us with
Antique Vaccines [Flu Fighters Take a Guess 'and
Hope It Has the Guts to Grow the Right Antigens'],"*
Los Angeles Times *(December 19, 2004).*

"That was no way to start the week. It was a Monday morning of windshields scraped with credit cards. Of radiators that split and hemorrhaged **superannuated** anti-freeze. Of emergency brakes that (like that kid in *A Christmas Story* who couldn't get his tongue off the flag pole) couldn't loosen their grip on rotors. Of pipes that froze, leaving just enough water to entice sleepyheads into showers and then run out while the shampoo was foaming on their scalps."

"Op/Ed: Just a Hint of Real Winter,"
Star News Online *(December 21, 2004).*

Telling the Story

THEME 5

raconteur

fabulist

apologue

anecdote

recapitulate

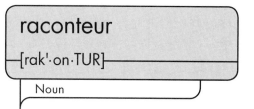

raconteur

[rak'·on·TUR]

Noun

1. a person skilled in telling stories or anecdotes in an entertaining or clever way: "My wife is the raconteur of the family, so I'll let her take the story from here."

ORIGIN

Approximately 1828; from Middle French, *raconter*: to relate; from Old French (*re*: the prefix re- + *aconter*: to count, to tell).

BONUS WORD Related antonym

laconic: brief and to the point

IN ACTION

"From the brother of Frank ('Angela's Ashes'), himself a noted **raconteur**, a memoir of an Irish rogue's life in New York City . . .

"Malachy McCourt is the embodiment of a certain Irish type; a talker, a drinker, a wit. It's very easy to picture him sitting next to you in some pub, swallowing his Johann Barleycorn (whiskey) and holding court. Still, as lovable a rapscallion as McCourt may be in real life, the **raconteuring** doesn't equal literary style. The average chapter length here is only about four pages, which, while creating the sense of a fast read, never allows anything or anyone to be described or pondered over in any real depth."

Lucy Grealy. "Lucy Grealy Reviews A Monk Swimming by Malachy McCourt," Salon.com (May 21, 1998).

fabulist
—[FAB·yah·list]—

Noun

1. a person who invents or writes fables
2. one who tells tales, especially fanciful or false tales: "Scott has been a fabulist since the fifth grade, when he convinced his mother to double his allowance to keep pace with what he called 'localized inflation' brought on by the exorbitant allowances of his peers."

ORIGIN
Approximately 1593; from French, *fabuliste*; from Latin, *fabula*: fable, from *fari*: speak, tell.

BONUS WORD   Related synonym

braggadocio: vain and empty boasting

IN ACTION

"'I've always used my writing to imagine my future,' says Maupin, 56. Or, as Gabriel Noone, the Maupin-like narrator of 'The Night Listener,' puts it, 'I'm a **fabulist** by trade, so be forewarned: I've spent years looting my life for fiction. Like a magpie, I save the shiny stuff and discard the rest; it's of no use to me if it doesn't serve the geometry of the story.'"

Bob Minzesheimer. "'Listener' Tells Tales from Maupin's Life," USA Today (November 7, 2000).

"Diego Rivera had a wilder life than Matisse and produced less important art, a balance wisely reflected in Marnham's entertaining biography. Rivera had a lifelong involvement with Marxist and Mexican politics, countless lovers, famous scandals, and a soap opera of a marriage (actually two marriages) to Frida Kahlo. He was also a **fabulist** of Marquézian proportions, spinning incredible yarns about his days as a student cannibal or a fighter with Emiliano Zapata."

> Jacob Weisberg. "Lives of the Artists: Is Biography Good for Painting?" (book review of Dreaming with His Eyes Open: A Life of Diego Rivera, by Patrick Marnham), Slate.com (January 10, 1999).

"Every writer is necessarily a critic—that is, each sentence is a skeleton accompanied by enormous activity of rejection; and each selection is governed by general principles concerning truth, force, beauty, and so on. . . . The critic that is in every **fabulist** is like the iceberg—nine-tenths of him is under water."

> Thornton Wilder (1897–1975). U.S. novelist and dramatist. Writers at Work, First Series, ed. Malcolm Cowley (1958).

apologue

[AP·ah·log']

Noun

1. a short moral story or fable, especially one featuring animals or inanimate objects as characters: "Victor always felt a connection with the wolves and other villainous animals of his childhood apologues, much to the chagrin of his mother."

ORIGIN

Approximately 1555; from Latin, *apologus*; from Greek, *apologos* (*apo*: the prefix *apo-* + *logos*: speech, narrative).

BONUS WORD   Sound

epilogue: a passage added at the end of a work

IN ACTION

"'I wonder, does he wear a star?' thought she, 'or is it only lords that wear stars? But he will be very handsomely dressed in a court suit, with ruffles, and his hair a little powdered, like Mr. Wroughton at Covent Garden. I suppose he will be awfully proud, and that I shall be treated most contemptuously. Still I must bear my hard lot as well as I can—at least, I shall be amongst gentlefolks, and not with vulgar city people': and she fell to thinking of her Russell Square friends with that very same philosophical bitterness with which, in a certain **apologue**, the fox is represented as speaking of the grapes."

*William Makepeace Thackeray (1811–63). English
novelist born in Calcutta, India. Vanity Fair (1848).*

"Andersen's fairy tales have the quaintness, the simplicity, the naturalness, of the primitive folk story, with a humor, a pleasant irony of their own. He was a born story-teller, and there are a dozen little masterpieces to be selected from his several collections. The 'Steadfast Tin Soldier' is one of the earliest as it is one of the best. It was published in 1835, when its author was already a full-grown man,—but a man who had preserved the power to see the world as a little child sees it.

"This is an **apologue**, a fable, a parable, if we so choose to take it. But it is real also, however fanciful the invention. It has the childlike ingenuousness of the folk-tale, so rarely caught by writers who have forgotten how they felt when they were young. A large part of the effectiveness of the story is due to the certainty with which the author keeps to the chosen key."

Brander Matthews (1852–1929).
"Notes to 'The Steadfast Tin Soldier' by
Hans Christian Andersen," The Short-Story (1907).

anecdote

[AN·ik·dote]

Noun

1. a short account of an interesting incident, especially a biographical one: "If only Raul had known, as a naked, tender little two-year-old, that all of his misadventures would someday be transformed into an arsenal of anecdotes for his parents to exploit at family gatherings, he would have behaved differently."
2. (plural, *anecdotes* or *anecdota*) previously undivulged details of a historical sequence or passages of a biography

ORIGIN

Approximately 1686; from Medieval Latin, *anecdota*; from Late Greek, *anekdota*: things unpublished (referring to the memoirs of Procopius, which consisted primarily of court gossip); from Greek, *anekdotos*: unpublished (*an*: not + *ekdotos*: published).

BONUS WORD   Synonym

aphorism: a short pithy instructive saying

IN ACTION

"'The family's doing well,' Mr. Bush said not long ago in Little Rock, Ark., a sure sign that he was about to begin a dog **anecdote**. 'Barney the dog is in great shape. Spot, the dog who was born in the White House when Mother and Dad were there, is getting a little up in the years, but she's doing well, too. She's used to the confines of the South Lawn. And I invite her every morning into the Oval Office to start my day.' Spot, the president continued, 'makes herself comfortable on the new carpet.' (Pause) 'That's why Barney's not invited in the morning.'

"The crowd laughed, as it always does."

Elisabeth Bumiller. "President Shifts Focus from Daughters to Dogs," New York Times *(June 24, 2002).*

"'Speaking of children's sermons, here's a funny little story for you,' Lundegaard said. 'This pastor was talking to a group of kids and, to illustrate a point, he asked: Does anybody know what's small, furry, has a bushy tail, and runs up trees looking for nuts? All the kids were silent but, finally, one little boy said, Well, I know the answer is Jesus, but it sure sounds like a squirrel to me!'

"Lundegaard then laughed good-naturedly for 15 to 20 seconds.

"'That's a good one!' he added. 'Isn't that a cute one?'

"Lundegaard's wife, homemaker Patty Lundegaard, who has heard the humorous **anecdote** an estimated 1,400 times over the course of their 26-year marriage, groaned audibly."

"Area Pastor Likes to Inject a Little Humor into His Sermons," Onion.com *(October 11, 2000).*

recapitulate

[ree'·kah·PICH·ah·layt']

Transitive Verb, Intransitive Verb

Transitive Verb

1. to repeat briefly the primary points: "He hands out an outline that will recapitulate the highlights for you, but there is still no substitute for actually showing up for class."
2. (as in biology) to mimic stages of evolution of the species during the embryonic development of the individual organism

Intransitive Verb

3. to summarize

ORIGIN

Approximately 1570; from Late Latin, *recapitulatus*, past participle of *recapitulare*: to sum up; from Latin, *re*: the prefix *re-* + *capitulum*: heading, diminutive of *caput, capit-*: head.

BONUS WORD   Origin

decapitate: to cut off the head of

IN ACTION

"*Theories, Models, Methods, Approaches, Assumptions, Results, and Findings* (also the show's title) consists of two clear glass vitrines, each about the size of a refrigerator laid on its back. Both have scores of Ping-Pong balls being whipped around by blowers. These lottery-like machines **recapitulate** our lives: We're tossed all over, everything is chaos, yet a hidden metaphysical calculus—the sum of gravity, bounce, chance, and air—might explain it all. Visually, it's hypnotic, constantly changing. Some of the balls are damaged, a few are stranded, all are aging. The animating force is ever present but never visible."

Jerry Saltz. "The Pursuit of Happiness," (art review of Damien Hirst), Village Voice *(October 11–17, 2000).*

Audio pronunciations for the words in this pack can be found on our website: www.vocabvitamins.com/book/pack5.

ST__L__N V__W__LS!!

Someone had the audacity to steal all our vowels. Please put them back using these clues.

Th__m__ 1: D__wn M__m__ry L__n__

1.	l__th__	amnesia
2.	__ __d__t__c	photographic
3.	mn__m__n__c	clue
4.	__ __ld l__ng syn__	good old days
5.	__nn__ls	archives

Th__m__ 2: Byg__n__s __nd H__s-B__ __ns

1.	__nt__b__ll__m	before the war
2.	q__ __nd__m	once
3.	__bs__l__t__	dated
4.	__nt__q__ __ty	ancient times
5.	__nt__d__l__v__ __n	before the Flood

Th__m__ 3: H__r__t__ St__y!

1.	__mm__m__r__ __l	before memory
2.	p__rd__r__bl__	permanent
3.	__nv__t__r__t__	enduring
4.	__m__r__nth__n__	undying
5.	p__r__nn__ __l	continual

Th__ m__ 4: __n th__ P__st

1.	pr__ m__ rd__ __l	prehistoric
2.	h__ __ ry	aged
3.	__ rch__ __c	ancient
4.	__ rstwh__ l__	bygone
5.	s__ p__ r__ nn__ __t__ d	out-of-date

Th__ m__ 5: T__ ll__ ng th__ St__ ry

1.	f__ b__ l__ st	teller of tall tales
2.	r__ c__ nt__ __ r	storyteller
3.	__ p__ l__ g__ __	fable
4.	__ n__ cd__ t__	short story
5.	r__ c__ p__ t__ l__ t__	paraphrase

[vo‘cab]
VITAMINS

PACK 6

IN PURSUIT

THEME 1
Sparks Flying   SIMILAR TO:

firebrand	troublemaker, instigator
coruscate	radiate, shine
phosphorescence	glow, light
incendiary	inflammatory
scintillate	sparkle, flicker

THEME 2
Honey-Tongued   SIMILAR TO:

blandish	flatter, coax, persuade
cajole	urge, wheedle
blarney	smooth talk, baloney
flummery	flattery, pudding
inveigle	butter up, manipulate

THEME 3
Love, Union, and Romance   SIMILAR TO:

gallivant	wander about, cruise
uxorious	doting, devoted
coquette	flirt
misogamy	hatred of marriage
banns	engagement announcement

THEME 4
Diamonds and Pearls   SIMILAR TO:

lustrous	radiant, brilliant
opalescent	pearly, milky
nacreous	mother-of-pearl
diamantine	hard, brilliant, like a diamond
iridescent	shimmering, rainbow-colored

THEME 5
Love to the Limit   SIMILAR TO:

ardent	passionate, burning
infatuation	crush, attraction
furor	commotion, frenzy
monomania	obsession, preoccupation
idolatry	worship, reverence

Sparks Flying

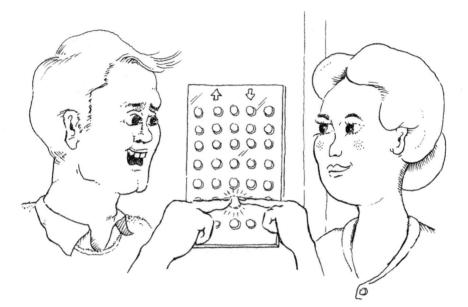

firebrand

[FIER·brand']

Noun

1. a person that stirs up mischief or strife, as by aggressively promoting a cause; an agitator: "We needed a real firebrand to step in and turn our little advocacy group into a thorn in their side."
2. a piece of burning wood

ORIGIN

Approximately 1200; from English, *fire* + *brand*.

BONUS WORD Synonym

rabble-rouser: agitating leader, demagogue

IN ACTION

"Old acquaintances crop up in surprising new guises. The dizzy blonde I despaired of turns out to be raking in millions as co-producer of Mamma Mia! The mild-mannered colleague has emerged as the **firebrand** activist for fathers' rights, the founder of Fathers Direct. I discovered last week that an old boyfriend whom I had deemed a shooting, hunting, fishing type, the kind of man who kept an elephant's foot as wastepaper bin (though purchased from a flea market rather than shot on safari), has become a great philanthropist in the environmental cause."

Cristina Odone. "Diary: My Hunter Goes Green,"
Observer (May 2, 2004).

"Polish **firebrand** Andrzej Lepper, whose nationalist Self-Defense party tops popularity rankings, was quoted Wednesday as saying he believed Nazi dictator Adolf Hitler's early policies were good.

"'At the beginning of his activities, Hitler had a really good program,' Lepper told the Zycie Warszawy newspaper. 'I don't know what happened to him later . . . who had such influence over him that he moved toward genocide.'"

*Katarzyna Mala. "Polish **Firebrand** Praises Hitler's 'Early' Policies," Reuters (April 14, 2004).*

coruscate

[KOR·ah·skayt']

Intransitive Verb

1. to give off flashes of light; to sparkle; to glisten: "On a sunny afternoon, the massive diamond ring would coruscate on her finger like a lighthouse."
2. to show brilliant virtuosity

ORIGIN

Approximately 1725; from Latin, *coruscatus*, past participle of *coruscare:* to flash, to glitter.

BONUS WORD Origin

obfuscate: to make obscure or unclear

IN ACTION

"It was, of course, an education in itself to work with [Vladimir Nabokov] even by correspondence. I remember one page coming back with a long list of Russian synonyms for verbs depicting light in the margins, with their English equivalents attached: glimmer, glow, gleam, shine, twinkle, sparkle, dazzle, **coruscate**, and so on. There were little lessons on verbs of motion (a complicated business in Russian) and extensive instruction on botany, zoology, entomology, and every possible aspect of natural history."

Michael Scammell. "The Servile Path: Translating Vladimir Nabokov," Harper's Magazine (May 2001).

 "The apex of Osaka's nightlife, where neon **coruscates** off the Dotombori canal, is Ebisu-bashi, a dazzling area to wander around, if only to check out the wild youth fashion."

Jan Dodd, et al. The Rough Guide to Japan (2001).

phosphorescence
[fos'·fah·RES·ahns]
Noun

1. continued emission of light after exposure to and removal of radiation
2. emission of light without sensible heat: "After the particularly grim winter, Kim's pale complexion actually had an unnatural phosphorescence."

ORIGIN
Approximately 1796; from Latin, *Phosphorus*: the morning star, from Greek, *Phosphoros*: Lucifer, from *phos*: light + the suffix *-escent*.

BONUS WORD Antonym

igneous: like or suggestive of fire

IN ACTION

"Bill Elford of Sea Otter Kayaking on Salt Spring Island offers stargazing tours by lunar light. 'It's a great time to check out the marine and bird life,' Elford says. 'Seals, porpoise and stoic blue herons are just a few of the live acts that regularly perform.'

"This harbor show is accompanied by the moon rising over Mount Parke on Mayne Island, and the sparkle of **phosphorescence** provides a living light show."

> Jane Cassie. "British Columbia Hosts a Star-Studded Line-Up," HelloBC.com (March 2004).

". . . And it is a strange thing that most of the feelings we call religious, most of the mystical outcrying which is one of the most prized and used and desired reactions of our species, is really the understanding and the attempt to say that man is related to the whole thing, related inextricably to all reality, known and unknowable. This is a simple thing to say, but a profound feeling of it made a Jesus, a St. Augustine, a Roger Bacon, a Charles Darwin, and an Einstein. Each of them in his own tempo and with his own voice discovered and reaffirmed with astonishment the knowledge that all things are one thing and that one thing is all things—plankton, a shimmering **phosphorescence** on the sea and the spinning planets and an expanding universe all bound together by the elastic string of time."

> John Steinbeck (1902–68). U.S. author.
> Log from the Sea of Cortez (1951).

"In youth the human body drew me and was the object of my secret and natural dreams. But body after body has taken away from me that sensual **phosphorescence** which my youth delighted in.

Within me is no disturbing interplay now, but only the steady currents of adaptation and of sympathy."

Haniel Long (1888–1956). U.S. author, poet, and journalist. Interlinear to Cabeza de Vaca *(1936).*

incendiary

—[in·SEN·dee·er'·ee]————————————

Adjective, Noun

Adjective

1. starting or capable of starting a fire: "According to Jamie's fire-building strategy, one must build a miniature wood teepee, with the most incendiary materials in the center."
2. containing highly flammable substances that ignite on impact: "an incendiary bomb," "an incendiary agent"
3. of or involving the deliberate burning of property; involving arson: "an incendiary fire"
4. tending to excite or inflame, especially unrest; inflammatory: "incendiary speeches"

Noun

5. a person who deliberately sets fire to property; an arsonist
6. an incendiary agent, especially a missile or bomb
7. a person who excites or inflames factions or sedition; an agitator; an exciter

ORIGIN

Approximately 1402; borrowed from Latin, *incendiarius*, from *incendium*: fire, from *incendere*: to set on fire (*in-*: in + *candere*: to light, to glow).

| BONUS WORD | Related |

demagogue: orator who appeals to audience passions

IN ACTION

"Despite Pentagon protestations to the contrary, they are only a slender slice of this land—young, disproportionately minority, largely from modest socioeconomic strata (words less **incendiary** than, say, 'working class,') and with generally fewer educational opportunities than the students in my classes.

"I remember when I was called up for my physical, being put on a bus in Canton, Ohio, and taken to the induction center in Cleveland. . . . That bus was America on its way to war—a cross section of rich and poor, black and white, college-educated and high school dropouts. It is what every war waged by a democracy should look like."

Ted Gup. "A Draft Makes War Personal,"
San Francisco Chronicle (May 2, 2004).

"Panicked, ladies? . . . **Incendiary** title aside, Lia Macko and Kerry Rubin, both 32, are not trying to scare you. The authors of 'Midlife Crisis at 30: How the Stakes Have Changed for a New Generation—And What to Do About It,' have a theory about a 'no name' problem that college-educated women share somewhere around age 30. In a nutshell, it's this: 'The lives women are living feel out of sync with the lives they thought they'd be living,' explains Rubin, a producer on CNN's 'American Morning' show. 'All these women feel like their professional and personal lives are on a collision path.' More and more, the authors say, major decisions about marriage,

motherhood and career are converging at the same
time, leaving some women stressed and confused."

*Kristin Dizon. "Thirty, Flirty and—Panicking?
Women's Midlife Crisis,"* Seattle Post-Intelligencer
(May 2, 2004).

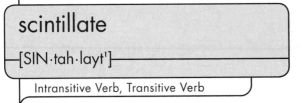

scintillate

[SIN·tah·layt']

Intransitive Verb, Transitive Verb

Intransitive Verb
1. to emit sparks; to flash: "Only in complete darkness can
   you see that common man-made fabrics scintillate when
   rubbed together."
2. to sparkle or flicker, as the stars
3. to be lively and dazzlingly clever

Transitive Verb
4. to emit (flashes or sparks)

ORIGIN
Approximately 1623; from Latin, *scintillatum*, from past
participle of *scintillare*: to sparkle, from *scintilla:* spark.

BONUS WORD   Sound

titillate: to excite

IN ACTION

"Very often a bright planet becomes visible over
the horizon, but it may be thought of as a bright
star rather than being recognized as a planet. And
typically a distinction will be made that suggests
that a planet, which reflects light, does not twinkle,

or **scintillate**, while stars, which are a source of light, do. While this may be a fair generalization our atmosphere does interfere with light from any source, and depending on meteorological conditions even reflected light from a planet may twinkle.

"A better, though more time consuming, method of telling the difference between a star and a planet would be to observe the object in question for a period of several days, perhaps even a few weeks. And if, after a period of several days, the object's position has changed with respect to the stars in that direction then it is more than likely a planet."

Kayne Crison. "Planets Continue Their Heavenly Dance," Casa Grande Valley Newspaper (April 7, 2004).

Honey-Tongued

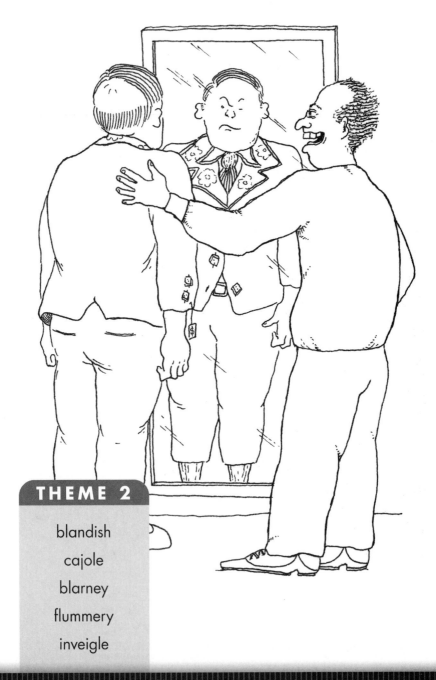

248

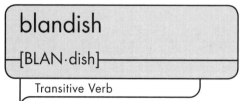

blandish
[BLAN·dish]

Transitive Verb

1. to coax or persuade by flattery; to cajole: "In the last phase of their recruitment process, the executive team decided to blandish Joanna with an evening of fine dining."

ORIGIN

Approximately 1340; borrowed from Old French, *blandiss-*, stem of *blandir*; from Latin, *blandiri*: to flatter, from *blandus:* flattering, smooth-tongued, bland.

BONUS WORD   Related

sycophant: one who tries to please to gain advantage

IN ACTION

"The New York century—the 20th century, that is—was based on the idea that the city was the center of finance, media and art, the aggregate of American talent and vitality, the flagship of the world's most powerful economy. 'NYC . . . Capital of the World,' the Giuliani-era signs proclaimed. In this context, the nation's love affair with New York in the rapacious 90's made sense. TV shows, mass-market magazines and a mayor with decidedly provincial tastes all combined to present New York, once the 800-pound gorilla of cities, as a cuddly chimp.

"As a writer fascinated with New York above all else, I found myself at a loss. Amid the Nasdaq uptick, the hordes of emigres from Ontario and Ohio, the easy **blandishments** of beef carpaccio and tuna tartare, New York was no longer the city of stories, but rather, to borrow the buzzword of the Internet age, a city of 'content.' That New York is gone now. Two years of tragedy was all it took to wipe out the image of the World City nonpareil. But in its place, once again, we find a city deserving of our love and grace. We live again in a city worthy of narration."

Gary Shteyngart. "The City of Stories Again,"
New York Times Magazine (October 5, 2003).

cajole

[kah·JOEL]

Transitive Verb

1. to influence with flattery or gentle but persistent urging; to coax; to wheedle: "She didn't sound very excited about the trip, but I'm sure that I'll be able to cajole her into coming along."

ORIGIN

Approximately 1645; borrowed from French, *cajoler*: to persuade by flattery; possibly a blend of Middle French, *cageoler*: to chatter like a jay, from *geai, jai*: jay, and Old French, *gaioler*: to cage.

BONUS WORD   Related

immure: to imprison

IN ACTION

"Now, know this: You can swear you won't. You can warn the children you won't. You can swear an oath on the sainted soul of your mother-in-law that you won't. But you WILL walk out of the Disney on Ice venue with some plastic trinket or bauble. It is part of a hitherto-unknown agreement, some sort of unspoken, unholy pact between the Mouse-ites and your little Mini-Mes: The Warriors of Walt provide the polymer plunder and the kids do the rest. They'll beg, plead and **cajole**. They'll do their version of reasoning. They'll go face down in a pile of spilled popcorn, wailing and kicking. They'll do, in short, whatever is necessary. Just accept it: They will win and you will lose."

Jeff Wisser. "It's a Joyous Jungle for Kids, but
Parents, You'll Pay a Price for 'Ice,'"
Chicago Sun-Times (October 2, 2003).

blarney

[BLAWR·nee]

Noun

1. artfully flattering talk: "John's blarney was charming and even made her blush, but it didn't make her like him any more."
2. humbug; nonsense; rubbish

ORIGIN

Approximately 1766; from Lady Blarny, a smooth-talking character in Oliver Goldsmith's *The Vicar of Wakefield*, her name being a literary contrivance in allusion to the Blarney Stone, which is supposed to bestow skill in flattery to those who kiss it.

BONUS WORD Related

beguile: to charm

IN ACTION

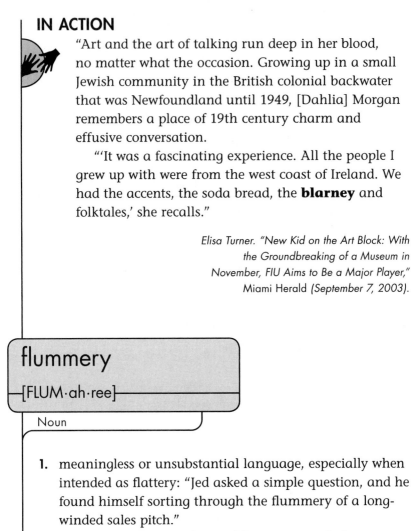

"Art and the art of talking run deep in her blood, no matter what the occasion. Growing up in a small Jewish community in the British colonial backwater that was Newfoundland until 1949, [Dahlia] Morgan remembers a place of 19th century charm and effusive conversation.

"'It was a fascinating experience. All the people I grew up with were from the west coast of Ireland. We had the accents, the soda bread, the **blarney** and folktales,' she recalls."

Elisa Turner. "New Kid on the Art Block: With the Groundbreaking of a Museum in November, FIU Aims to Be a Major Player," Miami Herald (September 7, 2003).

flummery

[FLUM·ah·ree]

Noun

1. meaningless or unsubstantial language, especially when intended as flattery: "Jed asked a simple question, and he found himself sorting through the flummery of a long-winded sales pitch."
2. a sweet, bland custard or pudding once made from strained oatmeal or flour

ORIGIN

Approximately 1623; from Welsh, *llymru:* soft jelly from sour oatmeal.

BONUS WORD Sound

flummox: to confuse

IN ACTION

"I walk west along 36th, then double back and come east again. The whole way I'm getting socked by wake turbulence. Except it's from trucks, not planes, as the sidewalks here are dangerously skinny. There are hundreds of bellowing vehicles but not a single other pedestrian in view. One more reason to hate Florida, I think to myself. . . .

"To my right is a store, Tally-Ho Airline Uniforms, and another one called Oshkosh Pilot Shop. Across the street a gigantic, windowless brown building rises like the wall of a canyon, marked only by a huge sign that declares simply, in an oversize jolt of meaningless **flummery**, 'AeroThrust.'"

> Patrick Smith. "Ask the Pilot: The Airport City of Miami
> International—a Metropolis for Airline Geeks to
> Savor," Salon.com (March 21, 2003).

"Perhaps a good reason why [Theodore Roosevelt] grasps things so quickly and correctly is that he looks for and tries to get at the underlying principles of them; deals with them on the elementary basis of right and fitness, divested of all the conceit and the **flummery** which beset so many things that come to the Executive of a great nation."

> Jacob A. Riis (1849–1914). Danish-American
> journalist and social reformer. "XI. What He Is Like
> Himself," Theodore Roosevelt, the Citizen (1904).

inveigle

[in·VAY·gahl, in·VEE·gahl]

Transitive Verb

1. to win over by charm, flattery, or deception; to ensnare; to lure
2. to obtain by persuasion or cajolery: "Carolyn had the money, but she preferred to inveigle tickets from her friends in the industry."

ORIGIN

Approximately 1494; from Middle French, *aveugler*: to delude, to make blind, from *aveugle*: blind; from Latin *ab-*: without, away from + *oculus:* eye.

BONUS WORD　Sound

inveigh: to complain bitterly

IN ACTION

"'We're really just weekend cricketers,' says an apologetic Amer Afzaluddin, 20, an engineering student at the University of Michigan-Dearborn. And while it's true that most of the team's 18 members—only 11 play at a time—are professional men who spend their weekdays behind desks, the grade of game that is played here is nothing to be ashamed of. Afzaluddin, in fact, was a member of the U.S. National Team that copped the America's Cup tournament in 2002.

"And what they lack in on-field brilliance, these players make up for with their expansionist plans. Like those long-ago soccer enthusiasts, they are determined to **inveigle** their way into the American consciousness.

"'We'll have youth camps next summer,' says team captain Muhammad Yousaf, 33, who works in quality/reliability at Ford. 'This is the way we must begin—get people involved when they are young. This is how baseball and basketball do it. We must do it, too.'"

David Lyman. "Slowly Bowling 'Em Over: Cricket— Baseball's Older Brother—Draws Small but Ardent Following," Detroit Free Press (September 15, 2003).

 "The hard truth is that long before the last school bell tolls, money has already **inveigled** itself into our identities. Some of us will idealistically try to rise above money's unseemly effects; others are already on the road to becoming money addicts. Either way, we've learned we can't get along without it. The age of innocence is over."

Kevin Kelleher. "Get Them While They're Young," Salon.com (June 12, 1998).

Love, Union, and Romance

THEME 3

gallivant

uxorious

coquette

misogamy

banns

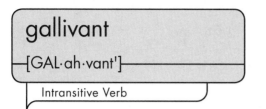

gallivant

—[GAL·ah·vant']—

Intransitive Verb

1. to wander about in search of pleasure, amusement, or diversion: "We have a few hours before the show tonight, so I suggest we gallivant about the city and see what kind of trouble we can get into."
2. to flirt; to play around with others amorously

ORIGIN

Approximately 1819; a humorous alteration of English, *gallant*; from Old French, *galant*: courteous, from present participle of *galer*: to make merry.

BONUS WORD   Synonym

traipse: to walk or tramp about

IN ACTION

"Darth Vader, or at least the latest actor to play the 'Star Wars' good guy-turned villain-turned good guy again, might opt to be Darth Fader-From-View. 'I don't find Hollywood interesting, so I'm thinking about studying architecture instead,' Hayden Christensen told the *London Sun*. Hey, no disrespect to architects, but do they get to **gallivant** around a pretend galaxy, smooching princesses and smiting enemies . . . for millions of dollars?"

Chuck Yarborough. "Forget the Dark Side,
He Wants the Out Side," Cleveland Plain
Dealer (May 25, 2005).

Over the pallor of only two faces
Passes the **gallivant** beam of the trams;
Shows in only two sad places
The white bare bone of our shams.
A little, bearded man, pale, peaked in sleeping,
With a face like a chickweed flower.
And a heavy woman, sleeping still keeping
Callous and dour.

> D. H. Lawrence (1885–1930). English author.
> "Embankment at Night, Before the War,
> Outcasts," New Poems (1918).

uxorious

[uk·SORE·ee·ahs, ug·ZORE·ee·ahs]

Adjective

1. doting upon, foolishly fond of, or submissive to one's
   wife: "It was clear to all that Jeremy adored his wife,
   which was generally wonderful, but his uxorious
   pampering in public situations would irritate his friends
   to no end."

ORIGIN
Approximately 1598; borrowed from Latin, *uxorius*: of or
pertaining to a wife, from *uxor:* wife.

BONUS WORD　Related

cosset: to treat with excessive indulgence

IN ACTION

"[Alfred Hitchcock] died in 1980 at the age of 80 and,
since then, the public perception of him has revolved
around contradictory images: the spooky, eccentric

Englishman, the Peeping Tom obsessive, the romantic, the cruel practical joker educated by Jesuits, the **uxorious** husband, the maestro of imagination with the tidy mind."

Anne Simpson. "Don't Keep Us in Suspense. Who Was Hitch?" Scotland Herald (May 2, 2005).

"**UXORIOUSNESS**, n. A perverted affection that has strayed to one's own wife."

Ambrose Bierce (1842–1914). American satiric writer. The Devil's Dictionary (1911).

coquette

[koe·KET]

Noun, Intransitive Verb

Noun
1. a seductive woman who flirts lightheartedly to win admiration and affection: "I leave you for one moment at the bar, and you find some pretty little coquette to chat up?"

Intransitive Verb
2. to talk amorously; to flirt

ORIGIN
Approximately 1669; borrowed from French, feminine of *coquet*: male flirt; from Old French, *coq*: cock + *-et*: -et, from similarities to a cock's gait.

BONUS WORD   Related

desultory: jumping from one thing to another

IN ACTION

"George Bizet composed the musical personality behind the ultimate **coquette** in his famous opera, *Carmen*. Carmen [is] 'seductive, arrogant, and flirtatious. She [needs to] change a lover with every day to be happy.'"

Steve Ettinger. JCarreras.com.

"After weeks of teasing, flirting, and false promise, spring—the **coquette** of the four seasons—finally delivered blue skies, mild temperatures, and buds in bloom."

Susan Bush. "Bloomin' Monday,"
iBerkshires.com (May 9, 2005).

"As one young starlet asked, with annoyance and pretension, 'What has Marilyn got? And how can I get it?' A large part of the answer lies in Miss Monroe's attitude toward herself. Along with her very evident feminine charms goes a genuine delight in being sexually attractive—an attitude that makes attractiveness seem as natural as sunlight. No amount of connections and calculated exploitation of beauty could achieve the same effect. Miss [Grace] Kelly is a symbol in a very different way. The heroines she plays take the sexual initiative in a remarkably overt way, but always as perfectly proper young ladies. It is as if a not-nice girl, when in love, would behave otherwise and no well-bred wife would act otherwise toward her husband. Female interest in physical love becomes respectable and proper, as if no one had ever thought it vulgar and immodest in a good woman. The nice girl as **coquette** or flirt is archaic and coy."

Delmore Schwartz (1913–66). U.S. poet and critic.
"Survey of Our National Phenomena," The Ego Is Always
at the Wheel: Bagatelles, New Directions (1986).

misogamy

[mi·SOG·ah·mee]

Noun

1. extreme lack of comfort with or hatred of marriage:
"Terry's misogamy was further fueled watching the
relationships of several of her friends deteriorate shortly
after marriage."

ORIGIN

Approximately 1656; from Greek, *misos*: hatred + *gamos:*
marriage.

BONUS WORD Related

unfettered: not subject to restrictions

IN ACTION

"Card, who becomes Dr. Marshall's best youth
organizer, is a mere eighteen when he forfeits his
studies at Fisk to face head on the acrimonious hatred
of white racism, segregation, church bombings, and
murder of young children and colleagues. He is a
disciple who, like his leader, must face the pervasive
fear of hovering death, which is forever kept in the
forefront by small-town sheriffs and supremacist
resisters of his voter registration efforts who murder
with impunity.

"Card is disabled, and his erratic, almost neurotic
behavior (years after the movement he can fall asleep
only when fully dressed) and life of drug abuse, AA,
bitterness, and **misogamy** are the legacies of the
living nightmare and abuse he experienced."

Wilfred D. Samuels. Book review of Julius Lester's And All Our
Wounds Forgiven, *African American Review (spring 1997).*

ON THAT NOTE

Could Atlanta, the ancient Greek huntress and runner, have been a **misogamist**? The young woman would challenge each of her suitors to a race, refusing to marry anyone who could not outrun her. She even allowed the men to take a head start or run naked while she ran in armor, but she always won the race and thus remained single.

Only Hippomenes was able to outrun the unwed beauty, with the clever use of three golden apples given to him by Aphrodite. As the two ran, Hippomenes dropped the golden fruit one by one. Unable to resist such a prize, Atlanta stooped and even ran back to pick them up, confident from past successes that she would be able to make up the time. Hippomenes took full advantage, winning the race and her hand in marriage.

Confirmed Bachelor

INGREDIENTS
1½ oz gin
1 tsp grenadine syrup
½ tsp lime juice
1 egg white
crushed ice

DIRECTIONS
In a shaker half-filled with crushed ice, combine all of the ingredients. Shake well. Strain into a cocktail glass.

SERVE IN
Cocktail glass

banns

[banz]

Noun

1. an announcement of a proposed marriage, given three times in the parish church of each party
2. any public notice of a proposed marriage issued in church or by a church official: "My mouth dropped as the name of my old high school sweetheart was announced in a banns at the morning's service."

ORIGIN

Approximately 549; from Middle English, *ban*: proclamation.

BONUS WORD   Related

clarion: loud and clear

IN ACTION

"As a philanthropist in general, and a friend to the Polynesians in particular, I hope that these Edens of the South Seas, blessed with fertile soils and peopled with happy natives, many being yet uncontaminated by the contact of civilization, will long remain unspoiled in their simplicity, beauty, and purity. And as for annexation, I beg to offer up an earnest prayer—and I entreat all present and all Christians to join me in it—that the **banns** of that union should be forbidden until we have found for ourselves a civilization morally, mentally, and physically higher than one which has culminated in almshouses, prisons, and hospitals."

Herman Melville (1819–91). U.S. author. Omoo:
A Narrative of Adventures in the South Seas (1847).

She sings as sweetly as a nightingale:
Say that she frown; I'll say she looks as clear
As morning roses newly wash'd with dew:
Say she be mute and will not speak a word;
Then I'll commend her volubility,
And say she uttereth piercing eloquence:
If she do bid me pack; I'll give her thanks,
As though she bid me stay by her a week:
If she deny to wed; I'll crave the day
When I shall ask the **banns**, and when be married.
But here she comes; and now, Petruchio, speak.

William Shakespeare (1564–1616).
English dramatist and poet. [Petruchio in]
The Taming of the Shrew (1594).

"'It's my belief, sir, that you have not the power or
the right to separate those two,' Dobbin answered in
a low voice; 'and that if you don't give your daughter
your consent it will be her duty to marry without it.
There's no reason she should die or live miserably
because you are wrong-headed. To my thinking, she's
just as much married as if the **banns** had been read
in all the churches in London.'"

William Makepeace Thackeray (1811–63).
English novelist born in Calcutta, India.
Vanity Fair (1848).

Diamonds and Pearls

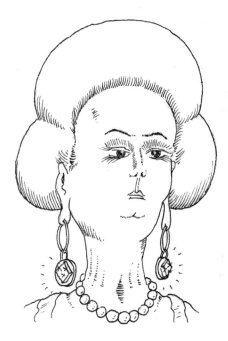

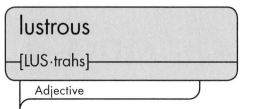

lustrous

[LUS·trahs]

Adjective

1. reflecting a sheen or glow: "a lustrous satin"; "Jack's prize possession was his lustrous yellow Mini Cooper with racing stripes."
2. brilliant; radiant: "a lustrous example for others to follow"

ORIGIN

Approximately 1601; borrowed from Middle French, *lustre*; from Italian, *lustro*: splendor, brilliancy, from *lustrare*: to illuminate; from Latin, *lustrare:* to spread light over.

BONUS WORD   Origin

lackluster: lacking brilliance or vitality

IN ACTION

"The defense was **lustrous**. Not only were there no errors, but not a single ball was bobbled. And Carlos Beltran, Scott Rolen and Albert Pujols all made spectacular plays.

"By the time Jeff Kent broke up the scoreless game with a home run in the ninth, my disappointment for the Cardinals was submerged in a happy awe at how beautiful baseball could be."

Rick Casey. "Confessions of a Native Cardinal Fan,"
Houston Chronicle *(October 21, 2004).*

"In shape, it is perfectly elliptical. In texture, it is smooth and **lustrous**. In color, it ranges from pale alabaster to warm terra cotta. And in taste, it outstrips all the lush pomegranates that Swinburne was so fond of sinking his lyrical teeth into."

Sydney J. Harris. "Tribute to an Egg,"
Majority of One (1957).

opalescent

[oe'·pah·LES·ahnt]

Adjective

1. reflecting a milky or pearly light from the interior; having an opaline play of colors: "Using the simplest of materials, Cindy would create breathtaking opalescent lamps."

ORIGIN

Approximately 1813; from Latin, *opalus*; possibly from Greek, *opallios*; possibly from Sanskrit, *upala-s*: gem, opal + *-escent*: resembling, characterized by.

BONUS WORD Antonym

subfusc: devoid of brightness or appeal

IN ACTION

"The round rice-flour skins are dry and come in packages of about 35. Delicate and **opalescent**, they are reminiscent of a paper moon. In order to make them pliable, one must soak them briefly in hot water. Truong explains that there are several thicknesses of skins available, but the packages do not indicate this. To the uninitiated there are two sizes: thin and thinner.

"The traditional filling includes lettuce, aromatic herbs, shrimp, a slice of pork belly, and rice-stick noodles."

Debra Samuels. "Spring Rolls: A Fresh Approach to Appetizers," Boston Globe (October 20, 2004).

"[Amira] Casar's features are conventionally beautiful, but her most striking feature is her **opalescent** skin—she's lit to glow softly in the dark."

J. Hoberman. "Gray Anatomy," Village Voice (October 12, 2004).

"A fibrous outer husk covered in thick hair-like flukes encases the soft and **opalescent** fruit inside. Getting to the meat of a rambutan is like peeling away a barnacle to find a milky ball, like a blind eye, inside. The spines make it look like some cross between a chestnut and a sea monster, or an alien pod with cracked light-colored fissures along the surface, turning pink."

Steve and Lisa Alcazari. "Strange Fruit: An Odd Spiky Fruit Conjures Images of a Trip to Thailand, and Some, um, Other Unusual Things," Hartford Advocate (October 21, 2004).

nacreous

—[NAY·kree·ahs]——————

Adjective

1. consisting of or resembling mother-of-pearl: "In the window stood an antique chess set with nacreous white pieces and black pieces of dark carved stone."

ORIGIN

Date unknown; from English, *nacre*: the iridescent internal layer of a mollusk shell + *ous*; *nacre* possibly borrowed from Arabic, transliterated as *naqur:* hunting horn, from the similarity in shape to a mollusk.

BONUS WORD   Related

bijou: a small and delicately worked piece

IN ACTION

"Each section complements its computer-generated and photographic imagery with detailed explanations about how these spectacles are created—and while some may be a bit scientific for those of us who prefer to classify clouds by what they look like, even the technical elements can sometimes entice with the related gee whiz factor. (**Nacreous** clouds, visible up to two hours after sunset due to their extreme altitude, are composed of ice crystals at temperatures around minus 85 degrees C.)"

Jim Regan. "Keep Your Head in the Clouds,"
Christian Science Monitor (September 29, 2004).

"A close look at an abalone shell reveals two layers, both made of calcium carbonate but organized into different microstructures with different properties. The rough outside layer derives from a mineral form known as calcite. But it is the aragonite form found in the inner, **nacreous** layer that makes the shell remarkably resistant to breakage."

Ivan Amato. "Mollusk Teaches Ceramics to Scientists,"
Science News (December 9, 1989).

diamantine

[die'·ah·MAN·tien]

Adjective

1. consisting of diamonds or resembling diamonds: "After chemically bleaching his teeth, Daniel's usually bright smile turned diamantine and almost painful to behold."

ORIGIN

Approximately 1625; borrowed from Medieval Latin, *diamantem*; from Latin, *adamantem:* the hardest metal, diamond.

BONUS WORD　　Origin

adamant: unsusceptible to persuasion

IN ACTION

"The San Franciscans danced 'Etudes' with mounting abandon. Yet no one turned its exuberant passages into mere circus tricks. Cast in the ballerina role, Yuan Yuan Tan paid careful attention to stylistic nuances. Some scenes require the lightness of early-19th-century Romantic ballet, and in these Ms. Tan looked airy and capricious. But when the choreography evoked the grandeur of late 19th-century Russian ballet, her dancing acquired a **diamantine** glitter."

Jack Anderson. "From Nasty to Elegant, a Company on Display" (dance review), New York Times (October 23, 1998).

iridescent

[ir'·i·DES·ahnt]

Adjective

1. varying in color when seen in different lights or from different angles: "iridescent oil slick," "iridescent glass"; "In the sleepy summer afternoon, the dragonflies stirred the heat with the flight of their iridescent bodies."
2. lustrous or brilliant in effect or appearance

ORIGIN

Approximately 1796; from Latin, *iris*: rainbow (genitive *iridis*) + English suffix *-escent*: resembling, characterized by.

BONUS WORD   Sound

incandescent: emitting light as a result of heat

IN ACTION

"The bankrupt, graffiti-slathered, mugger-ravaged metropolis of the 70's, a cliché that lingered long after it bore only the faintest shred of accuracy, has emerged as an **iridescent** playland, with avenues lined with shops and bars, along which pretty young women might, and do, tromp about in six-inch stilettos. But has this happy turn for the city prompted the death of the street-smart New Yorker, once as large an urban figure as the opinionated cabby?"

Joanna Smith Rakoff. "Is New York Losing Its Street Smarts?" New York Times (October 24, 2004).

"When she was younger—working as a model in Boston, where she was born—my mother was so beautiful that people often stopped to stare. Her entrance into any room delivered a knockout punch:

She was 5-foot-10 and had big breasts and a tiny waist. She knotted her black hair in a chignon, painted her full lips crimson and would flash her startling green eyes like **iridescent** almonds. Her beauty brought her lots of attention from men: Doors were opened, cigarettes lit, promises made and later broken. Beauty was my mother's trump card in life, and I was not surprised that she wouldn't accept her changing face—that she wanted time to stand still."

Anne Levine. "Face-Off [What Do You Do When Your Mother Won't Let You See Her Grow Old?]," Salon.com *(January 13, 1998).*

Love to the Limit

THEME 5

ardent

infatuation

furor

monomania

idolatry

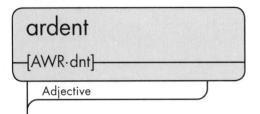

ardent

—[AWR·dnt]——————————

Adjective

1. expressing or having warmth, usually applied to a
   passion or affection; passionate; as ardent love, feelings,
   zeal, or hope: "Teddy didn't have much contact with his
   father as a child, and he always carried a wistful, ardent
   love for him."
2. characterized by intense enthusiasm or devotion; fervent;
   torrid; zealous.
3. glowing, shining, or burning like fire; fiery; as ardent
   eyes, fever, or liquor.

ORIGIN

Probably before 1425; from Old French, *ardant*; influenced
by Latin, *ardentem* (nominative *ardens*), present participle of
ardere: to burn.

BONUS WORD   Related

evince: to give expression to

IN ACTION

"But the magic of those first three films finally
proved too delicate to sustain. They're hermetic,
timeless-seeming, and that's a difficult standard to
live up to; not even the most **ardent** lovers, or the
most dedicated filmmakers, can make time stand
still forever. Jacques Demy was the sort of artist
who ventured outside the Neverland of his private,
idiosyncratic imaginative landscape at his peril."

Terrence Rafferty. "Jacques Demy: A New Wave
Auteur Without the Rough Edges," New York Times
(November 11, 2001).

"'I think he understands that Pakistan's future lies in modernism, it lies in being progressive, it lies in being in the mainstream of the rest of the world,' said Talit Massod, a retired general and an **ardent** supporter of Musharraf.

"Musharraf came to power in a 1999 military coup that unseated President Nawaz Sharif, who had been democratically elected."

> Joanne Levine. "A Delicate Balance: President Musharraf Tries to Please Pakistanis and U.S.," ABC News.com (October 8, 2001).

infatuation

[in·fach'·oo·AY·shahn]

Noun

1. a foolish and usually extravagant passion, love, or admiration: "Despite all of our incompatibilities and everything that my rational mind tells me, I just can't seem to shake my infatuation for Jeannette."
2. an object of extravagant, short-lived passion: "Comic books were my chief infatuation throughout junior high school—to the absolute dismay of my English and history teachers."

ORIGIN

Approximately 1649; from English, *infatuate* + suffix *-ion*; from Latin, *infatuare*: to make a fool of (*in-*: the prefix *in-* + *fatuus*: foolish).

BONUS WORD   Related

avidity: great eagerness or enthusiasm

IN ACTION

"Historians, by education and inclination, are practitioners of the long view. But Mr. Post and many fellow members of the Society for the History of Technology, who gathered in San Jose, Calif., last month, agreed that Sept. 11—coming at the end of an extraordinary, decade-long **infatuation** with technology—may have a lasting impact on a nation known for its technological optimism.

"Airliners and the mail became weapons, while skyscrapers became targets, and all of it shook the belief that America's technological supremacy could shield it from a troubled world. But terrorism is not the only reason the American faith in technology is being questioned. The collapse of the dot-com bubble and the precipitous slide in technology stocks on Wall Street has also had a sobering effect."

Steve Lohr. "A Time Out for Technophilia,"
New York Times (November 18, 2001).

"There are few people who are not ashamed of their love affairs when the **infatuation** is over."

François, Duc De La Rochefoucauld (1613–80).
French writer and moralist.
Sentences et Maximes Morales (1678).

furor

[FYOOR·or, FYOOR·ahr]

Noun

1. a general outburst of excitement or commotion; an uproar; public disorder: "Carlos loved the quieter side of New Orleans, and he avoided the furor of Mardi Gras at all costs."

2. violent anger or madness; fury; frenzy: "This is not the time to experiment, Thomas—I don't want to see their faces in furor, as you march out with a coy smile and a whole baked ostrich for their Thanksgiving dinner."

3. a fashion or fad adopted enthusiastically by the public; a craze

4. a state of intense excitement or euphoria

ORIGIN

Probably before 1475; borrowed from Latin, *furor*, related to *furia*: rage, passion, and from *furere:* to rage.

BONUS WORD Synonym

torrid: extremely hot

IN ACTION

"The deadly seven are Iran, Iraq, Syria, Libya, Cuba, North Korea, and Sudan. The State Department counterterrorism report emphasizes that Sudan is a leading harborer of international terrorists—but that nation has been overlooked in the recent media **furor** about this malevolent network."

Nat Hentoff. "The War on the Bill of Rights,"
Village Voice (September 26–October 2, 2001).

"For the first time, artists routinely portrayed the pharaoh in informal situations—being affectionate with Nefertiti or playing with his children. They also painted scenes of life and nature—wheat rippling in the wind, farmers plowing, birds taking flight. In truth, Akhenaten unleashed a creative **furor** that gave rise to perhaps the finest era of Egyptian art."

Rick Gore. "Pharaohs of the Sun,"
National Geographic (April 2001).

monomania

[mon'·ah·MAY·nee·ah, mon'·ah·MAYN·yah]

Noun

1. a pathological concentration of interest upon one particular idea or subject, as in paranoia
2. an exaggerated or obsessive zeal for or interest in one idea or subject; possession; mania: "Anita pursued her career as a stage actress with such a relentless monomania, that she couldn't help but be at the right place at the right time—to people in the industry, it seemed that she was in all places, at all times."

ORIGIN

Approximately 1820; from New Latin *mono* (borrowed from Greek, *mono*, from *monos*: single, alone) + *mania* (from Greek, *mania*: madness, related to *mainesthai*: to rage).

BONUS WORD　Origin

logomania: pathologically excessive talking

IN ACTION

"To be number one, it takes **monomania**. Focusing on nothing else; 100 hours a week doing virtually anything to win. It will be tough for nice guys to finish first. Mitch Kapor called it the 'kingdom of the doomed,' and he left the industry. The fun went out of it. It's like Star Wars, 'to defeat you I must become you.' There have been victories. Apache is a piece of server software that's on more than half the web servers out there. It was written by a University of California Berkeley drop-out. He wrote it and gave it to the world for free. Everyone from Microsoft to IBM is using it. Products come along born from a pure motivation, love of the technology. But can it grow into a company that takes down Microsoft a peg or two? I doubt it."

Gary Rivlin. "Barbarians at the Gates:
In Pursuit of the Microsoft Headman,"
ABC News.com (August 19, 1999).

"There is nothing in the world so enjoyable as a thorough-going **monomania**."

Agnes Repplier (1858–1950). U.S. author and
social critic. "The Decay of Sentiment,"
Books and Men (1888).

idolatry

[eye·DAWL·ah·tree]

Noun

1. the religious worship of idols, images, or anything that is not God
2. blind or excessive attachment or veneration for something: "I never understood my sister's idolatry of Justin Timberlake, despite her repeated efforts to convey his merits as a vocal visionary and an ideal prom date."

ORIGIN

Approximately 1250; borrowed from Late Latin, *idololatria*; from Greek, *eidololatreia* (*eidolon*: image + *latreia*: service or worship).

BONUS WORD   Related

infallible: incapable of failure or error

IN ACTION

"The art of government is the organization of **idolatry**. The bureaucracy consists of functionaries; the aristocracy, of idols; the democracy, of idolaters. The populace cannot understand the bureaucracy: it can only worship the national idols."

> George Bernard Shaw (1856–1950).
> Anglo-Irish playwright and critic.
> "Maxims for Revolutionists: Idolatry,"
> Man and Superman (1903).

Like most so-called geniuses, Jordan was blessed with enormous natural ability, then worked his fanny off. And he became the greatest basketball player that anyone had ever seen.

"However, directors Jim Stern and Don Kempf, and writer Jonathan Hock, take their praise to the point of pagan **idolatry**. Given the tone of the movie, you'd think that Jordan wasn't God, but put in long hours of intense concentration and physical labor to become Him."

> Paul Tatara. "He Shoots, He Always Scores"
> (movie review of Michael Jordan to the Max),
> CNN.com (May 30, 2000).

Audio pronunciations for the words in this pack can be found on our website: www.vocabvitamins.com/book/pack6.

Twisted Analogies

In these twisted analogies, each word is somehow related to its partner. Figure out what the relationship is, and then find a word pair on the right with a similar relationship. To make it easier on yourself, put the word pair into a sentence. For example, night:dawn can match book:last page because *night ends with dawn* and a *book ends with the last page*. Word pairs 1–5 will find their match in only a–e and so on.

1. dark:coruscate
2. calm:incendiary
3. firebrand:trouble
4. abyssal ocean depths: phosphorescence
5. eyes:scintillate

    a. door:open
    b. lightning:forest fire
    c. desert:wildflower
    d. laughter:morose
    e. quiet:beep

6. flummery:blushing
7. blandish:donkey
8. cajole:give in
9. inveigle:business deal
10. Jon's mouth:blarney

    f. refrigerator:cold
    g. bribe:border crossing
    h. expound:cat
    i. insults:teeth gritting
    j. sales pitch:purchase

11. gallivant:scenic route
12. misogamy:lonesome
13. uxorious:wife
14. banns:engagement
15. coquette:cocktail bar

    k. obituary:death
    l. commute:direct route
    m. mollycoddle:child
    n. student:library
    o. polygamy:exhausted

16. diamantine:sinking

17. iridescent:magical

18. dirty:lustrous

19. raw oyster:opalescent

20. nacreous:toilet seat

p. rice pudding:milky

q. broken:whizzing along

r. marble:basement floor

s. deserted:haunted

t. foamy:floating

21. workaholic entrepreneur: monomania

22. infatuation:obsession

23. idolatry:respect

24. furor:bang

25. long stem:ardent

u. abhorrence:dislike

v. small:large

w. chill:zzzzz

x. plastic:cheesy

y. steam engine:steam

[vo'cab]
VITAMINS

PACK 7

CUPID'S FAULT

THEME 1

Adversaries

SIMILAR TO:

estrange	separate, alienate
rancor	bitterness, spite
antagonist	adversary, opponent, rival
inimical	harmful, hostile
enmity	hatred, animosity

THEME 2

In a Drunken State

SIMILAR TO:

obstreperous	loud, noisy
vociferate	yell, utter, cry
discombobulate	confuse, disconcert
emotive	emotional, feeling, passionate
pandemonium	chaos, clamor, ruckus

THEME 3

My Head Is Spinning

SIMILAR TO:

vertiginous	dizzying
rotary	turning, spinning
vortex	whirlpool, spiral
gyral	spinning, circular
whirligig	revolving toy

THEME 4

Fleeting and Flimsy

SIMILAR TO:

ephemeral	short-lived, fleeting
fugacious	temporary, brief
evanescent	vanishing, vaporous
incorporeal	without a body, airy, insubstantial
gossamer	sheer, thin, gauzy

THEME 5

Curses and Curses

SIMILAR TO:

execration	curse, denouncement
anathema	ban, censure
malediction	swearing, slander
expletive	obscenity
imprecation	damning, cursing, evil eye

Adversaries

estrange

[i·STRAYNJ]

Transitive Verb

1. to keep at a distance, withdraw, or withhold; to arouse enmity or make hostile; to alienate or make indifferent: "You would never think that a disagreement about relish to ketchup proportions on a hot dog could possibly estrange two close friends."
2. to remove from customary environment or associations: "Whenever relatives come to visit, my mother shifts into 'hyperactive hostess mode,' and I feel estranged in my own house!"

ORIGIN

Probably before 1475; from Middle French, *estrangier*: alienate; from Vulgar Latin, *extraneare*: to treat as a stranger; from Latin, *extraneus*: foreign or strange.

BONUS WORD   Antonym

espouse: to take in marriage

IN ACTION

"U.N. Secretary-General Kofi Annan, diplomats said, also tried to avert a veto and pushed Palestinian President Yasser Arafat at the Amman summit to continue negotiations and not **estrange** himself from the new U.S. government. His plea worked for about 12 hours only."

"U.S. Vetoes U.N. Observer Force for West Bank, Gaza," CNN.com (March 28, 2001).

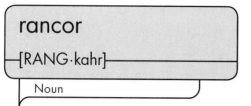

rancor

[RANG·kahr]

Noun

1. a feeling of deep-seated, bitter resentment or ill will; intense malice or hatred: "In order to truly understand the motives behind her actions, try to step into her skin for a moment, and feel the rancor that his behavior had caused."

ORIGIN

Probably before 1200; from Old French and directly from Late Latin, *rancor*: bitterness; from Latin, *rancere*: to be rotten or to stink.

BONUS WORD Synonym

bile: bitterness or digestive juice

IN ACTION

"'Despite all the violence and **rancor**, peace is possible in the region,' he said.

"'Each side has to address the fears and deeds of the other. If you can take away the fears, you can begin to build hope and trust again. If you have hope and trust and you have an environment that fosters that, you can produce peace,' said Ross."

"Former Mideast Peace Envoy Says There's Still Hope," CNN.com (March 31, 2001).

"If you are not already dead, forgive. **Rancor** is heavy, it is worldly; leave it on earth: die light."

Jean-Paul Sartre (1905–80). French novelist, dramatist, philosopher, and political activist. "The Devil and the Good Lord," act 1, Gallimard (1951).

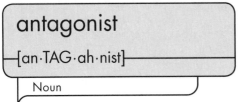

antagonist

—[an·TAG·ah·nist]—

Noun

1. one who contends with another; an adversary or opponent; someone who offers opposition.
2. the principal character in opposition to the protagonist of a drama or other literary work: "I knew I was in for trouble when, as a child, I never sided with Spider-Man or Captain America—but always with their bitter, scheming antagonists."

ORIGIN

Approximately 1599; from Late Latin, *antagonista*; from Greek, *antagonistes*: opponent or rival, from *antagonizesthai*: to contend.

BONUS WORD   Related

protagonist: the principal character

IN ACTION

"Last week, Purdue Pharma said that it was working to develop a painkiller like OxyContin that would also contain a compound to combat abuse. These narcotic **antagonists** do not affect a drug if it is taken normally. But if an abuser crushes a drug tablet and injects or snorts the powder an **antagonist** will block its opiate effect and reduce its appeal."

Barry Meier. "Maker Chose Not to Act to Reduce Abuse of OxyContin," New York Times (August 13, 2001).

"Perhaps one of the most compelling recent illustrations of the power of open source comes not with Linux but with XML. The markup language was created, says Jon Bosak, chair of the W3C's XML coordination group, 'In large part by a desire to ensure that the Web of the future would not be dominated by standards controlled by a single vendor or nation.' And despite XML being 'free,' plenty of companies make buckets of money selling cutting-edge products or services that draw on XML. Even Microsoft, open source's most aggressive **antagonist**, has put XML at the center of its sweeping .Net strategy."

"Analysis: Why Care About Open Source?"
CNN.com (July 10, 2001).

inimical

{i·NIM·i·kahl}

Adjective

1. adverse or harmful in effect; detrimental or damaging: "Love has kicked me in the butt once again, and I'm beginning to believe that it is all together inimical to my health."
2. having the disposition or temper of an enemy; not friendly; hostile (usually applied to private, rather than public, hostility).

ORIGIN
Approximately 1643; from Late Latin, *inimicalis*; from Latin, *inimicus*: unfriendly (*in* + *amicus*: friendly).

inimitable: defying imitation

IN ACTION

"Even more frightening, cable providers could just rope off certain parts of the Internet that they feel are immoral or **inimical** to their interests. It's a free-speech issue that's got people in many quarters upset, from the ACLU and the Consumers Union to a host of ISPs."

> Francine Russo. "The Incredible Shrinking Internet: When Cable Monopolies Rule the Web, Everyone Loses," Village Voice (November 1–7, 2000).

"What is wanted—whether this is admitted or not—is nothing less than a fundamental remolding, indeed weakening and abolition of the individual: one never tires of enumerating and indicting all that is evil and **inimical**, prodigal, costly, extravagant in the form individual existence has assumed hitherto, one hopes to manage more cheaply, more safely, more equitably, more uniformly if there exist only large bodies and their members."

> Friedrich Nietzsche (1844–1900). German philosopher, classical scholar, and culture critic.

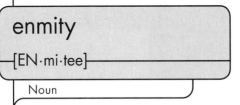

enmity

[EN·mi·tee]

Noun

1. a state or feeling of intense hostility or ill will, often used to describe a mutual hatred: "Despite the repeated efforts of friends and relatives to talk them into a reconciliation,

the two stubborn brothers refused to address the enmity between them."

ORIGIN

Approximately 1300; from Vulgar Latin, *inimicitatem*; from Latin, *inimicus*: enemy.

BONUS WORD Antonym

amity: state of friendship

IN ACTION

"In the millisecond before Ms. Johnson replied, the woman eyed her up and down, studying both outfit and body with cool precision. 'Oh, you're soooo thin,' the woman trilled, scarcely concealing the **enmity** inside the compliment."

Nelson Mui. "Ms. Perfect Opts Out,"
New York Times (August 19, 2001).

"India accuses Pakistan of arming and training Muslim separatists operating in Kashmir, a charge Islamabad denies. More than 30,000 people have been killed in separatist violence in Jammu and Kashmir since 1990, authorities say.

"But the war-torn region has been the focus of **enmity** between India and Pakistan for nearly all of the two nations' half-century existence. Two of three wars fought between the two were set off by the conflict."

"Attack Kills 17 Police, Wounds 6 in Jammu and
Kashmir," CNN.com (March 2, 2001).

In a Drunken State

obstreperous

[ob·STREP·ahr·ahs, ahb·STREP·ahr·ahs]

Adjective

1. noisily and stubbornly defiant: "Nestor was so obstreperous that his mother would avoid bringing any potentially contentious issues into their conversations."
2. noisily and aggressively boisterous; clamorous: "an obstreperous clamor," "the obstreperous city"

ORIGIN

Approximately 1600; borrowed from Latin, *obstreperus*: clamorous, noisy, from *obstrepere*: to oppose noisily (*ob-*: against + *strepere*: to make a noise).

BONUS WORD   Origin

obstinate: resistant to guidance or discipline

IN ACTION

"The first item for correction is the idea that corrections columns are easy. There are many challenges to writing such a feature—which is why I believe I am still the only pundit-type person who writes one. There's the issue of admitting that you're wrong, which is never easy. There's the logistical problem of combing through lots of angry e-mails to find the legitimate criticisms (you people don't make this any easier by burying your criticisms at the bottom of long essays and labeling your subject headers things like 'My dog is named Rex'). There's the issue of booze. And then there's this pesky issue of research.

"As many of you know, I work alone in my house. My only staff is an **obstreperous** couch . . . and a belly who increasingly feels the need to press the space bar on my keyboard himself. This makes some questions very hard to deal with."

Jonah Goldberg. "Goldberg File: Corrections Galore!" *National Review* (May 26, 2000).

"A lunatic may be 'soothed,' . . . for a time, but in the end, he is very apt to become **obstreperous**. His cunning, too, is proverbial, and great. . . . When a madman appears thoroughly sane, indeed, it is high time to put him in a straight jacket."

Edgar Allan Poe (1809–49). U.S. poet, critic, and short-story writer. [The superintendent of the asylum, on rebellion in the madhouse, in] "The System of Doctor Tarr and Professor Fether," *Graham's Magazine* (1845).

vociferate
[voe·SIF·ah·rayt']

Transitive Verb, Intransitive Verb

Transitive Verb
1. to utter or cry out in a loud voice, especially vehemently: "For the fourth delivery in a row, the cook proved unable to hold the mayonnaise, and this time Ben marched down to the restaurant to vociferate his displeasure."

Intransitive Verb
2. to utter or cry out something with vehemence

ORIGIN
Approximately 1599; from Latin, *vociferari*: to shout, to yell, from a lost adjective, *vocifer*: lifting one's voice (*vox*, genitive *vocis*: voice + *ferre*: to carry).

BONUS WORD   Origin

equivocate: to be deliberately ambiguous

IN ACTION

"They soon arrived at the door of this house, or cottage, for it might be called either, without much impropriety. Here Jones knocked several times without receiving any answer from within; at which Partridge, whose head was full of nothing but of ghosts, devils, witches, and such like, began to tremble, crying, 'Lord, have mercy upon us! surely the people must be all dead. I can see no light neither now, and yet I am certain I saw a candle burning but a moment before.—Well! I have heard of such things.'—'What hast thou heard of?' said Jones. 'The people are either fast asleep, or probably, as this is a lonely place, are afraid to open their door.' He then began to **vociferate** pretty loudly, and at last an old woman, opening an upper casement, asked, Who they were, and what they wanted? Jones answered, They were travellers who had lost their way, and having seen a light in the window, had been led thither in hopes of finding some fire to warm themselves."

Henry Fielding (1707–54). English novelist and dramatist. "Book VIII. Containing About Two Days: X. In Which Our Travellers Meet with a Very Extraordinary Adventure," The History of Tom Jones (1917).

"The blackbirds—three species of which consort together—are the noisiest of all our feathered citizens. Great companies of them—more than the famous 'four-and-twenty' whom Mother Goose has immortalized—congregate in contiguous tree-tops and **vociferate** with all the clamor and confusion of a turbulent political meeting. Politics, certainly, must be the occasion of such tumultuous debates, but still, unlike all other politicians, they instill melody into their individual utterances and produce harmony as a general effect."

Nathaniel Hawthorne (1804–64). American novelist and short-story writer. "Buds and Bird-Voices" [essay], (1846).

discombobulate

[dis'·kahm·BOB·yah·layt']

Transitive Verb

1. to throw into a state of disconcerting confusion; to disorient: "Bart had been working almost every waking hour for months, and social situations or any time not dedicated to productive tasks were beginning to discombobulate him."

ORIGIN

Approximately 1916; origin uncertain; possibly an alteration of English, *discompose.*

BONUS WORD   Synonym

discomfit: to make unsettled or confused

IN ACTION

"'I'm OK,' I said. The real answer was probably too complicated for a stadium conversation.

"'You seem in pretty solidly high spirits.'

"That was a big compliment coming from someone who had regularly made it a goal in college to make me worry less.

"But I did feel OK. Being at the game made me feel normal, and it was nice to be spending time in San

Francisco after a week of feeling **discombobulated** in Houston."

Alicia Parlette. "Alicia's Story: Cancer, Despair, Hope, Faith," San Francisco Chronicle (June 9, 2005).

"So, it was a surprise after *My Own Private Idaho* and the tediously **discombobulated** *Even Cowgirls Get the Blues* (1993) to see [Gus] Van Sant move to slicker and more disciplined studio projects: the tart black comedy *To Die For* (1995); the blue-collar-savant blockbuster *Good Will Hunting* (1997); and the taxidermist's reproduction of *Psycho* (1998), which afforded the director the least freedom imaginable."

David Edelstein. "Sand Trap: Gus Van Sant's Desert Folly. Plus: All the Real Girls," Slate.com (February 14, 2003).

emotive

[i·MOE·tiv]

Adjective

1. of or pertaining to emotion
2. showing, eliciting, or characterized by emotion: "Using emotive pleas that were impossible to resist, Linda obtained sizable commitments throughout the office for her charitable walks."

ORIGIN

Approximately 1735; formed from English, *emotion* + suffix -*ive*; *emotion* from Old French, *emouvoir*: to stir up; from Latin, *emovere*: to move out, to remove (*e-*: out + *movere*: to move).

BONUS WORD   Antonym

unflappable: marked by extreme calm and composure

IN ACTION

"Klein is a friendly, unassuming guy, keen to emphasize that My Real Baby was a group effort. To that end he introduces me to a small crew of engineers and coders standing around in the 'Toy Bay' with a robot named It: an 18-inch-high mechanical torso with arms retooled from a snake robot and a bare-bones but expressive face. iRobot's first **emotive** robot, built before Bit, It responds to my greeting with California surferese: 'Excellent!'"

Erik Davis. "Congratulations, It's a Bot!"
Wired.com (September 2000).

"[B]ecause stem cell research is such a contentious and highly **emotive** area, it will impact on some people's attitudes. It will further reinforce the attitudes of those who are already opposed to the field, and will probably shift the positions of those who are a bit ambivalent."

Dr. Stephen Minger. "Op/Ed: The Fall of a Scientific
'Rock Star,'" BBC News (January 10, 2006).

pandemonium

[pan'·dah·MOE·nee·ahm]

Noun

1. a chaotic and extremely noisy place: "The convention hall was a hopeless pandemonium, with hundreds of booths competing for attention, each with its own dramatic slogans, bright video displays, and pressing sales teams."
2. wild uproar or chaos

ORIGIN

Approximately 1779; from New Latin, *Pandemonium*: the palace built by Satan as the central part of hell, referenced in *Paradise Lost*, an epic poem by John Milton (Greek, *pan-*: all + Late Latin, *daemonium*: evil spirit).

BONUS WORD   Origin

Pandora: in Greek mythology, the first woman

IN ACTION

"The scene quickly devolved into **pandemonium**, with the launched hamster tumbling humorously in mid-air several times before landing at the foot of the sofa and fleeing in shock. A frantic, living-room-wide search for Harry ensued and, after extensive search efforts behind the sofa, under the recliner, and behind the bookcase, the hamster was found between the vertical blinds and the sliding glass door, shaken but alive. As of press time, Harry was resting in his cage, his condition described as 'skittish but stable.'"

"Hamster Thrown from Remote-Control Monster Truck,"
Onion.com (March 22, 2001).

My Head Is Spinning

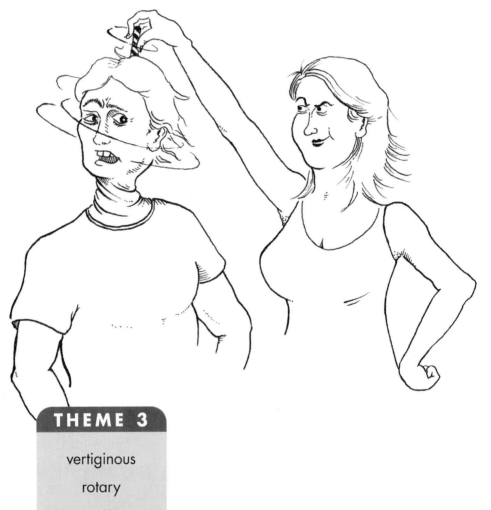

THEME 3

vertiginous

rotary

vortex

gyral

whirligig

vertiginous

[vahr·TIJ·ah·nahs]

Adjective

1. turning round; whirling; revolving: "vertiginous motion"; "There is no way you are getting me into that evil, nauseating, vertiginous amusement ride."
2. affected with vertigo; giddy; dizzy
3. tending to cause vertigo: "a vertiginous climb up the face of the cliff"
4. inclined to change frequently or suddenly; unstable

ORIGIN

Approximately 1608; from Latin, *vertiginosus*: suffering from dizziness, from *vertigo*: vertigo, from *vertere:* to turn.

BONUS WORD Related

planar: involving two dimensions

IN ACTION

"Other popular looks in the poll included the gamine haircut, styled by Leonard's of Mayfair, that transformed Twiggy into the 'Face of '66' and Catherine Zeta Jones' black shiny tresses. The Queen, whose hairstyle has hardly changed during six decades, was number nine.

"Sinead O'Connor's shaven head was also popular, just making the poll at number 18. And at number 14 was the cartoon character Marge Simpson's **vertiginous** blue bouffant."

Kate Morris. "Big Hair: The Celebrity Styles That Went Global," Independent *(November 26, 2004).*

"The journey to the sanatorium is much the same for me as it was for Hans Castorp. When I change at Landquart to connect to Davos, my tattered copy of the novel proves a useful guidebook. 'Here,' Mann writes, 'after a long and windy wait in a spot devoid of charm, you mount a narrow-gauge train; and as the small but very powerful engine gets under way, there begins the thrilling part of the journey, a steep and steady climb that seems never to come to an end.' It still thrills. The squat red train grinds around **vertiginous** alpine bends, skirts the trees, edges up snow-covered slopes. It's only at Davos-Dorf that the confluence between fiction and reality comes to a sudden end."

Matthew Sweet. "A Last Gasp on Magic Mountain [The Alpine Sanatorium Immortalised in Thomas Mann's Classic Novel Is About to Close Its Doors After 150 Years. Matthew Sweet Takes the Air at the Davos Valley Retreat]," Independent (November 25, 2004).

rotary
[ROE·tah·ree]

Adjective, Noun

Adjective
1. relating to or characterized by rotation: "rotary dial"; "This rotary salad spinner is a brilliant use of centrifugal force for culinary gain."

Noun
2. a machine or part of a machine that rotates around an axis
3. a road junction at which traffic streams circularly around a central island; a traffic circle; a roundabout: "The accident blocked all traffic at the rotary."

ORIGIN

Approximately 1731; borrowed from Medieval Latin, *rotarius*: pertaining to wheels; from Latin, *rota*: wheel.

BONUS WORD Related

pirouette: rapid spin of the body

IN ACTION

"'We had health departments with **rotary** phones and without beepers,' said Dr. Georges Benjamin, executive director of the American Public Health Association, which advocates providing more resources for the nation's public health system.

"Benjamin recalled that when the anthrax attacks occurred and he was Maryland's top health officer, 'our capacity to pull all the state health officials in the country on the phone at one time was zero, we didn't even have the numbers.' That has been fixed as public health officials reached out to one another."

Frank James. "Flu Crisis Exposes Large
Gaps in Bioterrorism Readiness,"
Chicago Tribune (November 28, 2004).

"Felix Wankel. It's one of those names that conjures up images of crooked yellowing teeth, creased chalk-stripe suit, scurf on the shoulders—and halitosis.

"The inventor of the **rotary** engine hopefully possessed none of those distinguishing features, but he was a genius.

"German-born Wankel has been described as one of the automotive world's greatest thinkers, yet he possessed neither an engineering degree nor a driving licence."

Mike Torpey. "New Mazda Has Style,"
Liverpool Daily Post (November 26, 2004).

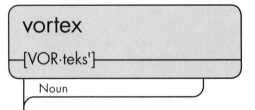

vortex

[VOR·teks']

Noun

1. a powerful circular current of water, usually the result of conflicting tides; a whirlpool
2. a place or situation that seems to swamp or engulf everything else: "As it has happened with so many actors, he was swept up in the vortex of Hollywood."

ORIGIN

Approximately 1652; borrowed from Latin, *vortex*, variant of *vertex*: an eddy of water or air, from *vertere*: to turn.

BONUS WORD Sound

vertex: the highest point

IN ACTION

"That's when the thousands of lasers, black lights, electroluminescent wire and LED outfits, vehicles, structures and art projects are in full effect. And in this respect, Burning Man 2004 was no exception. All around the playa, wildly lit up bar cars, domes and costumes attract the eye.

"From nearly anywhere on the playa, Nate Smith's Singularity Machine can be seen, a tall, swirling **vortex** of fire that stops most participants in their path."

Daniel Terdiman. "Bright Lights, Burning City,"
Wired.com (September 7, 2004).

"Investigators are now focusing on something known to pilots as 'wake turbulence.' When a plane is heavy and traveling at a relatively slow speed, as would normally be the case just after takeoff, the steep deck angle required to maintain lift helps propagate a kind of twin-forking roil of air that trails behind the aircraft like an invisible wake from a ship. Two **vortexes**, one from each wingtip, are spun away like sideways tornadoes.

"Whether taking off, landing or cruising straight ahead, the **vortexes** are always there, but their strength becomes exacerbated under certain combinations of aircraft speed, weight and deck angle."

P. Smith. "Turbulence Can Kill [Investigators Are Suggesting That Flight 587 May Have Become Fatally Entwined in the Jet Wake of Another Plane. Stranger Things Have Happened]," Salon.com (November 16, 2001).

gyral

[JIE·rahl]

Adjective

1. moving in a circular path or way; whirling: "Ten minutes into the final exam, Jasmine was still on her bike, propelling herself toward campus with a frenetic gyral motion."
2. relating to or associated with or comprising a convolution of the brain: "the gyral sulcus"

ORIGIN
Approximately 1745; from English, *gyr-*, variant of *gyro-*: ring, circle, from Greek, *gyros*: ring, round + suffix *-al*.

BONUS WORD Origin

spirogyra: freshwater algae

IN ACTION

"Not more than five miles eastward from the camp, while trundling over a stretch of stony ground, I am accosted by a couple of Koordiah shepherds. . . . With a growl more like the voice of a wild animal than of human beings, one draws his sword and the other picks up a thick knobbed stick that he had dropped in order to the better pinch and sound my packages.

"Without giving them time to reveal whether they seriously intend attacking me, or only to try intimidation, I have them nicely covered with the Smith & Wesson. They seem to comprehend in a moment that I have them at a disadvantage, and they hurriedly retreat a short distance, executing a series of **gyral** antics, as though expecting me to fire at their legs. They are accompanied by two dogs, tawny-coated monsters, larger than the largest mastiffs, who now proceed to make things lively and interesting around myself and the bicycle. Keeping the revolver in my hand, and threatening to shoot their dogs if they don't call them away, I continue my progress toward where the stony ground terminates in favor of smooth camel-paths, about a hundred yards farther on."

Thomas Stevens. Around the World on a Bicycle *(1984).*

"The American systems of grids and rectangles stands in sharp contrast to the devious British who move in **gyratory** arcs, curves and circles frequently interrupted by dead ends leading nowhere. Put in simpler terms, this simply means that almost anywhere in North America, a motorist can, even without a map, make three consecutive right (or even left) turns and come back to where he started. In Britain, there is practically no chance of returning to one's starting point."

Norman Berdichevsky. "Two Peoples Divided By
Common Road Signs—British-American Differences,"
Contemporary Review (October 1995).

whirligig
[HWUR·li·gig', WUR·li·gig']

Noun

1. a conical child's plaything tapering to a steel point on which it can be made to spin
2. a large mechanical apparatus with seats for children to ride on; a carousel; a merry-go-round; a roundabout: "Blue spent the last month building a large whirligig with flashing red lights that illuminated on each revolution."
3. anything that whirls around or in which persons or things are whirled about.

ORIGIN
Approximately 1425; from Middle English, *whirlegigge* (*whirlen*: to whirl + *-gigge*, spinning top, something that rotates, possibly of Scandinavian origin).

BONUS WORD Synonym

trundle: small wheel or roller

IN ACTION

"Thus the **whirligig** of time brings in his revenges."

*William Shakespeare (1564–1616). English dramatist
and poet. [Feste, marking the comeuppance afflicted
on Malvolio, in]* Twelfth Night *(1601).*

"The intellect is a very nice **whirligig** toy, but
how people take it seriously is more than I can
understand."

*Ezra Pound (1885–1972). U.S. poet and critic. [Letter
(undated) to Pound's mother, quoted in]* A Serious
Character, *by Humphrey Carpenter (1988).*

Fleeting and Flimsy

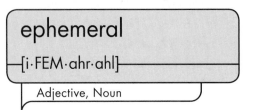

ephemeral

[i·FEM·ahr·ahl]

Adjective, Noun

Adjective

1. enduring for a very short time only; short-lived: "Credit cards can provide an ephemeral sense of wealth, but you'll come down hard in thirty days, when the bill arrives."
2. existing or lasting no longer than a day, as with certain insects or plants; diurnal: "The ephemeral female mayfly lives for only five minutes as a fully developed, reproductive insect."

Noun

3. a markedly short-lived thing: "I'm sure that he finds you very attractive, but don't pin all your hopes on the ephemeral."

ORIGIN

Approximately 1576; from Greek, *ephemeros*: short-lived (*ep*: the prefix *epi-*: on or upon + *hemerai*: day).

BONUS WORD   Origin

ephemeron: something short-lived

IN ACTION

"I'm not a romantic. We fall in love for **ephemeral** and unknowable reasons. What I hold onto is the fact that I loved my husband passionately from the moment I saw him. (I was romantic then.) And now he is the father of the children I love more passionately than I could have believed possible. Between us we have built houses and gardens. We've made a complex and bracing life. A life that is never boring."

Clea MacAllister. "The Thrill Is Gone,"
Salon.com (July 12, 2001).

"The people who make that system work are usually invisible too. They don't live in Manhattan; for the most part these are bridge-and-tunnel, Island-and-Jersey jobs, often pretty well paid, but never compensated with the kind of glamour that attaches to even the most **ephemeral** of Manhattan's knowledge industry occupations."

Bill McKibben. "New York's True Heart,"
New York Times (October 7, 2001).

"Curse this moribund, woeful orb, where all that is beautiful and good is so cruelly **ephemeral**!"

T. Herman Zweibel. "My Son, My Son!"
Onion.com (April 12, 2000).

fugacious
[fyoo·GAY·shahs]

Adjective

1. passing away quickly; fleeting or flying away: "Many people are afraid of the little green mounds that come with their sushi until they feel the spicy but fugacious rush that makes wasabi uniquely palatable."

ORIGIN
Approximately 1635; from Latin, *fugax*, from *fugere*: to flee.

BONUS WORD   Origin

fugue: a musical form using a repeated theme

IN ACTION

"Restless, shifting, **fugacious** as time itself is a certain vast bulk of the population of the red brick district of the lower West Side. Homeless, they have a hundred homes. They flit from furnished room to furnished room, transients for ever—transients in abode, transients in heart and mind. They sing 'Home, Sweet Home' in ragtime; they carry their lares et penates in a bandbox; their vine is entwined about a picture hat; a rubber plant is their fig tree."

O. Henry [William Sydney Porter] (1862–1910).
American short-story writer. "The Furnished Room,"
The Four Million (1906).

"No other mineral was liquid, highly inflammable, and **fugacious** in character. This last quality, operators soon learned, built up a strong pressure for rapid exploitation. Failure to drill on one piece of property could result in serious losses to wells on adjoining land. No later than the summer of 1860, petroleum producers also had ample confirmation of the unpredictable nature of petroleum supply. Repeatedly they saw production expand overnight to levels well beyond their most liberal estimates of needed storage and handling facilities."

Harold F. Williamson.
The American Petroleum Industry (1959).

evanescent

[ev'·ah·NES·ahnt]

Adjective

1. liable to vanish like vapor or become imperceptible: "In times of chaos or heated conflict, it seems that the firm moral boundaries that usually keep people in check become evanescent."

ORIGIN

Approximately 1717; from Latin, *evanescentem*, present participle of *evanescere*: to vanish (*e*: out + *vanescere*: to vanish, from *vanus*: empty).

BONUS WORD　Sound

effervescent: bubbly or marked by high spirits

IN ACTION

"Mr. Coxe's face grew perceptibly paler. His feelings, if **evanescent**, were evidently strong."

Elizabeth Cleghorn Gaskell (1810–65).
English novelist. Wives and Daughters (1865).

"Nobody thinks it's silly to invest two hours' work in two minutes' enjoyment; but if cooking is **evanescent**, well, so is the ballet."

Julia Child (1912–2005). American cooking teacher.

"We talk sometimes of a great talent for conversation, as if it were a permanent property in some individuals. Conversation is an **evanescent** relation,—no more. A man is reputed to have thought and eloquence; he cannot, for all that, say a word

to his cousin or his uncle. They accuse his silence
with as much reason as they would blame the
insignificance of a dial in the shade. In the sun it will
mark the hour. Among those who enjoy his thought
he will regain his tongue."

Ralph Waldo Emerson (1803–82). U.S. essayist, poet,
and philosopher. "Friendship," Essays (1841).

incorporeal

[in'·kor·PORE·ee·ahl]

Adjective

1. without material form or substance; not corporeal:
   "An incorporeal sense of dignity and pride seems to be
   pushing Americans forward to resume their lives in the
   face of fear."

ORIGIN
Approximately 1530; from Latin, *incorporeus* (*in*: the prefix
in-: not + *corporeus*: consisting of a body, from *corpus*,
genitive *corporis*: body).

BONUS WORD   Origin

corpulent: excessively fat

IN ACTION

"Though I could not but suspect, I was still surprised
to discover that they were a mass of correspondence—
daily almost, it must have been—from Linton
Heathcliff: answers to documents forwarded by
her. The earlier dated were embarrassed and short;
gradually, however, they expanded into copious
love letters, foolish, as the age of the writer rendered

natural, yet with touches here and there which I thought were borrowed from a more experienced source. Some of them struck me as singularly odd compounds of ardour and flatness; commencing in strong feeling, and concluding in the affected, wordy way that a schoolboy might use to a fancied, **incorporeal** sweetheart. Whether they satisfied Cathy, I don't know; but they appeared very worthless trash to me."

Emily Brontë (1818–48). English novelist.
Wuthering Heights (1847).

"To say that God is an **incorporeal** substance, is to say in effect there is no God at all. What alleges he against it, but the School-divinity which I have already answered? Scripture he can bring none, because the word **incorporeal** is not found in Scripture."

Thomas Hobbes (1588–1679). British philosopher.
"An Answer to Dr. Bramhall," English Works, ed.
Molesworth (1839–45).

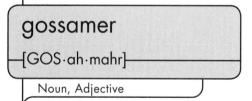

gossamer
[GOS·ah·mahr]

Noun, Adjective

Noun
1. an extremely fine-textured, sheer, gauzelike fabric
2. something fine-textured, sheer, or delicate
3. fine filaments from a cobweb, usually floating in the air or suspended on low bushes or grass
4. a thin and waterproof outer garment, usually for women

Adjective

5. light, thin, tenuous, or delicate; sheer: "Tim was still physically robust, but the surgery had left him with a gossamer voice."

ORIGIN

Before 1300; from Middle English, *gossumer*, probably from *gos*: goose + *sumer* or *sumor*: summer. A reference to the threads spun especially in fields of cut grain or stalks in autumn, when geese are in season.

BONUS WORD Synonym

diaphanous: so thin as to transmit light

IN ACTION

"There is something in the unselfish and self-sacrificing love of a brute [an animal], which goes directly to the heart of him who has had frequent occasion to test the paltry friendship and **gossamer** fidelity of mere Man."

Edgar Allan Poe (1809–49). U.S. poet, critic, and short-story writer. "The Black Cat" (1843).

"Mr. Yosses shows a **gossamer** touch with his lemon-raspberry soufflé, topped with verbena sauce and served with a clean, highly concentrated strawberry sorbet. It's light and elegant. The fruit flavors are deployed with pinpoint precision. This is a civilized dessert, presented in a quiet, adult setting."

William Grimes. "Citarella the Restaurant: Now They'll Even Cook It for You," New York Times (October 3, 2001).

"A wisp of **gossamer**, about the size and substance of a spider's web."

Monica Baldwin. [On encountering modern lingerie after twenty-seven years as a cloistered nun.] I Leap over the Wall: A Return to the World After 28 Years in a Convent (1950).

Curses and
Curses

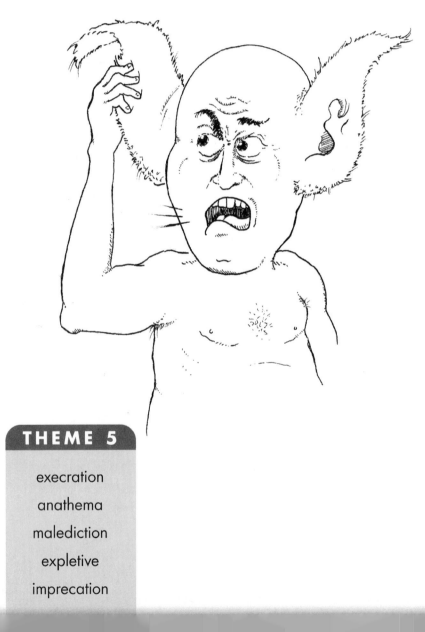

execration

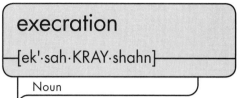

[ek'·sah·KRAY·shahn]

Noun

1. the act of cursing or denouncing; the expression of utter detestation: "Sally considered execration to be an act of spiritual cleansing and used it along with other calming techniques like deep breathing."
2. a curse
3. something cursed or detested

ORIGIN

Approximately 1382; from Old French, *execration*; borrowed from Latin, *execrationem*, from *execrari*: to hate, to curse (*ex-*: out + *sacrare*: to devote, either to holiness or destruction, from *sacer*: sacred).

BONUS WORD Sound

excretion: waste matter discharged from the body

IN ACTION

". . . I cannot help being astonished at the furious and ungoverned **execration** which all reference to the possibility of a fusion of the races draws down upon those who suggest it, because nobody pretends to deny that, throughout the South, a large proportion of the population is the offspring of white men and colored women."

Fanny Kemble (1809–93). British actor and abolitionist. Journal of a Residence on a Georgian Plantation in 1838–1839 (1863).

"The council's slender support does not guarantee its overthrow by a democratic revolution. Brutality and ruthlessness regularly defeat widespread peaceful opposition. The Bolshevik Revolution succeeded for 75 years in the Soviet Union by practicing and inculcating terror and fear. The reviled and reptilian military thugs in Myanmar hold an iron-grip on power despite virtual universal support for Nobel Peace Prize icon and National League for Democracy leader Aung San Suu Kyi. Saddam Hussein's widespread **execration** was no match for his indiscriminate wretchedness, torture, and general barbarism."

> Bruce Fein. *"Commentary: Revolt or Revolution?"*
> Washington Times *(January 28, 2004).*

anathema

[ah·NATH·ah·mah]

Noun

1. a curse or ban issued from a religious authority, usually accompanied by excommunication: "anathemas against unbelievers"
2. a forceful denunciation or curse: "Instead of yelling the anathema, she pronounced it slowly and quietly, dramatically amplifying its power."
3. one that is cursed, denounced, or excommunicated by a religious authority
4. someone or something that is loathed or intensely disliked: "the notion was anathema to his peers," "she is an anathema to me"

ORIGIN

Approximately 1526; from Greek, *anathema*: something dedicated or devoted, usually to evil, related to *anatithenai*: to set up (*ana-*: up + *tithenai*: to set, to place).

BONUS WORD   Related

peccant: liable to sin

IN ACTION

"James and Alice met for the first time, through their children, when they were both legally separated. They started living together with the three children over three years ago. James works with Air Malta and Alice with another parastatal company.

"Their families' reaction has been different. For Alice's mother the living arrangement is **anathema**. A deeply religious woman, she put pressure on Alice to stay with her husband, and when she failed there, insisted that Alice should never have a relationship again. James' family, on the other hand, have welcomed Alice with open arms."

> Gillian Bartolo. "Cohabitees Beyond the Pale,"
> Malta Independent (February 22, 2004).

malediction

[mal'·i·DIK·shahn]

Noun

1. a curse, or a proclamation of evil against another; an execration: "One malediction, cruelly placed by a close relative, would continue to haunt Dana for many years."
2. slander or evil talk

ORIGIN

Approximately 1447; borrowed from Latin, *maledictionem*: speaking evil of, from *maledicere*: to speak evil of, to curse (*male*: badly + *dicere*: to say).

BONUS WORD   Origin

malevolence: wishing evil to others

IN ACTION

"SAGITTARIUS (Nov. 22–Dec. 21)

"Most of us have had curses cast on us. But unlike how they're portrayed in novels and films, the real thing is rarely an act of black magic conjured by a bad wizard. Rather, it's a negative declaration about our potential delivered by a person we love or trust. For instance, when I was 21 years old, my astrology teacher smacked me with this paralyzing prophecy: 'You will never be known for who you really are.' I've fought that whammy ever since. Your own curse may have been hurled by a parent who said you would never succeed, or an ex-lover who asserted that you'll never have a decent relationship. But whatever **malediction** you've had to bear all this time, Sagittarius, I want you to know that the cosmic forces are now aligned to help you banish it for good."

Rob Brezsny. "Free Will Astrology,"
Village Voice (June 6, 2001).

"Throughout the game, the player must use ancient Egyptian rituals and concoct potions to heal those afflicted by the **malediction** and conquer evil entities. They must also enlist the help of various people and gods to unravel this mystery, save the Pharaoh and rescue Egypt. As well as an engaging and compelling story, gamers will also get to experience some of the wonders of ancient Egypt as they travel along the Nile and explore locations and monuments such as: Pi-Ramses, Memphis, and the labyrinth of Ptah.

Stephen Coleman. "The Egyptian Prophecy,"
IGN.com (February 17, 2004).

"With its history of failed presidential hopefuls and the Massachusetts Supreme Court's recent demand that the state legislature establish gay marriage, maybe the state's name has become a **malediction**, as powerful as the curse of the Babe Ruth that haunts the Boston Red Sox."

Jim Geraghty. "Don't Mess with Massachusetts: Is Bashing the Bay State Really Going to Help Bush?" National Review (February 17, 2004).

expletive

[EK·spli·tiv]

Noun, Adjective

Noun

1. an exclamation, especially one that is profane or obscene: "Susan was convinced that learning how to drive a stick shift required regular use of expletives."
2. a word or phrase that conveys no independent meaning but is added to fill out a sentence or metrical line (as in poetry) or fulfill a grammatical function (as *there* in "There are five books on the table.")

Adjective

3. added to fill up; superfluous: "expletive phrases"

ORIGIN

Approximately 1612; from Middle French, *expletif, expletive,* and directly from Late Latin, *expletivus*: serving to fill out; from Latin, *explere*: to fill out (*ex-*: out + *plere*: to fill).

BONUS WORD   Continuum

LESS RUDE . . .   . . . MORE RUDE
interjection   ⟶   expletive

interjection: an abrupt emphatic exclamation

IN ACTION

"There was also a potentially volatile incident last
year in which Tracy tried to lift Kevin Brown for a
pinch-hitter only to have Brown hurl an **expletive** at
him, grab a bat from the rack and calmly walk to the
plate to hit.

"'What was I going to do?' Tracy said, talking
about it for the first time. 'Tackle him on his way out
of the dugout? I wasn't going to make a scene in front
of the whole world.'"

> *Ross Newhan. "No Trace of Bitterness [Despite Being
> Faced with Job Insecurity and a Family Crisis, the
> Dodgers' Tracy Says That He Is Managing Just Fine],"*
> Los Angeles Times *(February 22, 2004).*

imprecation

[im'·pri·KAY·shahn]

Noun

1. the act of invoking evil upon someone: "Kim was
   amused by the portrayal of voodoo in the movie as a
   mix of imprecation and oddly placed bone jewelry."
2. a curse

ORIGIN

Approximately 1448; borrowed from Latin, *imprecationem*,
from *imprecari:* to invoke, to pray for (*im-:* in, within +
precari: to pray, to ask).

BONUS WORD Antonym

benediction: expression of approval or blessing

IN ACTION

"It's a tricky play, at times acerbic and wise, at others, cold and heavy-handed. (Before one of the characters gets around to deciding the fate of the Ekdals' unseen pet wild duck, you may feel like grabbing a gun and finishing it off yourself.) The challenge for a modern theater company is not to settle the controversies that 'The Wild Duck' foments, but to add psychological credibility to the men and women on each side of the argument.

"In his new adaptation of the play at his American Repertory Theater here, Robert Brustein, the theater critic and educator, for the most part accomplishes the task. He has provided an updated and sometimes even daring translation, imbuing the work with the invigorating clarity of a cloudless Scandinavian winter's morn. No longer does Dr. Relling, the Ekdals' cynical downstairs neighbor, conclude the play with what is often translated as a mild, muttered **imprecation**. Now, he spits the words 'Go to hell!' at the reeling Gregers. The overall effect is to give the work more blunt force and play down the all-too-obvious symbolism."

Peter Marks. "A Havoc of Meddling Fools Wrapped
Up in One Man," New York Times (January 8, 1997).

Audio pronunciations for the words in
this pack can be found on our website:
www.vocabvitamins.com/book/pack7.

The Search

Cupid can have a twisted sense of humor, sending us off in futile searches to find someone to love. At least in this search, you know exactly what you are looking for. Each word appears once.

n	u	j	u	n	k	t	b	b	g	c	q	l	e	b	q	f	k	g	x
g	d	z	f	u	h	e	v	p	e	v	i	t	o	m	e	d	g	f	i
o	f	s	l	n	t	s	i	n	o	g	a	t	n	a	s	q	y	q	v
o	j	u	e	y	p	i	y	w	d	l	t	v	a	l	h	r	r	o	h
w	r	o	t	a	r	y	s	m	u	i	n	o	m	e	d	n	a	p	x
a	l	r	a	s	g	e	u	b	k	e	e	e	e	d	k	k	l	x	o
l	a	e	r	o	p	r	o	c	n	i	c	x	h	i	y	c	q	z	i
i	c	p	e	a	v	b	n	m	a	b	s	x	t	c	h	l	r	q	u
k	i	e	f	o	m	n	i	m	p	r	e	c	a	t	i	o	n	k	s
k	m	r	i	o	i	t	g	k	m	x	n	n	n	i	q	x	t	a	r
p	i	t	c	o	y	d	i	i	e	u	a	a	a	o	d	w	k	z	a
f	n	s	o	t	x	s	t	c	g	a	v	s	d	n	z	r	u	a	o
u	i	b	v	a	o	o	r	c	n	i	e	p	h	e	m	e	r	a	l
d	d	o	w	k	g	a	e	g	z	y	l	e	g	w	u	m	m	w	o
e	x	p	l	e	t	i	v	e	g	n	a	r	t	s	e	a	n	d	p
k	w	l	w	i	k	v	b	f	u	g	a	c	i	o	u	s	y	r	u
f	n	v	o	r	t	e	x	h	h	n	c	e	m	h	l	s	s	k	w
g	p	n	s	z	u	i	z	i	c	p	p	d	e	q	w	o	h	z	d
e	n	d	x	g	a	o	a	o	d	a	w	i	u	z	u	g	o	k	l
p	r	t	p	z	h	m	r	q	g	n	y	m	x	c	z	d	r	q	x

1. anathema
2. antagonist
3. discombobulate
4. emotive
5. enmity
6. ephemeral
7. estrange
8. evanescent
9. execration
10. expletive
11. fugacious
12. gossamer
13. gyral
14. imprecation
15. incorporeal
16. inimical
17. malediction
18. obstreperous
19. pandemonium
20. rancor
21. rotary
22. vertiginous
23. vociferate
24. vortex
25. whirligig

PACK 8

THE CREAMY CENTER

THEME 1
At the Heart of It

SIMILAR TO:

archetype	original, prototype
epitome	ultimate, exemplar
pith	body, gist
quiddity	essence, substance
Zeitgeist	spirit of the time

THEME 2
The Bacon

SIMILAR TO:

emolument	salary, wages
guerdon	reward, compensation
lucre	profits, payoff, takings
pittance	small sum, peanuts
remunerate	repay, reimburse

THEME 3
The Space Between

SIMILAR TO:

antipodes	opposites
asunder	split, divided
hiatus	gap, interval
hyperborean	arctic, polar
ultramundane	beyond this world

THEME 4
The Cat's Pajamas

SIMILAR TO:

laudable	praiseworthy
palmary	principal, main
estimable	admirable, honorable
august	dignified, noble, venerable
meritorious	excellent, commendable

THEME 5
It's Universal

SIMILAR TO:

omnipresent	everywhere, universal
cosmopolitan	worldly, cultured
ecumenical	general, global
axiom	principle, truth, theorem
ubiquitous	universal, pervasive, everywhere

At the Heart of It

archetype

[AWR·ki·tiep']

Noun

1. an original model on which things of the same type are patterned; a prototype: "*X-Men* was the archetype of the modern comic book movie, successfully blending machismo with tights for the first time in the genre."
2. an ideal example of something

ORIGIN

Approximately 1545; from Latin, *archetypum*; from Greek, *archetypon*: pattern, model, from *archetypos*: original (*arche-*: first + *typos*: stamp, mold, model, type).

BONUS WORD   Synonym

prototype: a standard or typical example

IN ACTION

"Until now her characters have tended to be urban flotsam: intelligent women living in condemned council blocks, grimly aware of their marginal status. Lurking among them is a second Birch **archetype**, the charming, unreliable man, in whose net most of her female characters end up dismally ensnared. It says something for Birch's opinion of feckless, Bohemian gamma-males that Raff in 'Life in the Palace' dies prematurely of a stroke, while David, the egocentric failed poet of 'The Fog Line' ends up bludgeoned to death by his ex."

DJ Taylor. "Clamour of Ordinary Lives"
(book review of Turn Again Home, by Carol Birch),
Guardian (July 12, 2003).

"Other infamous episodes that have occurred during the couple's 18-month relationship include Tillich's August 1999 insistence that Jensen listen to all of side two of the Velvet Underground's *White Light/White Heat*, his January 1999 failure to talk Jensen into visiting the grave of Philip K. Dick during a Colorado road trip, and his ongoing unsuccessful efforts to get her to read Alan Moore's *Watchmen*, a 1986 postmodern-superhero graphic novel she described as 'a comic book about a big blue space guy' and that he calls 'nothing less than a total, devastating deconstruction of virtually every **archetype** in the genre's history.' . . .

"'You've got to realize, Bran is not just some airhead,' Tillich told Fuller over drinks at the Azusa Pacific student union. 'She's intelligent, involved, and culturally aware. So how the hell could she not know about Brando and Sheen's classic encounters in Kurtz's depraved jungle fortress? What in *Apocalypse Now* could possibly be unappealing to a smart, deep, complicated, interesting 22-year-old woman? It just doesn't add up.'"

> "Area Girlfriend Still Hasn't Seen *Apocalypse Now*," Onion.com (March 2, 2000).

epitome

{i·PIT·ah·mee}

Noun

1. an example highly representative of a type or class: "Barry may be the epitome of a new kind of athlete, able to use modern medical treatment and training techniques to maintain peak performance into middle age."

2. a brief summary or abstract of a written work

ORIGIN

Approximately 1529; from Latin, *epitome*: a summary; from Greek, *epitome*: an abridgment, from *epitemnein*: to cut short, to abridge (*epi-*: into + *temnein*: to cut).

BONUS WORD Synonym

paragon: model of excellence or perfection

IN ACTION

"Indifference, to me, is the **epitome** of evil."

> *Elie Wiesel (b. 1928). Romanian-born Jewish author.*
> U.S. News & World Report *(October 27, 1986).*

"The three-martini lunch is the **epitome** of American efficiency. Where else can you get an earful, a bellyful and a snootful at the same time?"

> *Gerald R. Ford (b. 1913). U.S. president.*
> *[On tax-deductible entertaining, to the National*
> *Restaurant Association.]* Speech *(May 28, 1978).*

"The **epitome** of toil is John Size, a modern phenomenon, who gave new meaning to the phrase 'working yourself to sleep'.

"Nobody in modern times arrived at Randwick in a more deprived state. Size wore a hat the Salvos wouldn't have accepted and had a couple of nags of similar status.

"Before long he had a social reputation of dozing off before the soup course because of exhaustion. Others, no doubt, put in the same hours, but without the results. Few rose so fast in reputation. When he went to Hong Kong, the experts said he wouldn't stand the social heat, which includes about 10 courses most days a week. Size did it his way and won his first two premierships there, a feat regarded as near-impossible.

"And should anybody feel success has changed, Size reports indicate he has already returned to his horses in Hong Kong after a long holiday—a week. Other trainers are expected back in August. Still, Size has upgraded his hats."

Max Presnell. *"Battlers Fighting to Keep the Wolves from the Door,"* Sydney Morning Herald *online (July 11, 2003).*

pith

[pith]

Noun, Transitive Verb

Noun
1. the central or most essential part of something; the heart: "Acme Widget Welders is our largest client and the pith of our business, so don't be shy with that corporate card when they come in tomorrow."
2. strength, vigor, or substance
3. importance

Transitive Verb
4. to remove the pith from (a plant stem)
5. to destroy the spinal cord of (an animal, as a frog), usually by inserting a needle into the vertebral canal as part of a laboratory experiment

ORIGIN
Before 1325; from Old English, *pitha*: pith of plants, essential part; cognate with Middle Low German, *pedik*, *peddik*: pith, and possibly with *pit*, *pitte*: pith, kernel.

BONUS WORD Related

pliant: capable of being influenced or flexed

IN ACTION

"The **pith**-filled stems of elderberry have been reamed out by generations of children for making popguns. The Chippewa name for elderberry means 'popgun-wood.' According to legend, Pan's flute was made from hollow stems of the European elderberry."

> *Wendy Wenck, North Carolina Botanical Garden.*
> *"Grow Elderberry to Please Butterflies, Birds and*
> *People," Herald Sun (Australia) (July 11, 2003).*

"The fact is that both the LEF and Ms. Greider have as priorities opening American drug markets as wide as possible. These are not the allies that pro-life members of Congress should be working with on issues of such great **pith** and moment. Their priority is not cheaper drugs for our seniors—the priority of the well-meaning members of Congress who support drug importation—but instead, to get easier access to abortion and to bizarre and untested therapies outside the country."

> *Jerry Falwell. Chancellor of Liberty University*
> *in Lynchburg, Virginia. "Editorial/Op-Ed:*
> *Choose Life, Not Drug Importation,"*
> *Washington Times (July 8, 2003).*

"These New England states, I do believe, will be the noblest country in the world in a little while. They will be the salvation of that very great body, the rest of the United States; they are the **pith** and marrow, heart and core, head and spirit of that country."

> *Fanny Kemble (1809–93). British*
> *actor and abolitionist (1847).*

quiddity
[KWID·i·tee]

Noun

1. the real nature or essence of something: "The blues from the jukebox captured the quiddity of my situation perfectly, and it helped to know that wherever he was, Muddy Waters was feeling my pain."
2. a trifling distinction; a quibble

ORIGIN

Approximately 1539; borrowed from Medieval Latin, *quidditas*: literally, whatness; from Latin, *quid*: what, neuter of *quis*: who.

BONUS WORD   Synonym

elemental: fundamental

IN ACTION

"Lest the advertising agency surrender all authority in auguring the 'brand essence' of a product, the last decade has seen a steep growth in a research approach called account planning. An uncertain hybrid of qualitative and quantitative analysis, it can seem to merge the worst impulses of the two: the fuzzy focus of the soothsayer and the info-hoarding of the retail statistician. Which is to say that account planning, to some extent, is the trend business by another name.

"Unlike the practical market researcher of old, the account planner conducts a search for the amorphous soul of a product, be it canned meat or tampons. It's a religious undertaking, filled with endless questioning and contemplation on the **quiddity** of the thing. The process is nothing less than a search for meaning—if a very small, canned, congealed meaning."

Michael Tortorello. "Trendspotting: How a Minneapolis Consulting Trio Discovered the 'Iconogasm,' and Other Tales from the Trendspotting Business," City Pages.com (February 25, 1998).

"Sebald's writing here, as in all his work, is nourished by precise detail, by the **quiddity** of the material world; but its scope derives from the largeness of his temporal imagination. In these poems, he seems to be writing as if from the vantage point of history or even geology itself—a majestic perspective within which all events are seen as interrelated and as transitory."

Eva Hoffman. "Curiosity and Catastrophe" (book review of After Nature, by W. G. Sebald), New York Times (September 22, 2002).

Zeitgeist

[TSITE·geyest', ZITE·geyest']

Noun

1. the spirit of the time; the general intellectual and moral climate or outlook of a period: "The vegetarian Zeitgeist had taken hold of Carolyn's circle of friends, but peer pressure was no match for her lust for steak."

ORIGIN

Approximately 1884; from German, *Zeit*: time, from Middle High German, *zit*, from Old High German + *Geist*: spirit, ghost.

BONUS WORD Antonym

anachronism: something seemingly displaced in time

IN ACTION

"Perennials like Michael or Sarah are not, to my mind, the nub of the issue. They don't explain why so many people seeking more adventurous names seem to hit upon the same ones. Why did I recently receive birth announcements from three couples who had never met, who lived as distant from one another as Maine, Minnesota and California, yet who had all named their sons Leo? How to account for the sudden spate of Natalies?

"I am not so smug as to think myself immune to first-name **zeitgeist**. A few years ago, I developed a sudden affection for Julia, which now hovers at 31, and then for Hannah, which is No. 3. Although I have never personally met a Madison (2), I have watched friends seduced by the seeming novelty of Alyssa (12), Olivia (10) and Dylan (24 among boys), only to discover that their children are destined to spend life with the initials of their last names appended to their first."

Peggy Orenstein. "Where Have All the Lisas Gone?"
New York Times (July 6, 2003).

"The pall of sequel overload is everywhere. Always keenly attuned to the pop **zeitgeist**, *Entertainment Weekly* has been running a poll on its Web site, asking fans to select 'What summer movie is the biggest disappointment so far?' Three of the four leaders are sequels."

Patrick Goldstein. "Retread Blockbusters Are
Generating Less Green [Second Time Not a Charm;
Originality of Finding Nemo Finding a Fan Base],"
Los Angeles Times (July 13, 2003).

The Bacon

THEME 2

emolument

guerdon

lucre

pittance

remunerate

emolument

—[i·MOL·yah·mahnt]——————

Noun

1. payment received for holding an office or having employment, usually in the form of salary, wages, or fees; compensation: "The post of neighborhood association treasurer, an office with no emolument and little prestige, nevertheless presents tangible opportunities to impact local quality of life."

ORIGIN

Approximately 1435; from Latin, *emolumentum*: profit, gain, originally: payment to a miller for grinding corn, from *emolere*: to grind out (*e-*: out + *molere*: to grind).

BONUS WORD Sound

emollient: having a soothing effect on the skin

IN ACTION

 "Your favor containing the question, as to whether I consider myself a 'new woman' is before me. As a rule I do not consider myself at all. I am, and always have been a progressive woman, and while never directly attacking the conventionalities of society, have always done, or attempted to do those things which I have considered conducive to my health, convenience or **emolument**. . . ."

Belva Lockwood (1830–1917).
U.S. lawyer and political activist.

 "Those who have been once intoxicated with power, and have derived any kind of **emolument** from it, even though but for one year, never can willingly abandon it. They may be distressed in the midst of all their power; but they will never look to anything but power for their relief."

Edmund Burke (1729–97). Irish philosopher, statesman, and political writer. A Letter to a Member of the National Assembly (January 19, 1791).

guerdon

[GUR·dn]

Noun, Transitive Verb

Noun

1. a reward or recompense; a requital: "After almost a decade of professional education, Clarence was finally ready to claim his guerdon from the corporate world."

Transitive Verb

2. to give a reward or recompense

ORIGIN

Probably fourteenth century; from Medieval Latin, *widerdonum*, related to Latin, *donum*: gift; alteration of Old High German, *widarlon widar*: back, against (related to the root *wi*: apart, in half + *lon*: reward).

BONUS WORD   Related

comeuppance: deserved fate

IN ACTION

Yet a rich **guerdon** waits on minds that dare,
If aught be in them of immortal seed . . .

William Wordsworth (1770–1850). English poet. "From the Dark Chambers of Dejection Freed."

"In racing it sometimes happens, despite all precautions, that some second or third string, put in to make the pace, will romp away from the whole field, including the animal which carried the rosiest hopes of the inspired pacemaker's owner. With some such mixture of exultation and rue as may fill that sportsman's bosom, the inhabitants of Great Britain and Ireland have just seen Mr WB Yeats victoriously flashing past the post, as the sporting reports say, for the Nobel Prize for Literature, a **guerdon** of the value of about 7,500 [pounds]."

"WB Yeats Wins the Nobel Prize,"
Guardian (November 4, 1929).

Love seeks a **guerdon**; friendship is as God,
Who gives and asks no payment.

Richard Hovey (1864–1900). U.S. poet and
dramatist. The Marriage of Guenevere (1895).

lucre
[LOO·kahr]

Noun

1. money, profits, or riches, often suggesting ill-gotten gains: "Glenn knew that there would be very little money in his art, but he took great pride in sticking to his vision and refused to succumb to the lucre of more compromised forms."

ORIGIN
Approximately 1390; borrowed from Latin, *lucrum*: gain, profit, which is related to the root *lau*: gain, profit.

BONUS WORD Synonym

specie: money in the form of coins

IN ACTION

"The timing couldn't be worse. Just after his break-up with Anne, Jimmie's wealthy grandfather croaks, leaving him an estate valued at a cool $100 million. The only condition is that he marry before the stroke of 6:05 on his 30th birthday. Of course, said birthday is a mere 24 hours away. Isn't that always the way with these sorts of things?

"*The Bachelor*, despite its predictable love-or-**lucre** dilemma, is not without its moments and, when it surrenders to the absurd Keaton-esque spirit that inspires it, can actually be very near delightful. An early scene set at a romantic, notoriously proposal-centric restaurant, for instance, is a neatly absurd riff on the clichés of courtship."

Mary Elizabeth Williams. Movie review of The Bachelor, Salon.com *(November 5, 1999).*

"For the Inner Circle, cracking software is a challenge. For the wannabe underground, collecting it is an obsession. For the software industry, it's a billion-dollar nightmare.

". . . warez world's leading citizens say that filthy **lucre** is beside the point. . . . Warez crackers, traders, and collectors don't pirate software to make a living: they pirate software because they can."

David McCandless. "Warez Wars," Wired.com *(April 1997).*

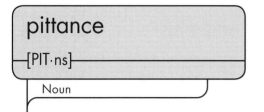

pittance

[PIT·ns]

Noun

1. a small or inadequate wage, allowance, or remuneration
2. a very small amount of something: "I had accepted the position hoping that Holly would mentor me, but she was way too busy, and the pittance of training I did receive hardly seemed worth it."

ORIGIN

Probably fourteenth century; borrowed from Old French, *pitance*: allowance of food to a monk or poor person (*pitie*: pity, from archaic Latin, *pietas*: pity, piety + the suffix *-ance*: state, condition).

BONUS WORD   Synonym

modicum: a small or token amount

IN ACTION

"But the census questions will capture nothing of Russia's transition from communism to capitalism, little of each individual struggle to survive that stormy voyage. It will not reflect, for example, that Ms. Sobrinina's work has moved from the public sector to the private, that she is now a property owner through privatization of the family apartment and that she has become a regular churchgoer.

"Nine years ago she quit her prestigious Soviet-era job as an instructor at an official linguistics institute, after inflation and the collapse of state funding turned her salary into a **pittance**. She tried her hand as a 'shuttle peddler,' hauling cheap consumer goods from Turkey to sell in Moscow, before landing a job with a private language academy. 'We went through years of poverty, extreme uncertainty, and adjustment,' she says."

Fred Weir. "What You Won't Find out from Russia's Census," Christian Science Monitor (October 17, 2002).

"The heart of good French cooking does not lie in haute cuisine. The great restaurants, wherever they are, can stay great, all fancy ingredients and cloches a go-go. But what matters is what happens in the back streets, all those little family-run places which are beginning to exist only in the nostalgic memories of wistful Francophiles. The young no longer want to go into the family business, earning a **pittance** while working long hours in a job that offers neither glamour nor independence."

Nigella Lawson. "Bless Butter, Cream and Simple French Fare," New York Times (October 16, 2002).

remunerate

[ri·MYOO·nah·rayt']

Transitive Verb

1. to pay a suitable equivalent for goods provided or services rendered, or to compensate for inconvenience or losses incurred; to recompense: "There is no shortage of opportunities to volunteer in this town, but I've had tremendous difficulty finding organizations that are willing to remunerate me for my time and efforts."

ORIGIN
Approximately 1523; back formation of English *remuneration*; from Latin, *remunerationem* (nominative *remuneratio*), from *remunerari*: to reward.

BONUS WORD   Continuum

POSITIVE IMPACT . . .   **. . . NEGATIVE IMPACT**

remunerate ———▶ requite ———▶ avenge

requite: to repay for or return something

avenge: to inflict punishment

IN ACTION

"Diplomats say that more alarming than such an appeal was a recent opinion poll conducted by Cairo's *Al-Ahram Weekly*. The paper said half of the respondents in the survey felt that United States 'deserved' the terrorist attacks of September 11, and that the U.S. war on terrorism was 'a war against Arabs and Muslims.'

"Egypt is one of the countries that Washington has promised to **remunerate**—to the tune of $1.5 billion in 'parallel aid'—for losses it is likely to suffer as a result of war against Iraq."

Andrew Borowiec. "Arab Media Echoes with Anti-U.S. Ire," *Washington Times* (October 16, 2002).

The Space Between

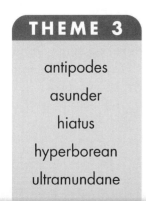

THEME 3

antipodes

asunder

hiatus

hyperborean

ultramundane

antipodes
[an·TIP·ah·deez']

Noun

1. any two places or regions on diametrically opposite sides of the earth, or people that are thus positioned (or people that live on these opposite sides): "E-mail enabled Greg to keep tabs on his former classmates from journalism school, despite various assignments that had literally made antipodes of his former roommates."
2. anything exactly opposite or contrary of another; an antipode

ORIGIN
Approximately 1375; borrowed from Latin, *antipodes*; from Greek, *antipodes*, plural of *antipous*: with feet opposite ours (*anti*: opposite + *pous*, genitive *podos*: foot).

BONUS WORD   Antonym

abutting: touching

IN ACTION

"At a time when the relationship between African-Americans and Jews is deeply fissured, 'The Color of Water' reminds us that the two groups have a long history of coexistence—sometimes within a single person. The author's mother, Ruth Shilsky, was born in Poland in 1920, the daughter of an Orthodox Jewish rabbi. She grew up in rural Virginia, hemmed in by anti-Semitism and small-town claustrophobia, and at the age of 18 she fled to the cultural **antipodes** of Harlem. There, four years later, she married a black man named Dennis McBride, and since her family promptly disowned her, she launched a second existence. . . . The lone Caucasian in her

Brooklyn housing project, she somehow raised 12 children without ever quite admitting she was white."

> James Marcus. "Sneak Peeks Nonfiction:
> The Color of Water," Salon.com.

"Have you ever eaten roo? Not many Australians have either, but we Aussies do insist on serving it in any restaurant we open overseas. You can try it with salad in downtown Manhattan at the newly opened Eight Mile Creek, recently praised by the *New York Times* for its fabulous food and restrained decor. . . . And all of this is made more exciting by the extensive **antipodean** offerings on the wine list."

> Christine Kenneally. "Throw Another Stereotype on the
> Barbie," Salon.com (February 25, 2000).

"In the futile critical exercise of contending which is the greatest American novel, choice ordinarily narrows down at last to 'The Scarlet Letter' and 'Huckleberry Finn'—a sufficiently **antipodean** pair and as hard to bring into comparison as tragedy and comedy themselves."

> Carl Van Doren (1885–1950). "Mark Twain,"
> The American Novel (1921).

asunder

—[ah·SUN·dahr]——

Adverb

1. into separate parts or pieces: "At one point during the storm last night, thunder rippled through so loudly I was sure it had torn our house asunder."

2. widely separated in space or direction; apart: "She threw the curtains asunder as soon as she woke up to let the sunshine pour into her room."

ORIGIN

Probably before 1000; from Old English, *on sundran* (*on*: on + *sundran*: separately, from *sunder*: apart).

BONUS WORD Origin

sundry: various

IN ACTION

"As Rte. 1 unwinds northward through the Olema Valley, its center line virtually traces the dreaded San Andreas Fault. On your left lies the Point Reyes Peninsula, which during the 1906 San Francisco earthquake jolted as much as 18 feet [5.5 meters] northwest, pulling roads and trees **asunder**."

"Marin County Scenic Drive," NationalGeographic.com
(October 25, 2001).

"But it's never too late to take advantage of a growing number of Web sites that help put **asunder** what church and state joined together. Just take a look at the cyberpromises. 'D-I-V-O-R-C-E doesn't have to be a bad experience,' coos Divorce USA Online. 'As easy as 1-2-3 you are free. . . . [E]verything you need to file your divorce today! Only $49.95.'"

Ioana Veleanu. "Make a New Plan, Stan:
Divorce Sites Offer 50 Ways to Leave Your Lover,"
Village Voice (June 7–13, 2000).

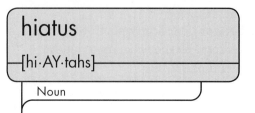

hiatus

[hi·AY·tahs]

Noun

1. a gap or an interruption in continuity; a break; an opening: "Amber was appalled to find no summer hiatus whatsoever in the professional world, and a paltry two weeks of annual vacation were hardly adequate consolation."

ORIGIN

Approximately 1563; borrowed from Latin, *hiatus*: gap, opening, from *hiare*: to gape, to stand open.

BONUS WORD   Sound

halitus: exhaled breath

IN ACTION

"NBC and TNT put the Knicks on **hiatus**: NBA fans, rejoice. The dreadfully boring New York Knicks have been dropped from four national TV broadcasts. 'Now, you often hear of soap operas or sitcoms being canceled by the networks,' the *New York Times*' Ira Berkow writes. 'But basketball games due to anticipated dullness?'"

> Bryan Curtis and Chris Suellentrop. "Sports Pages: Knicks Put on Hiatus," Slate.com (February 25, 2002).

"'Everybody owned Cisco and was making a killing,' says Rick BenSignor, Morgan Stanley's technical strategist, referring to the once high-flying stock, a poster child of the tech-led stock buying frenzy.

"[Rick] BenSignor remembers those freewheeling times and the ensuing carnage on Wall Street very well. He rejoined Morgan Stanley after a brief **hiatus** three days before Nasdaq topped out at its March 2000 peak."

"*Nasdaq Chart Tells Tale of Fear and Greed,*" Reuters
(March 10, 2002).

hyperborean
[hi'·pahr·BOR·ee·ahn, hi'·pahr·bah·REE·ahn]

Noun, Adjective

Noun
1. (as in Greek mythology, usually *Hyperborean*) one of a people who live beyond the source of the north wind, in a land of perpetual sunshine and abundance

Adjective
2. of or pertaining to the region beyond the north wind, especially its inhabitants
3. of or pertaining to or inhabiting a far northern or otherwise very cold region, as the Arctic: "Jim, our strained bladders would like to know if we will ever arrive at this hyperborean cabin of yours—and if it'll be equipped with modern plumbing."

ORIGIN
Date of origin uncertain; from Latin, *Hyperboreus*, from *Hyperborei*: the Hyperboreans; from Greek, *Huperboreoi*: beyond the north wind (*huper*: hyper, or beyond + *boreios*: northern or *Boreas*: the north wind, the north).

BONUS WORD Continuum

COLD . . .	. . . COLDER
algid ⟶	hyperborean

algid: chilly

IN ACTION

"You could have knelt down, damn it, Kinch, when your dying mother asked you, Buck Mulligan said. I'm **hyperborean** as much as you. But to think of your mother begging you with her last breath to kneel down and pray for her. And you refused. There is something sinister in you."

James Joyce (1882–1941). Irish novelist
and poet. Ulysses (1921).

"True, other fish are found exceedingly brisk in those **Hyperborean** waters; but these, be it observed, are your cold-blooded, lungless fish, whose very bellies are refrigerators; creatures, that warm themselves under the lee of an iceberg, as a traveller in winter would bask before an inn fire; whereas, like man, the whale has lungs and warm blood."

Herman Melville (1819–91). U.S. author.
Moby-Dick (1851).

ultramundane

{ul'·trah·mun·DANE, ul'·trah·MUN·dane'}

Adjective

1. extending or being beyond the world, or beyond the limits of our solar system or the whole universe: "As a prominent astrophysicist, Jonah possessed an extraordinary ability to analyze the ultramundane, but he had difficulty understanding his own children."

ORIGIN

Approximately 1545; from Latin, *ultramundanus* (*ultra*: the prefix *ultra-*: going beyond the limits of + *mundanus*: of the world, from *mundus*: world).

BONUS WORD Origin

mundane: ordinary or of this world

IN ACTION

"Mrs. Knollys had recovered from the first shock by this time, but the truth could no longer be withheld. The innkeeper could but nod his head sadly, when she told him that to recover her Charles was hopeless. All the guides said the same thing. The poor girl's husband had vanished from the world as utterly as if his body had been burned to ashes and scattered in the pathway of the winds. Charles Knollys was gone, utterly gone; no more to be met with by his girl-wife, save as spirit to spirit, soul to soul, in **ultramundane** place."

Frederic J. Stimson. "Mrs. Knollys," Mrs. Knollys and Other Stories *(1897).*

The Cat's Pajamas

354

laudable

[LAW·dah·bahl]

Adjective

1. worthy of being praised; commendable: "Despite the laudable efforts of his owners and several trainers, Biff's hatred of mailmen would persist to the end."

ORIGIN

Approximately 1425; borrowed from Old French, *laudable*; from Latin, *laudabilis*: praiseworthy, from *laudare*: to praise, from *laus*: praise, glory.

BONUS WORD   Origin

plaudit: enthusiastic approval

IN ACTION

"While the desire to be true to yourself is **laudable**, ethics primarily concerns the effects of our actions on others."

> Randy Cohen. "The Ethicist: Company Line," New York Times Magazine (July 11, 2004).

"When the parliament was set up, it was intended that staff would be treated fairly and that the parliament would be a shining example of working practices to the rest of the country.

"Yet sadly, the reality seems to be falling some way short of that **laudable** vision.

"An internal audit has revealed that one in eight members of staff claim that they have been subjected to bullying or harassment at work."

> "Opinion: Leading by Example," Scotsman (July 16, 2004).

palmary

[PAL·mah·ree, PAWL·mah·ree, PAW·mah·ree]

Adjective

1. preeminent; superior; principal; chief; worthy of the palm: "The palmary works in the field were required reading in the first year of the psychology program."

ORIGIN

Approximately 1655; from Latin, *palmarius*: deserving the palm, decorated with the palm of victory, from *palma*: palm tree, palm of the hand.

BONUS WORD   Origin

palmate: leaves that spread like fingers from a hand

IN ACTION

"But let us examine this principle a little more attentively—for it is the **palmary** one."

> *Sir Arthur Quiller-Couch (1863–1944).*
> *English poet and novelist. "I. Inaugural,"*
> *On the Art of Writing (1916).*

"Body-talk contrasting to speech, perceived as irony in the **palmary** case of the sartorial disguise of Odysseus, humble in speech but incongruently forward in proxemics, is probably as common as complementary messages. The mute messages of the body communicate sentiment while preserving deniability."

> *Donald Lateiner. Sardonic Smile (1998).*

estimable

[ES·tah·mah·bahl]

Adjective

1. capable of being estimated or valued: "estimable damage"
2. worthy of esteem or respect; deserving our good opinion or regard: "George loved working for a company that manufactured great products, paid well, and made an estimable effort to give back to the community."

ORIGIN

Approximately 1475; borrowed from Old French, *estimable*; from Latin, *aestimabilis*: worthy of estimation, from *aestimare*: to value.

BONUS WORD   Continuum

LESS RESPECT . . .   **. . . MORE RESPECT**

deplorable ⟶ quotidian ⟶ estimable

deplorable: worthy of condemnation

quotidian: commonplace

IN ACTION

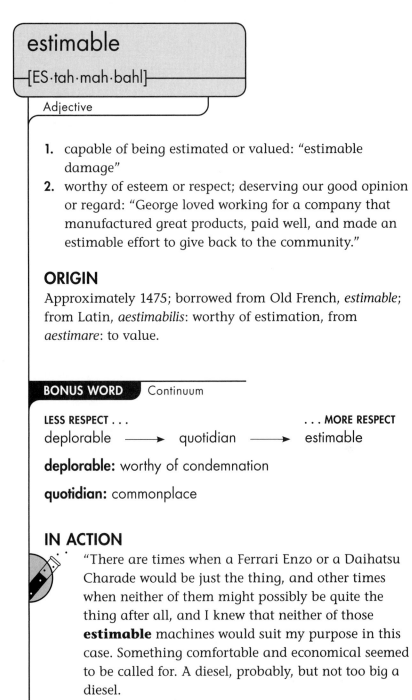

"There are times when a Ferrari Enzo or a Daihatsu Charade would be just the thing, and other times when neither of them might possibly be quite the thing after all, and I knew that neither of those **estimable** machines would suit my purpose in this case. Something comfortable and economical seemed to be called for. A diesel, probably, but not too big a diesel.

"Fortune smiled, birds sang, angels fluttered their eyelashes. The CARkeys road test schedule for the period came through, and there beside my name was the resounding phrase 'BMW 525d SE Touring'. I could hardly have chosen better myself."

David Finlay. "A Car for the Long Haul
[Road Test: BMW 525d SE Touring Steptronic],"
Carkeys.co.uk (July 19, 2004).

august

[aw·GUST]

Adjective

1. of a quality inspiring mingled admiration and reverence; having an aspect of solemn dignity or grandeur; sublime; majestic; grand; having exalted birth, character, state, or authority: "Even in old age and ill health, her august presence at any event was cherished."

ORIGIN

Approximately 1664; borrowed from Latin, *augustus*: venerable (assumed as a title by the Roman emperors), from *augus*: increase, from *augere*: to magnify, to increase.

BONUS WORD   Antonym

ignoble: lacking nobility in character or purpose

IN ACTION

Ancient of days! **august** Athena! where,
Where are thy men of might? thy grand in soul?
Gone—glimmering through the dream of things that were.

George Gordon Noel Byron (1788–1824).
British poet. Childe Harold's Pilgrimage (1818).

"Prayer is an **august** avowal of ignorance."

Victor Hugo (1802–85). French poet,
novelist, playwright, and essayist.
Intellectual Autobiography (1907).

meritorious
[mer'·i·TOR·ee·ahs, mer'·i·TOER·ee·ahs]

Adjective

1. deserving of reward or honor; worthy of recompense;
   valuable: "Such meritorious service should not go
   unrecognized."

ORIGIN

Approximately 1425; borrowed from Latin, *meritorius*:
serving to earn money, from *meritus*, past participle of
merere, mereri: to earn, to deserve, to acquire.

BONUS WORD Origin

meritocracy: a system with advancement based on ability

IN ACTION

"For years I lived in west Marin County, Calif., the
somewhat less chi-chi part of the famously flaky
and physically beautiful land just north of San
Francisco across the Golden Gate Bridge. West Marin
is dominated by the Point Reyes National Seashore
and numerous state and county parks or open space
preserves, as well as many large dairy farms.

"The region attracts an odd assortment of artists,
retirees, vacationers, rascals, drifters, bohemians,
day-trippers, surfers, freelance nutcases, farm workers
and cowpokes. Stir them all together and one of the

happy results is an endlessly entertaining stew of misbehavior, which is documented every week in the tiny *Point Reyes Light* newspaper, edited by David Vokes Mitchell. (The paper got some attention in 1979 for winning a Pulitzer gold medal for **Meritorious** Public Service for its coverage of the Synanon cult.)"

Douglas Cruickshank. "The Poetry of Rural Roguery,"
Salon.com (September 2, 1999).

"Unlike the custom in America, where originality is fundamental to gift selection, in Japan price is what counts—the occasion and relationship to the recipient dictates the amount. Food is the most popular gift. The Japanese depend on personal relationships to sustain them throughout their lives. Most feel that the time, money, and energy they spend on nurturing a network of professional and personal contacts are both essential and gratifying.

"That $95 luxury melon, presented to the patient but consumed by family members, becomes a welcome respite as they worry about illness. In a society that finds effort **meritorious**, time spent on a long line waiting to buy a limited edition gift adds to its intrinsic value. An exclusive, $20 assortment of petit fours becomes a coveted prize. Presented to a math tutor before a big exam, that box of little cakes (one of only 30 offered for sale at the depachika that day) demonstrates the parents' determination to have their child succeed, while acknowledging the importance of the tutor's role."

Elizabeth Andoh. "Choice Tables: Culinary
Delights Laid Out to Tempt Japan's Commuters,"
New York Times (April 25, 2004).

It's Universal

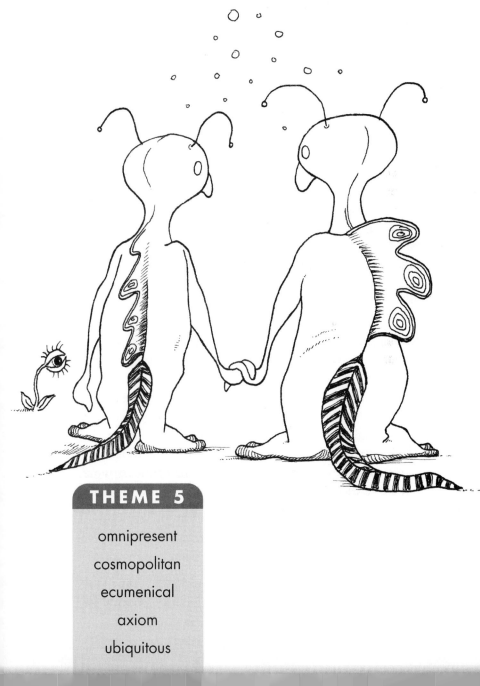

omnipresent

cosmopolitan

ecumenical

axiom

ubiquitous

omnipresent

[om'·ni·PREZ·ahnt]

Adjective

1. present in all places at the same time; ubiquitous:
    "During the spring months, Jason suffered immensely
    from omnipresent allergens."

ORIGIN

Approximately 1625; from Medieval Latin, *omnipresens*;
from Latin *omni-*, combining form of *omnis*: all + *praesens*,
present participle of *praeesse*: to be present.

BONUS WORD   Origin

omniscient: infinitely wise

omnipotent: having unlimited power

IN ACTION

"Next on her shopping list: Clothing in today's must-
have hues. Particularly eye-catching to Sanchez is
an aqua shade reminiscent of the signature blue on
Tiffany & Co. gift boxes and shopping bags.
    "'Tiffany blue can go anywhere,' said Sanchez,
who also has sprung for the cropped pants that are
omnipresent this season. 'For the first time in years,
I think the fashions for spring and summer are great.'"

Becky Yerak. "Trendy Hues Brightening
Fashion Retailers' Bottom Line," Chicago Tribune
(June 6, 2004).

"The Showtime glory days of the Lakers wouldn't have
had as much glitz and glam without **omnipresent**
coach Pat Riley, who guided the Lakers to four NBA

titles (1982, 1985, 1987, 1988). He's now the president of the Miami Heat, a young team that could be moving up the ranks in the Eastern Conference."

Joanne C. Gerstner. "Talking with . . . Pat Riley, Former Lakers Coach," Detroit News *(June 6, 2004).*

"She returned home, to the empty and dark room, and there, lonely and suffering, uttered a prayer to the God whom she had long since abandoned, yet who remained the God of her ancestors, praying that the spirit of goodness and mercy, **omnipresent** and all-pervading, would soften the hearts of those who decided Sasha's fate."

Anatoly Rybakov. [On a mother seeking the whereabouts of her son during the Stalinist era in the USSR, quoted in] New York Times *(March 14, 1987).*

cosmopolitan

[koz'·mah·POL·i·tn]

Adjective, Noun

Adjective

1. of worldwide scope or applicability: "Bailey was perpetually obsessed with issues of cosmopolitan relevance, often to the detriment of his college studies."
2. composed of people or constituent elements from many parts of the world
3. having an international sophistication; at home in any place

Noun

4. a sophisticated and well-traveled person; also, cosmopolite

ORIGIN

Approximately 1844; formed in English from *cosmopolite* + *-an*, patterned after *metropolitan*; *cosmopolite* borrowed from Greek, *kosmopolites* (*kosmos*: world + *polites*: citizen, from *polis*: city).

BONUS WORD   Antonym

parochial: relating to a parish

provincial: associated with a province

IN ACTION

"Freemasonry, whose date of origin is somewhere in the 16th or 17th century, purports to be (according to its adherents) a benign organization, albeit with a mystical element, which served for much of the 19th century to disseminate rationalist learning among its members in the days before public education: geometry, architecture, astronomy, and similar subjects. Its members aren't allowed to discuss politics or religion within the Lodge. As Brother Roscoe Pound, a Mason and current professor of jurisprudence at Harvard, puts it, 'Every lodge ought to be a center of light from which men go forth filled with new ideas of social justice, **cosmopolitan** justice and internationality.' All the same, Masons have been periodically accused of satanism, manipulation of global finance, and secret influence among the world's movers and shakers."

> Gary Indiana. "No Such Thing as Paranoia: On the Culture of Conspiracism," Village Voice (May 25, 2004).

"The movies, meanwhile, seem to be changing with the good times, away from pure escapism to more sophisticated stories.

"'There's a growing realization that there's this huge other market apart from the poor people in the rural areas: a **cosmopolitan**, English-speaking audience, in India and overseas, with a different taste,' said Raj Baronia, the executive editor of Indolink, a California-based company that runs several Web publications, including *Planet Bollywood.*"

Stefan Lovgren. *"Bollywood: Indian Films Splice Bombay, Hollywood,"* National Geographic News (January 21, 2004).

ecumenical

[ek'·yah·MEN·i·kahl]

Adjective

1. general or universal in scope, influence, or application: "Darrel's stories always had basic human emotions at their core, which helped their ecumenical appeal."

ORIGIN
Approximately 1575; from Latin, *oecumenicus*: general, universal; from Greek, *oikoumenikos*, from *oikoumene ge*: the inhabited world, from *oikos*: house.

BONUS WORD   Related

pantheism: the belief that God is present in everything

IN ACTION

"On this night, there seem to be no duds in the dubs, as the dancing begins to build. Groups of five or so break into synchronized moves so deft you'd think they were choreographed. It's more reminiscent of the line dancing of African bands like Ladysmith Black

Mambazo than American club dancing. The crowd goes crazy, as the moves become more intricate. Deathly serious, they are cool personified.

"With each passing hour, inhibitions start to melt. 'Girls Gone Wild' would have a field day here. The men are dressed in an island variation on hip-hop. Women favor anything short and tight. If you glance quickly at the crowd you'd swear that 70's mesh never left. Here, terry cloth rules, as do brand names. 'Corona' logos tattoo fannies. 'Sean John' decorates chests. Bandannas are de rigueur. Thongs are not (unless viewed through open mesh). Most of all, passa-passa is **ecumenical**. There are little girls wearing spike heels and dreadlocked men rocking in wheelchairs. 'Music dictates how our whole society lives,' says Yogie, as the walking dead start to teeter home. 'In Jamaica, everyone knows all the artists. Your bus driver could be a record producer here. Everyone could.'"

> Steve Garbarino. "The Other Side of Paradise," New York Times (May 30, 2004).

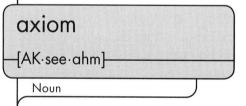

axiom

[AK·see·ahm]

Noun

1. an established principle that people accept as self-evidently true: "Joon tried to live his life according to a handful of moral axioms."
2. (as in logic) a proposition that is necessary to take for granted: "A thing cannot, at the same time, be and not be."

ORIGIN

Approximately 1485; from Latin, *axioma*; from Greek, *axioma*: something thought worthy or fit, from *axioun*: to think worthy or fit, from *axios*: worthy, weighty, from the lost noun *ak-tis*: weight, from *agein*: to weigh, to pull.

BONUS WORD Synonym

maxim: a succinct statement of a principle

IN ACTION

"The mating of thoroughbreds in quest of victory at the track has long been a sophisticated combination of art and informal science. Owners and breeders study thoroughbreds' family trees so closely, they are more likely to be able to list a horse's great-great-great grandparents than their own.

"Yet the ways genes recombine generation after generation are so unpredictable, the **axiom** long has been, 'Breed the best to the best and hope for the best.'

"Now, as 100 scientists at 25 laboratories around the world cooperate to map the horse genome for the first time, geneticists and a few figures in the traditional world of thoroughbred breeding are beginning to explore the ways genetic information might enhance the chances of breeding a champion."

Robyn Norwood. "Horse Breeding for Speed Getting Down to a Science," Los Angeles Times (June 5, 2004)

"Mr. Bush, who repeated his view that the United States and France are age-old friends that simply disagree on the Iraq issue, returned fire, especially when asked by a French journalist about an **axiom** first uttered by Thomas Jefferson, 'Everyone has two countries—their own and France.'

"'To paraphrase President Kennedy, there's America, and then there's Texas,' he quipped during the press conference at the Elysee Palace."

Joseph Curl. "Bush, Chirac Find Accord on Transfer of Power in Iraq," Washington Times (June 6, 2004).

ubiquitous

[yoo·BIK·wi·tahs]

Adjective

1. being or seeming to be everywhere, or in all places, at the same time; omnipresent; widespread: "Amelia rebelled against ubiquitous teen fashions by customizing her clothes and making her own jewelry."

ORIGIN

Approximately 1837; formed in English from *ubiquity* + *-ous*; *ubiquity* borrowed from Middle French, *ubiquite*; from Latin, *ubique*: everywhere, from *ubi*: where.

BONUS WORD   Antonym

bereft: sorrowful through loss or deprivation

IN ACTION

"Hardly a section of the country, urban or rural, has escaped the **ubiquitous** presence of ragged, ill and hallucinating human beings, wandering through our city streets, huddled in alleyways or sleeping over vents."

American Psychiatric Association. [Report on transfer of the mentally ill from institutional to outpatient care, quoted in] New York Times (September 13, 1984).

"So how did corporations become so powerful? Longer question. Longer answer.

"A number of big thinkers have been chewing on that question of late, mostly from the left side of the political stage. The interest is predictable. Corporations are **ubiquitous**. And some of the biggest have been caught cheating of late. Finding out who they are and how they got so powerful makes sense.

"Unfortunately, some of the analysis also has been predictable: The usual biz-bashing, IMF-hating, window-smashing dreck that does about as much for advancing progressive policy as getting naked and spelling out 'WTO' in the sands of Cancun did last year."

Alan T. Saracevic. "Insightful Books Put Ubiquitous Corporations Under a Microscope [Authors, Film Study Powerful Firms and How They Got That Way]," San Francisco Chronicle (May 30, 2004).

Audio pronunciations for the words in this pack can be found on our website: www. vocabvitamins.com/book/pack8.

Word Math

This is a word book, but we thought you could use some extra practice with your addition. Word meanings are given first, followed by the word math clue. Figure out each clue and add them up to get each word. Word segments that appear in parentheses can be added in as they appear.

1. ultimate, exemplar

   — — — + — — — —

   word root means "into" + a volume or a book

2. repay, reimburse

   — — + mune + — — — —

   again + (mune) + what you do on hotornot.com

3. principle, truth, theorem

   — — + — + — —

   wood chopper + self + meditating sound

4. admirable, honorable

   — — — + — — + — — — —

   when created + computer chat + can do

5. opposites

   — — — — + — — — + es

   when you are against + two peas go here + (es)

6. small sum, peanuts

   — — — + — — — — —

   the fruit part you don't eat + could intimidate if it had an s

7. worldly, cultured

— — — — — + — — — — + — — —

drink/magazine/space boss + almost a
Greek city-state + dark from the sun

8. dignified, noble, venerable

— — + — — — —

gold element symbol + strong wind

9. body, gist

— — + — —

special number that begins with 3 + Sylvester's sound

10. everywhere, universal

— — — — + — — — — — — — —

all + Christmas thing

11. profits, payoff, takings

— — — + — —

French male name + again

12. reward, compensation

— — + — — + — — —

fuel for runners + thinking sound + to put on

13. original, prototype

— — — — + e + — — — —

curved entranceway + (e) + what you do
at a keyboard

14. principal, main

— — — + — — — —

friend + famous virgin

15. arctic, polar

— — — — — + — — — — + an

overly active + dull + (an)

16. salary, wages

— — — + — — — — — + —

short for *emotional* + space or light + intersection type

17. praiseworthy

— — — — + — — — —

give praise + can do

18. essence, substance

— — — — + — — — —

Irish money + almost a song

19. excellent, commendable

— — — — — + — — + — + ous

ability + alternatively + self + (ous)

20. beyond this world

— — — — — + mun + — — — —

super + (mun) + big dog

21. gap, interval

__ __ + __ __ + __ __

quick greeting + directed + me and you

22. split, divided

__ __ + __ __ __ __ __

you like it + beneath

23. spirit of the time

__ __ __ __ + __ __ __ __ __

[from German] time + spirit

24. universal, pervasive, everywhere

__ + __ __ + __ __ __ __ + ous

you in text messages + both + with two weeks' notice you might do this + (ous)

25. general, global

ecu + __ __ __ + __ __ __ __

(ecu) + have Y chromosomes + Mac calendar program

[vo'cab]
VITAMINS

PACK 9

THE BAD
ONES

THEME 1
How to Get Fired

SIMILAR TO:

indolent	lazy, idle, inactive
flippant	flighty, breezy, offhand
impudence	nerve, boldness
sanctimony	outward piety
irreverence	boldness, disrespect, cheek

THEME 2
You Tyrant!

SIMILAR TO:

usurp	take over, displace
imperious	arrogant, overbearing
despot	tyrant, dictator
dogmatic	rigid, strict, authoritative
martinet	sergeant, disciplinarian

THEME 3
Shams and Imposters

SIMILAR TO:

dissemble	hide, conceal, falsify
prevaricate	distort, evade, lie
mountebank	scam artist, jokester, con man
quack	fake, sham, imposter
pinchbeck	fake, cheap substitute

THEME 4
El Macho

SIMILAR TO:

audacity	daring, courage, nerve
intrepid	fearless, brave
effrontery	arrogance, brazenness
temerity	recklessness, rashness
intractable	difficult, stubborn

THEME 5
Troublemakers

SIMILAR TO:

varmint	troublesome person or animal
recreant	coward, traitor
malefactor	wrongdoer, criminal
hellion	little devil
interloper	meddler, intruder, buttinsky

How to Get Fired

THEME 1

indolent

flippant

impudence

sanctimony

irreverence

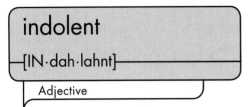

indolent

—[IN·dah·lahnt]——————————

Adjective

1. disinclined to work or exertion or conducive to inactivity; habitually lazy or idle: "No one in the family knew how to inspire the indolent youngster to apply himself."

ORIGIN

Approximately 1710; from Late Latin, *indolentem*: insensitive to pain; from Latin, *in-*: not + *dolentem*, from *dolens*: grieving, from *dolere*: to suffer pain.

BONUS WORD   Synonym

lackadaisical: lacking spirit

IN ACTION

"Traumatized by their father's death and furious at having to shoulder responsibilities they would not normally have to handle, Maya and Yair are less than ideal candidates for surrogate parents, but they have no choice. Maya, an aspiring singer and composer for a rock band that is moving to Tel Aviv, is itching to flee Haifa. (Her touching song for her father opens and closes the movie.) Yair, a once promising basketball player, has become an **indolent** high school dropout who contemptuously counters friendly overtures with his bitter, nihilistic rants about there being no God and no truth."

Stephen Holden. "Dad Dies, Leaving a Caldron of
Rage, Despair and Love" (movie review of Broken
Wings), New York Times (March 12, 2004).

"In the past three years, 29 suicide-bombings were perpetrated by youths under 18. Another 22 were killed while attacking Israelis. Forty other teens were arrested while trying to do likewise.

"Ascribing these statistics to occupation-engendered despair is intellectually **indolent** or demagogic. Palestinian youngsters are incessantly subjected to brainwashing in the media and classroom. Hate is inculcated in them. Even preschoolers are taught to aspire to martyr status. They grow in a culture that, rather than consecrating life, glorifies violent 'sacrificial' death."

"Opinion: Child Sacrifice," Jerusalem Post *(March 16, 2004).*

flippant

[FLIP·ahnt]

Adjective

1. showing inappropriate levity or casualness: "With all of us pressing him for answers, the assemblyman was not going to get away with flippant one-liners."

ORIGIN

Approximately 1605; possibly formed in English from *flip*: to move nimbly + *-ant*: to be in a specified state, analogous to adjectives like *rampant*.

BONUS WORD Continuum

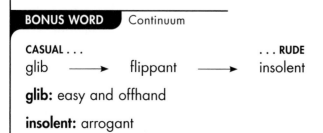

CASUAL . . .   . . . RUDE

glib ⟶ flippant ⟶ insolent

glib: easy and offhand

insolent: arrogant

IN ACTION

"To non-swimmers, lane swimming appears to involve far less personal contact than most sports. In fact, swimmers feel both more protected and more exposed by their watery surroundings, and have developed an elaborate etiquette to preserve the necessary illusion they are in their own private pool rather than sharing bath water with begrimed strangers.

"Novice lane swimmers, however, wear inappropriately skimpy or **flippant** togs [clothes], elbow slower swimmers in the face when passing, and attempt to make jocular conversation. They also visibly flinch when confronted by the looming clumps of hair and sticking plasters that roam public swimming pools like schools of spawning jellyfish (the hair is a mystery to us all: it looks nothing like human hair, and I've often wondered if perhaps lifeguards walk herds of llama through the deep end of the pool after closing time)."

Linley Boniface. "At Times, Life Can Go Swimmingly,"
Dominion Post (January 10, 2006).

"Frankly, it's day-to-day and touch-and-go whether I'd rather read Henry James or read about him. Ditto Joseph Conrad and, I fear, many other important writers—the drear fact is that many writers' lives are more interesting than their work, but this is not the case with Mark Twain, whose most casual journalism remains somehow crackly fresh. Others whose journalism has that imperishable, impeccably **flippant** quality would include Shaw, Stendhal, Vidal, and Waugh."

Larry McMurtry. U.S. screenwriter, novelist, and essayist.
"The Lives and Loves of Samuel Clemens,"
New York Review of Books (April 8, 2004).

impudence

[IM·pyah·dahns]

Noun

1. the quality of being shamelessly bold: "Her impudence may have insulted some along the way, but she built her company into a global empire."
2. a shamelessly bold action or statement

ORIGIN

Approximately 1390; borrowed from Latin, *impudentia*, from *impudentis*, from *impudens* (im-: not + *pudentis*, nominative *pudens*, from *pudere*: to cause shame).

BONUS WORD Sound

impotence: powerlessness

IN ACTION

"Friends said Seuss was a combination of the Cat and the Grinch—the saucy grouch. The Cat 'had an elegance about him and an **impudence**, standing there with one leg over the other, twirling his tail— that was Ted,' says his widow, Audrey Geisel. 'And, like the Grinch, he really never cared for Christmas. I was up that close to him, and I found him different people at different times, one with enormous personal humor and an adult naughtiness, too.'"

Maria Puente, Craig Wilson, and Mary Cadden.
"Why We Love Dr. Seuss (in a Few Words),"
USA Today (March 1, 2004).

"It was there in Manchester that I first met [Dwain] Chambers, on the periphery of the athletes' village. Top sprinters have an almost comic propensity to strut, but Chambers had taken the ritual to new levels of **impudence**. But somehow he defied ridicule. When you looked at him, his eyes stared back with the cold, incontrovertible conviction of a man destined for gold. I was impressed.

"Until the 100 metres showdown, that is. It was then that I realised that it was all an act. Chambers started as favourite and finished hobbling off the track, ostensibly on account of cramps, but perhaps he was just the victim of his own psychological inadequacy."

Matthew Syed. "Why This Was a Great Day for Athletics," Times Online *(February 26, 2004).*

sanctimony

[SANGK·tah·moe'·nee]

Noun

1. hypocritical or outward-facing devoutness: "Kim couldn't believe the sanctimony of her older sister imploring her to behave like a demure and sober 'lady.'"

ORIGIN
Approximately 1540; borrowed from Middle French, *sanctimonie*, and directly from Latin, *sanctimonia*: holiness, sacredness, from *sanctus*: holy, sacred.

BONUS WORD   Origin

sacrosanct: must be kept sacred

IN ACTION

"But even though [Gavin] Newsom's bold moves have surprised me, the way he made them and defended them has not. I also voted for him because of a gut sense of his personal decency, an intuition that, agree with him or not, he acts from a moral base, which I respect. When you disagree with him, it can be a little scary. I called him a '**sanctimonious** schoolboy' last year after we argued about his aggressive panhandling initiative, when he insisted opponents like me were basically saying it was fine to let the city's down-and-out continue to die on the streets. Ouch. Of course, it's **sanctimony** when you disagree with someone, but conviction when they're on your side."

Joan Walsh. "Winter of Love,"
Salon.com (February 26, 2004).

"Ah, the mid '90s. A time when Gen X'ers resigned to aestheticizing their shaky future suddenly found a bunch of weird, semi-lucrative jobs to fill. The Internet budded into boom, and new 'organizational cultures' buzzed about 'performance coaching.' It was a heyday for Landmark Forums. Office retreats encouraged ritualized atonement. *Jagged Little Pill* hit the stores just as perceived prosperity edged out hand-to-mouth scarcity. And when preternaturally preachy Alanis Morissette hooked up with Man in the Mirror Glen Ballard, pop **sanctimony** would never be the same. Recasting the verbosity of fellow Canadian avenging angel Joni Mitchell, Alanis spewed old-soul caveats, post-fem pep talks, and new age hellfire. The promise: If we came correct, good vibes would be kozmo.commed right to our doorstep."

Laura Sinagra. "Step by Step: Up in Canada,
Sk8ing Away on the Thin Strife of a New Day"
(music review), Village Voice (May 28, 2004).

irreverence

[i·REV·ahr·ahns]

Noun

1. a lack of proper reverence or respect: "Linda's irreverence to her teachers was beginning to affect her grades."
2. an action or a remark that is disrespectful

ORIGIN

Date uncertain; from Latin, *irreverentia* (*ir-*: not + *reverentia*: reverence, from *revereri*: to revere, *re-*: intensive prefix + *vereri*: to stand in awe of).

BONUS WORD   Sound

irrelevance: lack of relation to the matter at hand

IN ACTION

"Approach with all the skepticism and **irreverence** you want, but if there's a soft spot anywhere in your heart for Barbra Streisand, she will find it and make it grow during her appearance on Bravo's 'Inside the Actors Studio' tomorrow night at 8.

"She's charming, earnest, candid, unpretentious and anything but the Ms. Full of Herself that she's often said to be. Oh, she's not humble; let's not go goofy. But since the interview spans her life and career starting with birth and continuing through 'The Movie Album,' you get a renewed appreciation of how many conquests and triumphs she has had, how strong and uncompromising she has been and how much she has meant to popular culture."

Tom Shales. "Streisand: Nobody Is Gonna Rain on Her Parade," Washington Post *(March 20, 2004).*

"The Stanford Tree was making himself comfortable in a nearby chair . . . or as comfortable as a man can sit in a chair while wearing a giant tree costume. I don't know if the Tree is the best mascot in college basketball or the worst, but he's definitely the cockiest.

"'The Tree is known as the anti-mascot and a symbol of Stanford's **irreverence**, but at Stanford they think the Tree is cool,' said the Tree, a Stanford junior named William Rothacker. 'It's a cool student who gets picked. It's someone who's known as the biggest partier, that all the girls want to date.'

"When I expressed some doubt about chicks digging a guy in a tree costume, he insisted it isn't the costume. It's the mystique that comes with passing a selection process that requires 'a lot of nudity and getting yourself in trouble with the law.'"

Jim Caple. "Blest Be the Bracket That Binds," ESPN.com *(March 19, 2004).*

You Tyrant!

usurp

[yoo·SURP, yoo·ZURP]

Transitive Verb, Intransitive Verb

Transitive Verb
1. to seize and hold in possession (for example, powers, office, rights of another) by force and without right or legal authority; to arrogate; to appropriate
2. to take or encroach upon without right: "Seth had allowed his neighbor's garden to slowly usurp the back corner of his yard, but he resolved now to reclaim his territory with a pair of sharp shears."

Intransitive Verb
3. to unjustly seize or encroach upon the power, place, functions, or possessions of another

ORIGIN

Approximately 1325; borrowed from Old French, *usurper*; from Latin, *usurpare*: to make use of, to seize for use, from *usu-rapos*, from *usus*: use + *rapere*: *to seize.*

BONUS WORD Continuum

LESS FORCEFUL . . .   . . . MORE FORCEFUL
supplant   ———→   usurp

supplant: to take the place of

IN ACTION

"Though television arrived in this country in the late 1940s amid fears in Hollywood that it would **usurp** film's audience, those concerns obviously proved ungrounded.

"Television couldn't have been more different a medium. Whereas the movies were made to mesmerize hundreds gathered in the dark, television was pitched to families huddled in their living rooms and dens. Whereas the movies emphasized the extraordinary, television relied on the familiar."

Neal Gabler. "Meanwhile: U.S. Cultural Hegemony Lives on Movies, Not TV," International Herald Tribune (January 10, 2003).

"It is from quiet places like this all over the world that the forces accumulate which presently will overbear any attempt to accomplish evil on a large scale. Like the rivulets gathering into the river, and the river into the seas, there come from communities like this streams that fertilize the consciences of men, and it is the conscience of the world that we are trying to place upon the throne which others would **usurp**."

Woodrow Wilson (1856–1924). U.S. president. Address in Carlisle, England (December 29, 1918).

"You will find that reason, which always ought to direct mankind, seldom does; but that passions and weaknesses commonly **usurp** its seat, and rule in its stead."

Philip Dormer Stanhope, Fourth Earl of Chesterfield (1694–1773). British statesman and man of letters. Letter to his son (February 15, 1754).

imperious

[im·PEER·ee·ahs]

Adjective

1. domineering or haughtily overbearing: "Shane was a visionary leader, but ultimately, I found his imperious style stifling."

2. urgent or intensely compelling; imperative: "the imperious problems of the new age" (J. F. Kennedy)

ORIGIN

Approximately 1541; from earlier *imperiously*; possibly influenced by Middle French, *imperieux*; from Latin, *imperiosus*: commanding, from *imperium*: empire.

BONUS WORD Sound

empyrean: highest part of heaven

IN ACTION

The strange mixture [in Queen Victoria] of ingenuous light-heartedness and fixed determination, of frankness and reticence, of childishness and pride, seemed to augur a future that was perplexed and full of dangers. As time passed the less pleasant qualities in this curious composition revealed themselves more often and more seriously. There were signs of an **imperious**, a peremptory temper, an egotism that was strong and hard.

> Lytton Strachey (1880–1932). English biographer and critic. Queen Victoria (1921).

"The haughty and **imperious** part of a man develops rapidly on one of these lonely sugar plantations, where the owner rarely meets with anyone except his slaves and minions."

> Rutherford B. Hayes (1822–93). U.S. president. [Written while visiting a college classmate in Texas.] Diary (January 30, 1849).

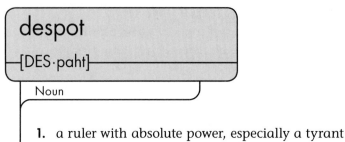

despot

[DES·paht]

Noun

1. a ruler with absolute power, especially a tyrant
2. someone who behaves in a tyrannical or oppressive manner: "Anne was the sole owner of the company, and without any counterbalancing voices, she was developing into a despot."
3. a minor emperor or prince of the Byzantine, Roman, or Ottoman empires

ORIGIN

Approximately 1585; from Italian, *dispoto*: a lord; from Greek, *despotes*: master (of a household), lord, from *des-*, akin to *domos*: house + *potes*, akin to *posis*: husband; akin to Sanskrit *dampati*: lord of the house. The negative sense came into widespread use during the French Revolution, when it was applied by revolutionaries to Louis XVI.

BONUS WORD   Antonym

magnanimous: noble and generous in spirit

IN ACTION

"When Bourne failed in his mission to kill the dictator, he instantly became expendable. With no memory, however he fails to realize that little detail. Now, he and the woman are on the run. In hot pursuit are the out-of-control CIA unit and the secret police of the **despot** Bourne failed to kill. Look for one of the best car chase scenes since 'The French Connection' (1971)."

Paul Clinton. "Review: 'Bourne Identity' a Nifty Throwback," CNN.com *(June 14, 2002).*

"Some scientists say it is only a matter of time before cloning technology is perfected, and some argue there could be situations where it is appropriate, as a substitute for in-vitro fertilization for infertile couples, for example.

"Even though cloning is a transplantation of an entire nucleus and not of specific genes—the principle behind genetic engineering—it is nonetheless an attempt to produce a child with specific traits.

"The idea of reproducing specific people, either as individuals or in hordes, has been expressed in popular culture to both sinister and comic effect.

"In Woody Allen's 1973 science-fiction comedy 'Sleeper', the character played by Allen finds himself 200 years in the future where he foils a plot to clone a deceased tyrannical **despot**, who was blown up by rebel forces, by stealing all that is left of the dictator—his nose."

"Cloning Myths Distort Reality," Wired.com
(December 31, 2002).

dogmatic
[dog·MAT·ik]

Adjective

1. relating to or resulting from an established doctrine or tenet
2. characterized by arrogant, authoritative assertion of unproved or unprovable principles: "We could appreciate Maria's beliefs, but it was difficult for us to buy into such a dogmatic position."

ORIGIN

Approximately 1678; from earlier *dogmatical*; probably borrowed from French, *dogmatique*; from Latin, *dogmaticus*; from Greek, *dogmatikos*, from *dogma*: opinion, belief.

BONUS WORD　　Sound

doggedly: with obstinate determination

IN ACTION

"A Harvard MBA and a **dogmatic** style might not be the surest path up the ladder anymore. Collins found that the CEOs who best handled innovation were often the least likely candidates.

"Collins: Of all the persistently good companies we studied in Good to Great, only one was led by a CEO who had an MBA. The most common academic background, oddly enough, was law. I asked one of the CEOs how law school helped prepare him to be a business leader, and he replied, 'It taught me to ask the right questions rather than come up with the right answers.'"

> *Joshua Macht. "What Makes a Great Leader?"*
> *Business 2.0 (August 2002).*

"Frum's account is generally complimentary, although he writes that [President George W.] Bush 'has many faults.'

"'He is impatient and quick to anger; sometimes glib, even **dogmatic**; often uncurious and as a result ill informed; more conventional in his thinking than a leader probably should be. But outweighing the faults are his virtues: decency, honesty, rectitude, courage and tenacity,' he wrote."

> *Associated Press. "Speechwriter Describes 'Axis of*
> *Evil' Origins [Former Aide Weighs in on Cabinet],"*
> *CNN.com (January 14, 2003).*

martinet

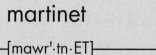

[mawr'·tn·ET]

Noun

1. a military officer who is a strict disciplinarian
2. someone who demands rigid adherence to rules, forms, and fixed methods: "I found it odd that someone so well known for his unorthodox playing style could be such a martinet as an instructor."

ORIGIN

Approximately 1779; developed from English, *Martinet:* a system of drill thought to be invented by the French general Colonel Jean Martinet (d. 1672).

BONUS WORD   Synonym

authoritarian: characteristic of absolute rule

IN ACTION

"'I'm a driving boss,' [George] Steinbrenner says, rapping the table for emphasis. 'I'm not an Eisenhower; I'm a Patton.'

"He once embodied the volatile side of Patton, a headline-grabbing, prospect-trading, manager-firing **martinet**, more feared than respected. But since returning in 1993 from a suspension for consorting with gamblers, Steinbrenner has learned how to win. He listens more and shows more restraint. The result: four World Series championships and expansion of his sovereignty to other sports and television.

"'As you get more powerful, you get smarter,' says Steinbrenner, who ranked No. 2 on the 2001 Power 100. 'At least you'd better.'"

Stuart Miller. "Boss Tops List of Most Powerful: Yankees' Steinbrenner All About Winning, and He Gets What He Wants," Sporting News (January 7, 2003).

"As a London bus operator turned novelist, Magnus Mills knows a thing or two about futility. After all, he used to drive around in circles for a living, and these days he writes novels that, if they don't sell well enough, get pulped back into paper on which to print more novels. Who better to write 'The Scheme for Full Employment,' his sly yet slender new absurdist satire about the irresolvable foolishness of the working world?

". . . 'Three to See the King' follows this structure, and so does 'The Scheme for Full Employment.' Of course, as surefire formulas go, it's hardly boy-meets-girl. But the prose is, if unadventurous, as amusing as ever, and Mills' workplace dialogue perfectly captures the lopsided power equation between squirming time-servers and the petty **martinets** who exploit them."

David Kipen. "Many Turns, Few Twists on His Road" (book review of The Scheme for Full Employment, *by Magnus Mills), San Francisco Chronicle (December 29, 2002).*

"On matters of intonation and technicalities I am more than a **martinet**—I am a martinetissimo."

Leopold Stokowski (1882–1977). American conductor. [Recalled on his death] (September 13, 1977).

Shams and Imposters

dissemble
[di·SEM·bahl]

Transitive Verb, Intransitive Verb

Transitive Verb
1. to hide or conceal under a false or misleading appearance: "Please don't dissemble your own career aspirations behind the facade of company necessity."
2. to feign; to make believe or make a false show of

Intransitive Verb
3. to disguise one's true nature, motives, thoughts, and so on, behind some pretense or false appearance

ORIGIN
Approximately 1413; from Old French, *dessembler*: to be different (from *des-*, *dis-* + *sembler*: to appear, to seem).

BONUS WORD   Origin

dissident: disagreeing, especially with a majority

IN ACTION

"He who knows not how to **dissemble** knows not how to reign."

> *Tiberius (42 B.C.–A.D. 37). Second Roman*
> *emperor, succeeded by Caligula.*
> *[Statement also used by Louis XI of France.]*

Perhaps it was right to **dissemble** your love,
But—why did you kick me down stairs?

> *J. P. Kemble (1757–1823).*
> *[Act I, scene 1, of] The Panel.*

prevaricate

[pri·VAR·i·kayt']

Intransitive Verb

1. to be deliberately ambiguous, unclear, or misleading in order to create a false impression or withhold information; to equivocate; to lie: "I know that you prevaricate to protect me, but please, mother, I am old enough to handle the truth."

ORIGIN

Approximately 1550; from Latin, *praevaricat-*, past participle stem of *praevaricari*: to walk crookedly, from *varus*: crooked, knock-kneed.

BONUS WORD   Related

subterfuge: deceptive device or stratagem

IN ACTION

"This was not because he was cowardly and abject, quite the contrary; but for some time past he had been in an overstrained, irritable condition, verging on hypochondria. He had become so completely absorbed in himself, and isolated from his fellows that he dreaded meeting, not only his landlady, but any one at all. He was crushed by poverty, but the anxieties of his position had of late ceased to weigh upon him. He had given up attending to matters of practical importance; he had lost all desire to do so. Nothing that any landlady could do had a real terror for him. But to be stopped on the stairs, to be forced to listen to her trivial, irrelevant gossip, to pestering demands for payment, threats and complaints, and to rack his brains for excuses, to **prevaricate**, to lie—

no, rather than that, he would creep down the stairs like a cat and slip out unseen."

Fyodor Dostoevsky (1821–81). Russian novelist and short-story writer. Crime and Punishment *(1866).*

From all the rest I single out you, having a message
  for you:
You are to die—Let others tell you what they please,
I cannot **prevaricate**,
I am exact and merciless,
but I love you—There is no escape for you.

*Walt Whitman (1819–92). U.S. poet.
"To One Shortly to Die,"* Leaves of Grass *(1855).*

mountebank

[MOUN·tah·bayngk]

Noun, Intransitive Verb

Noun
1. one who sells quack medicines, attracting customers with tricks, jokes, or stories, especially from a platform in public places
2. a flamboyant deceiver or charlatan: "I fell asleep late last night with the television on, and my dreams were haunted with visions of a plastic-smiled mountebank insistently peddling useless services and gadgets for three easy swipes of my credit card."

Intransitive Verb
3. to behave or act as a mountebank

ORIGIN

Approximately 1577; from Italian, *montambanco*, contraction of *monta in banco*: quack, juggler, literally, mount on bench (to be seen by crowd) (*montare*: to mount + *banca*: bench).

BONUS WORD Related

aver: to declare

IN ACTION

"As the motto around the place is, 'The more you drink, the better the magic,' the shows can be laughably mediocre. There's always one Eastern European **mountebank** sweating bullets as he pulls a pigeon from his rumpled tuxedo. And be prepared for lots of puns and ventriloquism."

Adam Gollner. "The Talk: House of Cards"
(travel review: The Magic Castle),
New York Times (May 15, 2005).

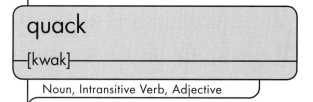

quack

[kwak]

Noun, Intransitive Verb, Adjective

Noun

1. an untrained or ignorant person who pretends to be a physician and who dispenses medical advice: "Your uncle Henry is the family quack, and he's famous for offering remedies that require yogurt."
2. a charlatan or an imposter; one who pretends to have skills or qualifications that they do not possess

Intransitive Verb

3. to act as a medical quack or a charlatan

Adjective
4. characteristic or befitting of a quack
5. falsely presented as having powers or attributes, especially curative powers

ORIGIN
Approximately 1638; shortening of English, *quacksalver*; from Dutch, *kwaksalver*, literally, hawker of salve; from Middle Dutch, *quacken*: to brag, to boast, literally, to croak.

BONUS WORD   Related

analgesic: medicine used to relieve pain

IN ACTION

"Sigmund Freud was a half baked Viennese **quack**. Our literature, culture, and the films of Woody Allen would be better today if Freud had never written a word."

Ian Shoales. Columnist, satirist, and "sneer artist."

"A **quack** doctor can kill you without a knife."

Chinese proverb

---

pinchbeck

[PINCH·bek]

Noun, Adjective

Noun
1. an alloy of copper and zinc that is used in cheap jewelry to imitate gold
2. a cheap substitute; something spurious, phony, counterfeit, or sham

Adjective

3. made of pinchbeck
4. serving as an imitation, sham, or counterfeit: "I'm not jealous at all of your pinchbeck title, because I think we both know who does the work around here."

ORIGIN

Approximately 1750; from Christopher Pinchbeck (1670?–1732), an English watchmaker.

BONUS WORD Synonym

spurious: intended to deceive

IN ACTION

"I love the past; the movies are always better there. When it comes to plays, though, I get more selective. Americans in general tend to take the past as a lump sum that's already been spent; any old coin you show them will do as a token of the whole bygone monetary system. Those of us who see the past as a living whole, continuous with the present, know too much to take the mechanically touted **pinchbeck** specimens as fair samples of the whole."

> Michael Feingold. "History's Mysteries [Theater: Two by Mamet; Look Back in Anger]," Village Voice (October 27–November 2, 1999).

"Where, in these **pinchbeck** days, can we hope to find the old agricultural virtue in all its purity?"

> Anthony Trollope (1815–82). English novelist.
> Framley Parsonage (1861).

El Macho

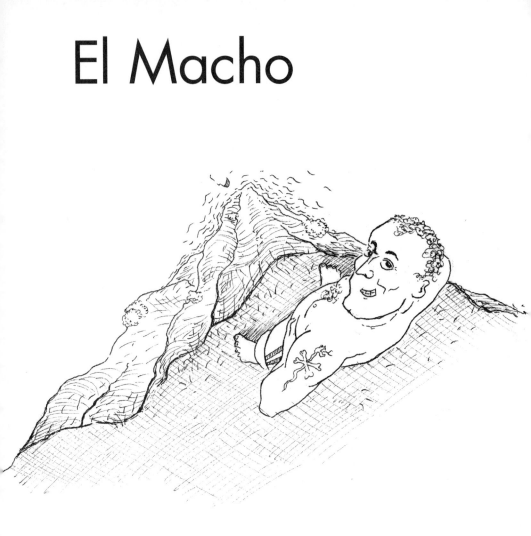

THEME 4

audacity

intrepid

effrontery

temerity

intractable

402

audacity
[aw·DAS·i·tee]

Noun

1. fearless daring or resolution; boldness
2. presumptuous or arrogant disregard of law or moral restraints: "She had the audacity to marry, divorce, and then remarry in the same year and in the same chapel."

ORIGIN
Approximately 1425; borrowed from Medieval Latin, *audacitas*: boldness; from Latin, *audax*: bold, from *audere*: to be bold.

BONUS WORD   Sound

edacity: frequently consuming a great deal

IN ACTION

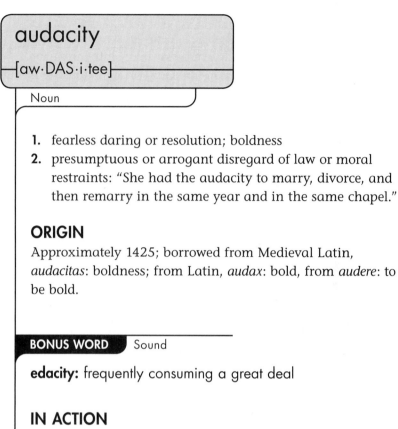

"The Google team dished up a fresh serving of its trademark **audacity** on Mar. 31 when it announced a new e-mail service known as Gmail. The service will offer users free e-mail with one gigabyte of storage—250 times as much as its nearest competitor. But it comes with a catch: a bold and controversial proposal to introduce advertising into e-mail. Google's computers will sift through correspondence and place related advertisements in the margins of e-mails. Gripe in an e-mail about your busted toilet, and the note is likely to come with an ad for plumbing supplies. It's classic Google: imaginative, provocative, and capable of obliterating the status quo."

"Google: Why the World's Hottest Tech Company
Will Struggle to Keep Its Edge,"
BusinessWeek Online (May 3, 2004).

"According to the governor, local governments are struggling financially not because of state and federal unfunded mandates, not because of reductions in aid to municipalities, not because we have an unfair tax system in the Commonwealth, but because teachers and municipal workers have the **audacity** to negotiate collective bargaining agreements that call for living wages (i.e., enough to be able to live in the community they serve) and affordable health insurance coverage."

James J. Palermo. "Opinion: Municipal Workers Aren't Overpaid," Boston Globe *(April 24, 2004).*

intrepid
[in·TREP·id]
Adjective

1. resolutely fearless and persistent; brave; courageous: "It took an intrepid spirit to emigrate to a new land without speaking the language or having any relations."

ORIGIN
Approximately 1697; borrowed from Latin, *intrepidus* (*in-*: not + *trepidus*: alarmed, agitated, possibly related to Greek, *trapein*: to press grapes).

BONUS WORD Origin

trepidation: a feeling of alarm or dread

IN ACTION

"Hershel Sarbin and Jim Brown are the site's 'Golf After 50 Editors' and, in rather dramatic fashion, they have penned a piece called 'Confronting your worst nightmare: Nocturnal leg cramps'.

"Now pay attention here, even if you are under 50, because you're going to have to confront your nightmare at some point. Sarbin and Brown start with some good news: 'Medical experts haven't figured out the exact cause, the best way to treat them, or how to prevent them.'

"But that's not going to stop our **intrepid** duo from having a go. They list a bewildering array of possible causes—lack of sodium, dehydration, alcohol, caffeine, tobacco, too much sugar, pinched nerves, prolonged sitting, flat feet, certain medications, diabetes, anaemia, hypoglycemia—and possible treatments. Then come the preventative measures."

Stephen Penman. "Golf: Top Tips to End the Nightmare That Cramps Your Style," Sunday Herald *(Scotland) (April 25, 2004).*

effrontery

[i·FRUN·tah·ree]

Noun

1. shameless and insulting boldness; presumptuousness; insolence: "The effrontery of his initial proposal set a bad tone, which persisted throughout the negotiations."

ORIGIN

Approximately 1715; borrowed from French, *effronterie*, from *effronte*: shameless; possibly from Late Latin, *effrontem*: barefaced, from *effrons* (*ef-*: out + Latin *frontem*, *frons*: forehead, front).

BONUS WORD   Synonym

chutzpah: unbelievable gall

IN ACTION

"For a species that is supposed to be finicky and clean, he has the grossest habits. When he eats, he sucks up his food, making a horrid slurping sound. But much of that food doesn't make it into his mouth, and he doesn't groom away the leftovers.

"Which means he stinks and must be bathed regularly—with a window screen on top of the tub so that he hooks his angry talons in the mesh instead of the eyeballs of the people who are bathing him.

"And I won't go into what happened after he ate a very long piece of string.

"His worst character flaw is how, in a houseful of self-professed cat people, he has the **effrontery** to act like a dog.

"When we go out for walks he likes to follow us up to Bloor St., howling as he goes."

Robin Harvey. "This Cat's So Bad He's Good
for Us [United Front Only Way to Cope with Jacko,
but We Wish He'd Stop Thinking He's a Dog],"
Toronto Star (April 24, 2004).

temerity

[tah·MER·i·tee]

Noun

1. reckless and unreasonable disregard of danger; rashness; heedlessness: "Either pride, temerity, or both caused the commander to rush into battle without proper reinforcements."

ORIGIN

Approximately 1387; borrowed from Latin, *temeritatem*: blind chance, accident, from *temere*: by chance, blindly, rashly; akin to Old High German, *demar*: darkness.

BONUS WORD Sound

timidity: shyness

tumidity: slight swelling

IN ACTION

"Ms. Siddiqi blames the **temerity** of the international aid agencies and the foreign forces for the failure to make progress outside the capital.

"'Donor countries are concentrating on Kabul,' she said, adding that 'it would help' NATO's tentative first effort at a presence outside Kabul 'if they would actually get out of their bases.' It's a view shared by others who have seen the operation in Konduz, marked by reticence instead of the haste and perseverance that are called for.

"'Now, there is a window to rebuild Afghanistan with the rule of law and an economy that offers some hope,' said General Richard Hillier, the Canadian currently in command of the NATO forces, 'but that window won't stay open forever.'"

Paul Koring. "Comment: And Now for Some Good News [Afghanistan Is Hardly a Picnic, but Paul Koring Looks Around and Sees Signs of Hope]," Globe and Mail (April 24, 2004).

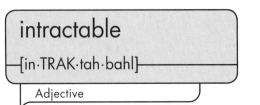

intractable

─[in·TRAK·tah·bahl]─

Adjective

1. not easily managed or directed; stubborn; obstinate: "Ken's intractable disposition made him a natural entrepreneur."
2. not easily shaped or manipulated: "intractable metal"
3. not easily cured or alleviated: "intractable pain"

ORIGIN

Approximately 1500; borrowed from Latin, *intractabilis* (*in-*: not + *tractabilis*: tractable, from *tractare*: to manage).

BONUS WORD Synonym

cantankerous: having a contrary disposition

IN ACTION

"So what do you do if you have nightmares about werewolves, humans supposedly turned into savage beasts? Bring one down with a bullet made of silver and rest easy. The supernatural essence of the legends led to the current pejorative meaning of silver bullet: 'a surefire, simple, instant solution to a seemingly **intractable** problem.'"

William Safire. American journalist, political analyst, and speechwriter for President Nixon (1969–73). "A Little Bit About That Silver Bullet . . ." (syndicated column) (April 24, 2004).

"Envy is as persistent as memory, as **intractable** as a head cold."

Harry Stein. "Thy Neighbor's Life," Esquire (July 1980).

Troublemakers

THEME 5

varmint

recreant

malefactor

hellion

interloper

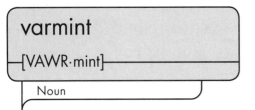

varmint

—[VAWR·mint]—

Noun

1. an irritating, obnoxious, or troublesome person: "Don't let me catch you cavorting with that varmint again, as he's liable to get you into trouble."
2. (usually in the Southern and South Midland United States) any wild animal, usually considered predatory, that is undesirable—for example, a coyote or bobcat

ORIGIN

Approximately 1539; American English dialectal variant of *vermin*; from Vulgar Latin, *verminum*: vermin, possibly including bothersome insects; from Latin, *vermis*: worm.

BONUS WORD Origin

vermin: a pest

IN ACTION

"The word 'later' took on new meaning for me now. 'Later' might never come; that T-word reverberated in my aching skull like a tennis ball and conjured up horror stories about typhoid fever epidemics wiping out whole populations. I thought of Typhoid Mary. Would I be Typhus Travis? More importantly, would I live?

"It turned out that typhus and typhoid, although both bacterial infections, are two different illnesses. My physician, Dr. Alejandro Fuentes at Mid-Valley Family Practice Associates in Weslaco, told me typhoid fever is spread through contaminated food and water. On the other hand, people catch typhus through insect bites such as fleas, ticks and lice.

"Great. It is now confirmed that I really am a flea-bitten **varmint**."

Travis Whitehead. "Weird Infection Plagues Reporter"
(commentary), Rio Grande Valley (TX) Monitor
(December 19, 2005).

recreant

[REK·ree·ahnt]

Adjective, Noun

Adjective
1. unfaithful or traitorous to a cause or principle
2. cowardly, craven; lacking even the rudiments of courage: "I apologized sincerely, but she seemed to think that I had been so recreant in her time of need, she could never trust me again."

Noun
3. an abject coward
4. a disloyal or faithless person; one who forsakes his or her cause, political party, religion, friend, and so on

ORIGIN
Approximately 1300; from Old French, *recreant*: yielding, giving, present participle of *recroire*: to yield in a trial by combat, to surrender allegiance (*re-*: again, back + Latin, *credere*: to believe).

BONUS WORD Sound

miscreant: a villain or heretic

IN ACTION

What a fool art thou,
A ramping fool, to brag, and stamp and swear
Upon my party! Thou cold-blooded slave,
Hast thou not spoke like thunder on my side?
Been sworn my soldier? bidding me depend
Upon thy stars, thy fortune, and thy strength?
And dost thou now fall over to my foes?
Thou wear a lion's hide! doff it for shame,
And hang a calf's-skin on those **recreant** limbs.

> *William Shakespeare (1564–1616).*
> *English dramatist and poet. [Constance in] The Life*
> *and Death of King John (1598).*

"Public officials must guard against entering into
a Faustian bargain with **recreant** employees lest
they jettison an intangible that cannot be valued in
dollars—public trust."

> *John A. Tuthill. "Op/Ed: It Is Newspaper's*
> *Duty to Expose WESD [Willamette Education*
> *Services District] Activities," Salem (OR)*
> *Statesman Journal (January 7, 2006).*

malefactor

[MAL·ah·fak'·tahr]

Noun

1. someone who has committed a crime or who has been
   legally convicted of a crime
2. one who does harm, especially toward another; an
   evildoer: "I wish I could catch the malefactors that have
   desecrated our bridge."

ORIGIN

Approximately 1440; from Latin, *malefactor*, from *malefactus*, past participle of *malefacere*: to do evil (*male*: badly + *facere*: to do, to perform).

BONUS WORD   Origin

malefic: exerting a malignant influence

IN ACTION

"EXCEPTION, n. A thing which takes the liberty to differ from other things of its class, as an honest man, a truthful woman, etc. 'The exception proves the rule' is an expression constantly upon the lips of the ignorant, who parrot it from one another with never a thought of its absurdity. In the Latin, 'Exceptio probat regulam' means that the exception tests the rule, puts it to the proof, not confirms it. The **malefactor** who drew the meaning from this excellent dictum and substituted a contrary one of his own exerted an evil power which appears to be immortal."

Ambrose Bierce (1842–1914). American satiric writer.
The Devil's Dictionary (1911).

hellion

[HEL·yahn]

Noun

1. a rowdy, troublesome, or mischievous person, especially a child: "Who would have thought that my second-grade class could have featured such a well-organized, devious band of hellions?"

ORIGIN

Approximately 1846; alteration (influenced by *hell*) of Scottish dialectal, *hallion*: a worthless fellow, scamp.

BONUS WORD   Antonym

cherub: statue of a plump angel

IN ACTION

"I want all **hellions** to quit puffing that hell fume in God's clean air."

> *Carry Nation (1846–1911). U.S. proponent of temperance and prohibition, famous for using a hatchet to smash saloons. [On smoking.]*

"A-Plus Attendance: Nicole Richie gets top honors here! Seriously, the 'Simple Life' **hellion** rarely missed a bash. *Teen People* party? Present! Celebrity poker game? Present! Lucky Strike bowling bash? Here! Can she keep her near-perfect attendance record next year? My money says yes."

> *Lara Morgenson. "Hollywood Party Girl: I Have to Thank My Caterer, Valets and All the Servers with Whom I Share This Award. . . .," E! Online (December 30, 2004).*

interloper

[IN·tahr·loe'·pahr]

Noun

1. somebody who interferes in the affairs of other people, especially for selfish reasons

2. somebody who intrudes in a place, group, or situation: "In such pristine and isolated wilderness, Nolan couldn't help but feel like a human interloper in an otherwise natural world."

ORIGIN

Approximately 1590; from Middle English, *enterloper*: an unauthorized trader, probably formed from the prefix *inter-, enter-*: between + *-loper*: as in *landloper*: vagabond, adventurer; from Middle Dutch, *landloper* (*land*: land + *loper*: runner, rover, from *lopen*: to run).

BONUS WORD Origin

interlard: to insert something foreign

IN ACTION

"'Namen?' she asked. Strauss and Eichenbronner, I told her. Hearing Eichenbronner, the older woman said to her younger friends, 'Hebräisch' and 'Jüdischer.'

"Immediately I became apprehensive. I had no idea how people would react to **interloping** Jews poking around their towns, their cemeteries, their history. I as much expected to be told to go away as to be helped. But the ladies did not seem the least bit uneasy. I went ahead.

"'Ja,' I said while pointing to Nina and me, 'Jüdischer.' I can remember as a kid thinking it better not to identify myself as a Jew, and even telling people that, yes, Strauss was German but that my family was Lutheran. Once I told my mother that I didn't feel Jewish at all. 'Tell that to Hitler when he comes back,' she said with uncharacteristic bluntness. And here we were, in Germany, telling complete strangers, the fathers of whom did who knows what in the war, that we were Jewish."

Robert L. Strauss. *"My Jewish Roots in Germany,"*
Salon.com *(September 18, 1999).*

"Wondering if your new Pentium 4-powered PC is moonlighting on the side? You should be. While your system is happily chomping away on 5 gigs of digital video, a freeloading **interloper** could be sucking excess processing power for its own dirty work.

"Like a leech feeding off its host, a simple kernel of code can tap into your PC or Web server undetected, then use it to solve complex mathematical equations."

Michael Behar. *"Parasitic Computing: Who's Using
Your Machine?"* Wired.com *(December 2001).*

Audio pronunciations for the words in
this pack can be found on our website:
www.vocabvitamins.com/book/pack9.

Heaven and Hell Pen Pals

In this exercise, opposites really attract. Match these pen pals, hailing from opposing ends of the moral spectrum but desperately wishing to share their respective experiences. Word pen pals 1–5 wish to correspond with only word pen pals a–e and so on.

1. dissemble
2. indolent
3. audacity
4. usurp
5. varmint

a. assiduous
b. endow
c. clarify
d. propriety
e. cherub

6. flippant
7. prevaricate
8. recreant
9. imperious
10. intrepid

f. elucidate
g. humble
h. careful
i. laureate
j. resolute

11. despot
12. malefactor
13. effrontery
14. mountebank
15. impudence

k. decorum
l. altruist
m. courtesy
n. paragon
o. Good Samaritan

16. temerity

17. quack

18. hellion

19. dogmatic

20. sanctimony

p. prudence

q. authentic

r. asceticism

s. angel

t. clement

21. intractable

22. pinchbeck

23. irreverence

24. martinet

25. interloper

u. genuine

v. obeisance

w. accommodating

x. colleague

y. mentor

Answer Key

Fill-in Frenzy!

1. fervid
2. jaunty
3. dudgeon
4. mawkish
5. qualms
6. impetuous
7. revelry
8. acrimony
9. simper
10. contrition
11. irascible
12. copasetic
13. irate
14. maudlin
15. chagrin
16. precipitant
17. mollify
18. apoplexy
19. confection
20. compunction
21. tempestuous
22. levity
23. ebullition
24. saccharine
25. expiate

PACK 2
Heads or Tails

1. recus**ant**
2. **ph**alanx
3. complici**ty**
4. **tru**culent

5. **be**llicose
6. succ**umb**
7. capitu**late**
8. **cas**tigate
9. rest**ive**
10. cab**al**
11. **pe**tulant
12. abdi**cate**
13. bera**te**
14. **exc**oriate
15. **acq**uiesce
16. **coll**usion
17. **co**terie
18. **se**dition
19. **pu**gilism
20. **fact**ious
21. lamba**ste**
22. **kow**tow
23. reb**uke**
24. **re**fractory
25. **upb**raid

PACK 3
Friend or Foe?

1. a
2. a
3. b
4. a
5. b
6. b
7. a
8. a
9. a
10. b

11. a
12. b
13. b
14. a
15. b
16. a
17. a
18. a
19. b
20. b
21. a
22. b
23. a
24. a
25. b

PACK 4
Antidote!

1. gregarious
2. paucity
3. pullet
4. innocuous
5. acumen
6. acerbic
7. allegory
8. paroxysm
9. trialogue
10. bifurcate
11. panegyric
12. acuity
13. necromancy
14. quadruped
15. univocal
16. quintessence
17. pusillanimous
18. mediocre
19. agoraphobia
20. egregious
21. necrosis
22. noxious

23. puerile
24. pernicious
25. poltroon

PACK 5
Stolen Vowels

Theme 1:
1. lethe
2. eidetic
3. mnemonic
4. auld lang syne
5. annals

Theme 2:
1. antebellum
2. quondam
3. obsolete
4. antiquity
5. antediluvian

Theme 3:
1. immemorial
2. perdurable
3. inveterate
4. amaranthine
5. perennial

Theme 4:
1. primordial
2. hoary
3. archaic
4. erstwhile
5. superannuated

Theme 5:
1. fabulist
2. raconteur
3. apologue
4. anecdote
5. recapitulate

PACK 6
Twisted Analogies

1. e
2. d
3. b
4. c
5. a
6. i
7. h
8. j
9. g
10. f
11. l
12. o
13. m
14. k
15. n
16. t
17. s
18. q
19. p
20. r
21. y
22. v
23. u
24. w
25. x

PACK 7
The Search

n	u	j	u	n	k	t	b	b	g	c	q	l	e	b	q	f	k	g	x
g	d	z	f	u	h	e	v	p	e	v	i	t	o	m	e	d	g	f	i
o	f	s	l	n	t	s	i	n	o	g	a	t	n	a	s	q	y	q	v
o	j	u	e	y	p	i	y	w	d	l	t	v	a	l	h	r	r	o	h
w	r	o	t	a	r	y	s	m	u	i	n	o	m	e	d	n	a	p	x
a	l	r	a	s	g	e	u	b	k	e	e	e	e	d	k	k	l	x	o
l	a	e	r	o	p	r	o	c	n	i	c	x	h	i	y	c	q	z	i
i	c	p	e	a	v	b	n	m	a	b	s	x	t	c	h	l	r	q	u
k	i	e	f	o	m	n	i	m	p	r	e	c	a	t	i	o	n	k	s
k	m	r	i	o	i	t	g	k	m	x	n	n	n	i	q	x	t	a	r
p	i	t	c	o	y	d	i	i	e	u	a	a	a	o	d	w	k	z	a
f	n	s	o	t	x	s	t	c	g	a	v	s	d	n	z	r	u	a	o
u	i	b	v	a	o	o	r	c	n	i	e	p	h	e	m	e	r	a	l
d	d	o	w	k	g	a	e	g	z	y	l	e	g	w	u	m	m	w	o
e	x	p	l	e	t	i	v	e	g	n	a	r	t	s	e	a	n	d	p
k	w	l	w	i	k	v	b	f	u	g	a	c	i	o	u	s	y	r	u
f	n	v	o	r	t	e	x	h	h	n	c	e	m	h	l	s	s	k	w
g	p	n	s	z	u	i	z	i	c	p	p	d	e	q	w	o	h	z	d
e	n	d	x	g	a	o	g	o	d	a	w	i	u	z	u	g	o	k	l
p	r	t	p	z	h	m	r	q	g	n	y	m	x	c	z	d	r	q	x

PACK 8
Word Math

1. epitome
2. remunerate
3. axiom
4. estimable
5. antipodes
6. pittance
7. cosmopolitan
8. august
9. pith
10. omnipresent
11. lucre
12. guerdon
13. archetype
14. palmary
15. hyperborean
16. emolument
17. laudable
18. quiddity
19. meritorious
20. ultramundane
21. hiatus
22. asunder
23. Zeitgeist
24. ubiquitous
25. ecumenical

PACK 9
Heaven and Hell Pen Pals

1. c
2. a
3. d
4. b
5. e
6. j
7. f
8. i
9. g
10. h
11. l
12. n
13. k
14. o
15. m
16. p
17. q
18. s
19. t
20. r
21. w
22. u
23. v
24. y
25. x

Index

About Vocab Vitamins

Vocab Vitamins Philosophy

Words are candies, tools, keys, weapons, delicacies, and packages. Many of us come to the study of words for only brief intervals, usually under pressure from a coming standardized exam. This is an odd, competitive context for learning, especially since words are meant for utility and enjoyment, not hoarding. Words can also be important tools for individual empowerment, as the word selections people make can have social and professional ramifications.

At Vocab Vitamins, we revel in the diversity of difficult words, avoid pretension like the plague, and never dumb things down. Come fortify your vocabulary with us and you will do better on tests, read with more joy and understanding, communicate more effectively, and generally amuse yourself with the English language.

About VocabVitamins.com

At our website, we provide an internet- and e-mail–based word learning service that begins with a word of the day and continues with a host of practice and quiz tools. If you like our book, you'll love VocabVitamins.com. Most of the content on these pages debuted first with our online community, and we're busy assembling and delivering new content there every day of the week.

We have specialized versions of Vocab Vitamins for:

- schools
- standardized exams

- businesses
- word lovers

Special Benefits for Book Owners

There's a special place in our hearts reserved for book owners. We'll have you over anytime for tea. Well, truthfully, we don't do tea all that often. So in lieu of tea, we've set aside a few special perks:

- A 6-month premium subscription to VocabVitamins.com for free with the purchase of this book. Yes, free.
- Additional book materials such as word pronunciations and bonus pages on VocabVitmamins.com.
- Practice makes permanent, and on VocabVitamins.com we have several tools to reinforce the words you've seen here.

Partnerships

If you work for an internet portal or publishing company and you like our approach, drop a note to bizdev@vocabvitamins .com. To incorporate a dynamically updating word-of-the-day content element in your site, contact us about syndication. For publishing partners, we can create a cobranded version of our premium online service using your brand and a customized curriculum.

About the Authors

Colin O'Malley and Julie Karasik started Vocab Vitamins in the year 2000 on the rickety fire escapes of New York's Hell's Kitchen and now operate the venture from the mostly sun-baked and occasionally fog-soaked Mission District in San Francisco. They live with a multi-thumbed feline named Gus, and by the time this book graces your fingers, they will have welcomed their first child.

LIBRARY
1800 STAGE B-C, 8-9...
2800 LAKE ST.
W.C.C. KRAMER-CITY
ACADEMY OF... 228